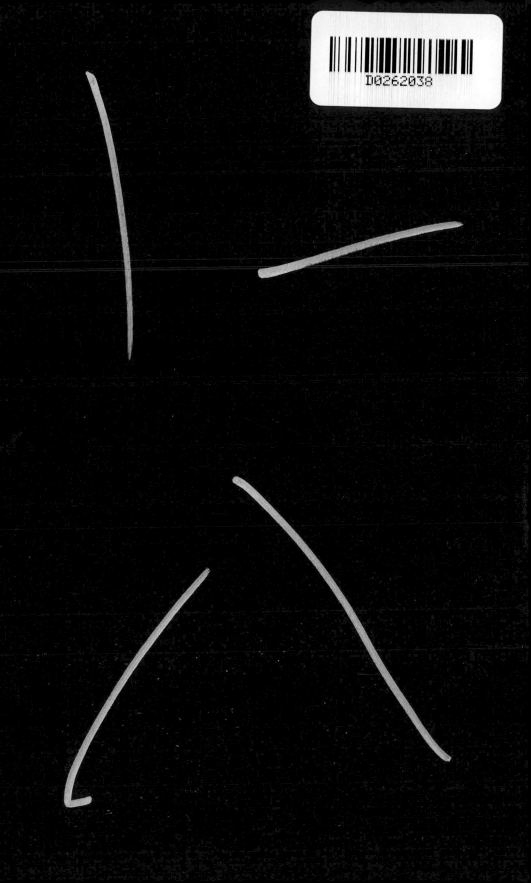

THE MAN IN THE WHITE SUIT

THE MAN IN THE WHITE SUIT

THE STIG LE MANS THE FAST LANE AND ME

BEN COLLINS

HarperCollins*Publishers*

HarperCollins*Publishers*
77–85 Fulham Palace Road,
Hammersmith, London W6 8JB

www.harpercollins.co.uk

First published by HarperCollins*Publishers* 2010

1 3 5 7 9 10 8 6 4 2

While every effort has been made to trace the owners of copyright material
reproduced herein and secure permissions, the publishers would like to
apologise for any omissions and will be pleased to incorporate missing
acknowledgements in any future edition of this book.

A catalogue record of this book is
available from the British Library

HB ISBN 978-0-00-732796-6
PB ISBN 978-0-00-733168-0

Printed and bound in Great Britain by
Clays Ltd, St Ives plc

Mixed Sources
Product group from well-managed
forests and other controlled sources
www.fsc.org Cert no. SW-COC-001806
© 1996 Forest Stewardship Council

FSC is a non-profit international organisation established to promote the
responsible management of the world's forests. Products carrying the FSC
label are independently certified to assure consumers that they come
from forests that are managed to meet the social, economic and
ecological needs of present and future generations.

Find out more about HarperCollins and the environment at
www.harpercollins.co.uk/green

All men dream, but not equally. Those who dream by night in the dusty recesses of their minds, wake in the day to find that it was vanity: but the dreamers of the day are dangerous men, for they may act on their dreams with open eyes, to make them possible.

T. E. LAWRENCE

Dad, thank you for every opportunity that life
brought through your guidance.

Mum, your moral compass is a shining light;
thank you for putting up with me.

CONTENTS

1

AUDITION

Intermittent shafts of sunlight sliced across the damp carriageway through the canopy of trees. Leaves spattered away from the spinning wheels. I still had plenty of time, but this journey was worth enjoying, so I kept pulling gears and cranked the stereo.

The suspension shuddered as I braked hard on the worn tarmac and rounded a long hairpin. The car was busy but my mind, as usual, was elsewhere. Was this a good idea? Who was this guy I was meeting? Where the hell was this place?

I glanced down at my complex route directions, then realised my turning was about to appear on a blind bend. I slowed to check for oncoming traffic before veering off down a track with no discernible markings.

My left thumb clicked at the handbrake button as I toyed with the idea of a sharp about-face. I topped a gentle crest and the view widened. Just past a field of grazing sheep lay a security entrance. Three feet and two inches to the right of the middle of nowhere.

The security guard spilt his tea and leapt to his feet as I pulled up at the gate. He emerged from his cabin and approached my window. 'Do you know where you're going?'

'Yes,' I lied.

'Who are you here with?'

That was a trickier one, but I dealt with it.

'Oh, OK, just follow the one-way system around.'

I drove into a vast expanse of clear skies, grass, concrete and airfield. The path ahead led to an old DC3 passenger plane. I followed the broken concrete track to the right. An office building stood amongst a haphazard collection of large green metal warehouses. I dropped down a ramp into a staging area in front of a much larger hangar. At the far end of it, on the edge of the airfield, lay a very dilapidated cabin with 'Production' daubed on its side. A Harrier Jump Jet was parked in the middle distance.

It seemed I'd arrived at the 'Studio'. With a little time in hand, I walked the site.

The airfield was as flat as a billiard table, with neat green fields surrounding the tarmac landing strips. I couldn't make out any kind of circuit in the sea of grey mist. A tired silver tree-line separated the earth from the clear blue sky.

The place must have had a real buzz in its glory days, first during the Second World War and then as a Harrier proving ground. On this still morning I could almost hear the banter of aircrew scrambling to their aircraft.

Now it felt like the Land that Time Forgot. Rusted control panels littered the area. Cracked concrete billets jostled with disused hangars and pebble-dashed Seventies monstrosities.

I paid an obligatory pre-match visit to the nearby loos. Two fresh pieces of graffiti read: 'Fuck Jeremy Clarkson' and 'Richard Hammond is a'. Sadly, Hammond's eulogy had never been completed. My laughter echoed down the deserted corridor. I felt like a madman.

I returned to the production hut and gave it the once over. A cardboard cut-out of a policeman stood guard at the window beside a larger cut-out still of John Prescott, an ironing board, a moth-eaten mini-sofa and a cluster of toxic coffee cups and Bic biros.

What the hell did they do here?

A worn chair overlooked a grubby telephone which sat, inert, on a filthy wood veneer table. A printed list of 'key contacts' was pinned to the wall, belying the cabin's absence of discernible function.

Room 2 was marginally better appointed, with a small TV set surrounded by VHS tapes but no player. A few photos of random celebrities decorated the flimsy, cobwebbed walls.

Room 3 contained a large hanging rail from which hung a gold sequin jacket, a flower power shirt and an enormous pair of jeans. A crate of Red

Bull lurked in the corner. The place stank of fags, mildew and *Eau de Man*.

With an uncertain recollection of my last tetanus jab, I opted to wait inside my car and nod off to some filthy hard house tunes.

I woke to the sound of rushing gravel as a small hatchback pulled up in front of me. I guessed this was my man by his silver hair and media issue denim jacket. I climbed out to greet him.

He hitched up his trousers and shuffled towards me like a glum but familiar uncle on a rare visit home. It was only 9.30, but his five o'clock shadow suggested he had already had a long day. He clasped a bursting folder of papers under one arm.

He looked in every direction but mine. I moved to shake his hand. With some reluctance he eventually reciprocated.

'Right …'

'Great to meet you, Andy.'

'Did you tell anyone you were coming?' he asked.

'No,' I said.

'OK, good.'

Andy explained that the track would open up for some fast laps at ten.

I had no idea of what the track even looked like, what car I would be driving or what test lay ahead, so it wasn't easy to prepare for what came next.

Andy unlocked a blue Ford Focus in the car park and it dawned on me that this underpowered front-wheel-drive affair would be his measuring stick of my performance. Years of racing experience in Formula 1 style machines went out the window; it was time to rely on a few bad habits.

Andy hunched over the wheel and drove us serenely around the track. But for the occasional steely-eyed glare at a corner, his eyes sparkled as if he was enjoying some private joke.

The silver fox indicated the areas I was 'not allowed to drive across', such as the white lines on the exit of the first corner, coming out of the second corner, and especially those marking the 'Hammerhead' chicane. I nodded respectfully, as you do on the headmaster's tour of the school grounds.

The track looked straightforward enough, and there were some ballsy fast corners in the middle that could be hairy in a proper car.

'This one sorts the men out from the boys,' Andy said with something approaching relish.

A riot of skid marks and freshly carved-up grass around the final corners did indeed suggest that the last two turns might be treacherous.

Andy's expression darkened again as he parked on the start line and he compressed his lips. 'You start each lap here, yeah, and I'll be timing you. Go across the line and then I'll reset so you can go again.'

'So it's not flying laps then?'

'No. Standing start every time.'

'How many do I get?' I asked.

'Um … we'll do a few. OK.'

Andy disembarked. I jumped into the driver's seat and clunk-clicked. The foam seat didn't give much, it felt upright and too close to the wheel. I shuffled it back for some leg-room, adjusted the steering higher and removed the valet paper from the foot-well. I gave the controls a quick once-over. A five-speed manual box and a fairly solid brake pedal.

I searched the dashboard for the traction control button and turned it off for the closest its 1.6 litres could get to maximum, unbridled acceleration. I envisaged making a few reconnaissance laps to learn the track, then posting a ballistic time.

As I looked up Andy was gesticulating with his right hand and brandishing a stopwatch with his left.

'*Shit*, hang on …'

I grabbed the gear-stick and jammed it into first gear, simultaneously gunning the engine to a respectable 4,000rpm. Andy's arm dropped and I didn't stick around to ask questions. Dumping the clutch, I lurched off the line, wheels spinning and clawing at the track.

Less revs next time …

The car felt tiny on the broad expanse of runway. I approached the first corner by positioning myself to the far right, then swung across to the left, leaving my braking till the last possible moment.

I heaved on the middle pedal and the ABS cut in immediately, reducing it to a vibrating waffle. The front tyres of the Focus were in protest all the way. I missed the middle point of the corner by a country mile, which cost me speed on to the short straight that followed. I planted the accelerator anyway.

The tyres howled with discomfort and wafts of burning rubber filled the cabin, replacing the sweet silicone smell of the new fabrics.

I pulled out of the gutter and lined up for a simple left-hand kink marked only by a white line as the surge of torque ran through the

Ford's engine. There was no need to release the throttle as we sped towards the next corner, marked by a wall of tyres, that Andy had called 'Chicago'.

I hit the brakes with a little more sensitivity and the front tyres responded by turning more gracefully in the right direction. I slapped the stick across to second and gradually soaked up the biting point of the clutch to let the torque of the engine-braking do its job. I snatched a tiny bit of the throttle mid-corner to keep up the speed before burying it again.

I proceeded down the middle of a gigantic runway and realised I had no idea where to go next. After a while, the straight began to run out. I noticed some unfriendly looking fencing in the scrub beyond for netting runaway aircraft. I didn't fancy tangling with it, but I didn't want to lose time being cautious either.

To my right was a braking marker, with some squiggly white lines adjacent. The notorious Hammerhead chicane.

I whipped across to the right-hand side and dived on the brakes. The ABS thought it was having an accident, then so did I as the rear end lost grip.

I flicked the steering left and right as the back swung around like a Beyoncé bootie shake. I accelerated to regain control and the powering front wheels dragged the squirming chassis into line, a trait unique to front-wheel-drive cars.

Messy, I'll get it right next time …

I sped down the straight towards the fast 'Follow Through' section. Without knowing how many laps I had to prove myself, I opted to try the corner flat out and see what gave.

I turned in towards the red-painted chevrons on the tarmac and felt the Ford's body lean heavily on to its wheel arches as the weight swung across the suspension. The wing mirrors were scraping the floor as I ran out wide towards the grass. Her ass wiggled as she dipped in and out of a small gully and I breathed again as we rejoined the tarmac.

I approached the Chicago tyre wall for the second time, remembering to hold it flat for the left, rather than braking to turn right. The level horizon made it hard to read the ground coming fast through the dashboard but I could see a seam where the taxiway joined the main runway. I aimed for the angular join, clobbered a storm drain and flew out the other side. A flurry of spray squirted out of the brimmed windscreen

washer reservoir as the impact weakened its bladder. The citrus taste in my mouth made me swallow for the first time since I started the lap.

The big challenge lay in the final two corners, which I couldn't even see because the runway was so wide and stretched so far into the distance.

I would be approaching 'Bacharach' at the car's terminal velocity. After my Hammerhead experience, I opted for a sensible approach and scoured the runway for signs of a corner. Suddenly, 100 feet to my left, an opening in the grass appeared.

The brakes groaned. The car pointed clumsily in the correct direction and travelled the breadth of the runway to finally join the corner, which abruptly tightened. The road quickly ran out and I dropped two wheels on the turf. Now I knew why this was skid mark central.

There was a short shoot to the final corner and I wondered if I could take it without braking. I dabbed the pedal anyway and was glad for it as the front broke away and the grass verge to the outside loomed into view, with Andy standing on it.

His trousers were bunching at the ankle again as he bent and fixed me with his stony gaze. He snapped down hard on his stopwatch as I crossed the line.

I pulled up alongside him and rolled down the window.

'What do you think?' he asked.

'I think I know which way the track goes now. What am I trying to beat?'

'We don't tell you the times.'

'What? Not even *my* times?'

'Nope. The old Stig's pretty fast round here though. He knew this place like the back of his glove. Can you go any quicker?'

'Absolutely. That's just my first go.'

A puff of smoke appeared from behind the wing mirror. A sniff in its direction confirmed the problem.

'Excuse me, I think the brakes are catching fire. I'll be back in a minute.'

I set off down the airstrip to cool the pins and assess the situation. This was unlike any qualifying session I'd done before. The rules seemed to be changing by the minute.

Without a time to beat I had to focus on maximising my personal performance. If I could put a lap together that I would struggle to repeat,

I'd bet it would beat whatever benchmark time Andy had for this car. The track was simple enough, if a little hard to make out, but my peripheral vision was dialled in. Now I just needed to master the rhythm. Just one, perfect, lap.

I lined up at the start and warned Andy to stand further back this time.

My second lap was much cleaner. I punished the front tyres less by braking lighter and earlier to carry more speed into every corner. I slammed across the finish line, ran a little wide and caught a glimpse of Andy pouncing on his stopwatch.

I rolled the window down and he leant against the door.

'How was that?' he asked.

'I don't know,' I grinned. 'You tell me!'

'You're not far off.'

That was when the adrenalin started. The early laps were just kitten play. To eke out the tiny fractions of speed in every corner, I needed one exceptional run. My mouth dried as blood surged around my body and I felt the elation of impending excellence. I was becoming quicker, stronger and more explosive with every heartbeat. I was a heartbeat away from bursting out of my shirt and turning green.

I made a perfect start. The short hairs prickled on the back of my neck. At the far end of the tunnel lay the first corner. I absorbed the view. As I closed in, I allowed my vision to loosen, blur and widen into the periphery. One all-seeing eye.

I braked late, skimming the gravel on the inside and loading the front tyres just enough to prevent the ABS from gate-crashing. I squeezed the throttle. The car remained steady, boring even. Perfect.

The process was repeated through Chicago and then Hammerhead, staying just within the tolerance of the front tyres, controlling every movement, stealing every ounce of throttle, every inch of tarmac.

I used as little steering as possible through the fast right, then the left, keeping the friction of the rubber to the bare minimum with the gas pedal welded to the floor. The tyres emitted a guttural howl as all four wheels skated at 100mph. Only two turns to go.

The speed ramped up as I shifted into top gear. The markers appeared on my right side, with the 100 first. I scanned left and found the corner. Not yet. Past the 50. Not yet. The final marker, an arrow board, was coming up fast.

I braked, the car dug in, then I immediately had to release the pressure to get the front wheels to turn. It was an impossible speed and the rear skidded away. I jammed the throttle open. The front wheels spun in third gear and I flipped a coin in my head: stick or spin. *Stick, you bastard.*

The car launched into the corner at an acute angle, cutting across the grass at its apex and bouncing over the concrete kerbing. I was out of control, but coping.

I slid across the narrow section of tarmac and dropped three wheels on the grass on the exit. I barely had time to get back on the black stuff to blat the brake and chuck it left for the last time.

I pitched her in a bit too quick, swiped the apex, slid wide and hit the mark where Andy had been standing. The verge projected the car sideways into the air but it no longer mattered to me. It could flip on to its roof and explode because we'd still cross the finish line just 25 feet away.

I crashed landed on the other side of the grass, the metal wheel rims ploughing first into the concrete then crunching through the gravel bed lining the edge. Rocks spewed in all directions.

'That one felt good,' I said.

Andy was scribbling notes in his little pad.

'Yeah. That one was faster.'

I thought to myself, *Yes, I've bloody got this!* but made no outward sign, since he hadn't either.

His brow furrowed. 'Do you think you can get any more out of it?'

'More?' That had me worried. I didn't think it had any, but it was worth a try.

I banged in another lap that was nearly as fast as my best, then conceded that I couldn't go any quicker.

'All right. Well, if you think that's it, we'll call it a day.'

Andy put his stopwatch back into his pocket. It seemed that our business had been concluded. He thanked me and said he would call me sometime.

I waited weeks for any suggestion that my performance was up to scratch, or that there was any work with these people that might pay the rent. Andy called and asked me to send him a commercial I'd done for Vauxhall which featured lots of precision sliding close to camera on snow and ice, just the kind of tradecraft he needed. 'Can you send the rushes too?'

'Sure, no problem,' I told him, not knowing what on earth he was talking about.

Rushes, I learnt, were the raw footage. By sifting through them, Andy could determine whether the director had had to edit around my driving or if I was consistently getting it right on the first take. His attention to detail knew no bounds. Only time would tell if I had a future with *Top Gear*.

2

NEED FOR SPEED

I flew along the tarmac, engine screaming. The rain lashed down from the swirling mass of cloud above. With the next corner approaching I checked the mirrors for the competition; they were nowhere in sight. My goal was ultimate speed and perfection, at any cost. Leaning on the brakes at the last possible moment and matching the revs with each down-change, I could feel the chassis squirming loosely as it struggled to find enough grip to cope with the braking forces.

Accelerated movement sharpened the senses, dulled reality, heightened perception, quickened the mind, slowed time, purified travel, transported my being into another world – the place where I wanted to live.

Down into third gear with just enough time to make the crest of the right-hander, the brakes released and we launched through the air, spearing sideways on the landing. It took every ounce of strength to shove the steering into full opposite lock until it banged on to the end of the rack stop. The slide continued, closer and closer to the fence line. I came off everything, released the throttle and hoped for the best. The limited friction of the sodden surface finally took a few crucial mph off my speed, as the slide balanced and the track plunged steeply. I adjusted the steering and cracked the throttle again. I felt unbeatable.

The bottom corner cut across a steep hill, creating a hefty amount of adverse camber. A challenge on a good day, the wet surface seriously reduced the grip and braking power available to make it through.

As I stretched my oversized rubber boot towards the brake, the tip of the toe caught on the bodywork and stuck for a nanosecond too long, causing the rear wheels to lock. Front and rear began to slide in a perfect but totally uncontrollable drift towards the woods.

I started to see strand after strand of barbed wire intertwined between the trees. The consequences of destroying the machine weighed heavily. Fifty miles per hour across wet grass into blades and bark became my immediate reality. Raw adrenalin surged around my system. Time slowed.

I made a split-second decision to save my own skin. I threw myself off and hit the deck hard. Clad in no less than three Barbour jackets and my mother's Hunter Wellingtons, I scrabbled at clumps of grass to divert my speeding body towards a friendly looking pine.

Meanwhile, the farm's one and only All Terrain Cycle thundered into a sizeable birch on fast forward, the barbed wire ripping the bodywork apart like a cheese-slicer.

My body cartwheeled across the slick grass and I came to rest in a bed of stinging nettles against the pine tree. I lay flat on my back with tree roots embedded in my shoulders, wheezing to get the wind back into my lungs. I glanced down to see my three pairs of socks dangling from my toes. They had been the only way to fit my ten-year-old feet reasonably snugly into the wellies. The boots themselves, cowards, were nowhere to be seen.

The elation of survival and the absurdity of my situation sank in. I was alone, crashed out at the bottom of a remote field in the corner of a tiny island on a planet the size of a speck of dust in the limitless universe. I burst out laughing.

I wiped the mud from my eyes and hobbled over to make a cursory inspection of the three-wheeled cycle. The bodywork was smashed around the wheel arches, the plastic speedometer was cracked and the foam seat, where I had been sitting just moments earlier, was slashed to pieces by the barbed wire. It looked really cool. Dad was going to kill me. But my addiction to speed was all his fault in the first place.

My father was more into cars than anyone I have ever known. He would watch Formula 1 on the TV religiously, snoring his way through the final laps on a Sunday afternoon. It was my cue to find something more interesting than watching a bunch of cars drone around a stretch of tarmac. And that something normally took the shape of a Lotus F1-styled pedal kart. It took me eighteen years to realise the connection.

The thrill of driving and risk taking had been instilled in me from an early age. No two journeys in my dad's car were ever the same, but they generally began with some kind of stunt and always broke the speed limit.

When I was four, Dad was a manager for a transport company and his star was rising. His gift was his ability to eye up a business and sharply turn it around. We all climbed aboard his Rover SD1 and headed over to his boss's place for lunch. It was a cool hatchback, shaped like a wedge of cheese with a hint of Ferrari Daytona around the kisser. Cooler still, I had the matchbox version in its racing livery.

Dad was decked out in a tan suit with ludicrous lapels that were très vogue in the Seventies. His colour blindness always guaranteed something special and today was no disappointment: a psychedelic paisley tie and a bright yellow shirt, dripping with Old Spice.

He came from a working-class background and was raised the hard way. When he earned a slot at the local grammar school, his mother had to dig deep to afford the uniform. Nan didn't take any crap. When it came to parting with her hard-earned, she bought the uniforms she liked most rather than the one for the institution my dad was actually attending. Sporting the cap from one school and a blazer and tie from two others, his first days at college were inevitably bloody, but he never lost his unique sartorial style.

My mother had swept her hair back in a chignon and boasted pearl earrings, elegant gold necklace and frilly blouse. Fabulous, darling. I sat in the back with my hair like a pudding basin, looking sharp in blue cords and matching jumper. Butter wouldn't melt.

Seeing us all in our Sunday finery triggered something in my old man. He shot me a knowing smile in the rear-view mirror.

'Hold on, Ben.'

I knew what that meant.

The lane to the house I grew up in was just over a quarter of a mile long and met the main road at a T-junction. The perfect drag-strip.

Dad dropped the clutch and tore away, laying a couple of thick black lines of bubbling rubber across our driveway. Once the G-forces had subsided, I leant forward to get a ringside view. The revving engine and the squealing tyres all but drowned out my mother's objections. She swatted him with her handbag, but there was no stopping him.

The hedgerows zoomed past. I cheered every gear change until the T-junction sprang into view. Everything went quiet.

I didn't need to be a driving expert for my four-year-old brain to register there was no way the car would stop in time for the corner using conventional means. Mum figured that too. She gave up with the handbag and emitted a high pitched 'Fuuuuuuuuuuck ...'

It took a lot to rattle Mum. When she was four years old she lived in Sutton, which lay along the German bombing run during the Second World War. Three of the houses she lived in were completely destroyed. By pure luck, her family had been out on each occasion. One summer's day she was playing in the garden when her mother screamed for her to come inside. Before she could move an inch, bullets from a low-flying aircraft strafed the garden walls and plant pots exploded either side of her. Mum went on to work in hot spots across the Middle East and around the globe as a Royal Navy nurse. She always held her nerve, but Dad's driving freaked her out every time.

Dad kept his foot on the gas until the very last moment. The ditch on the far side of the junction was only metres away. We were thrown forward as Dad yanked hard on the handbrake and spun the Rover sideways, skidding across the tarmac.

The car drifted to the edge of the verge bordering the ditch and my stomach flipped with the exciting prospect of crashing into it.

By careful judgement, or a stroke of luck, we just caressed the verge and straightened up. Disaster was averted. Mum recovered her necklace from between her shoulder-blades and we drove away giggling.

I'd never heard my mother swear before, so I treated this new word 'fuuuuuuuuuck' with great reverence. After a twenty-five-minute journey we arrived at our destination. Mum adjusted my shirt and tie as we approached the front door. We were greeted by the boss, his wife and finally his daughter.

'Ben, this is Stephanie.'

'Fuuuuuuuuuuck Stephanie,' I replied.

You could have heard a mouse fart. After a little smooth talking, my parents dug themselves out of it and I was allowed in for chipolatas and cake.

Dad kept his job with the company in spite of his feral offspring and we were invited back for a grander function a year later. The company was changing its vehicle fleet and new cars were dished out. I knew how

disappointed he was not to be in line for a new Jaguar XJS, like the one the boss had ordered for himself.

We piled into the Rover to the accompaniment of Dad's favourite driving soundtrack, the jangling guitar riffs from *The Good, the Bad and the Ugly*.

I was thoroughly briefed to avoid the swearing issue, but Dad was kicking off again about the Jaguar situation. Mum told him to put a sock in it.

I didn't talk much as a kid and they probably thought I wasn't listening. I felt detached from the absurdity of the everyday. I stared blankly at the blurred stream of green and yellow outside the window and dreamt of flying this low in a fighter jet. Secretly, I was in training.

We duly arrived at the party and made it past the introductions without a single thirteen-letter word. The do was well under way, with scores of business types mingling, networking and slurping their way up the corporate food chain. My old man was holding forth as ever, entertaining a group of young managers with a mixture of jokes and forthright discussions, interspersed by plenty of vigorous gestures and raucous laughter. Dad's laugh was infectious. His eyes creased and his broad mouth spread into the enchanting grin that epitomised his joie de vivre.

I was loitering around the food table like a time bomb waiting to explode. I was already programmed with the view that the world was populated by good guys and bad guys, and in this room full of small talk and grown-ups I decided to break free of my shyness and act on a judgement call.

The boss was breezing past when I caught his eye. He felt he had to stop and feign some interest.

'How is school then … uh … Ben?' he asked.

'Why can't my daddy have a Jaguar?' I replied.

He made some more talking noises that failed to make an impression on me, so I kicked him squarely in the testicles.

A small boy was ideally placed for such an attack. What I lacked in firepower was more than made up for by the accuracy gained from being at eye level with the target.

Judging by the way the boss's legs buckled as he doubled over, I'd properly rung the bell on his High Striker. The second pain-wave swept across him, tears welled in his eyes and he dropped to his knees, straining to get his breath back. Something about the bell-bottoms draped from

his parted legs on the Oriental rug made him look entirely ridiculous. The whole party erupted with laughter. The boss was as popular in the office as David Brent.

The importance of being truthful and standing up for myself had been instilled in me by my parents; I just added my own interpretation. Dad deserved that car and the boss was a troll under the bridge for suggesting otherwise. 'Truth Tourette's' has stuck with me ever since. I can't say that it's made life easy, but I've enjoyed busting a few balls.

Dad didn't get the Jaguar that time but he made up for it in later life. He changed cars as often as he emptied the ashtray. He must have owned about forty of the things. As soon as he could afford one, he bought it.

In spite of the love of cars that pervaded our family, my sole ambition was to be a fighter pilot. I wanted supersonic speed and the superhuman reflexes to go with it. I read endless accounts of Jump Jets winning in combat simulations against scores of faster but less nimble American F-14 Tomcats. My bedroom was littered with posters of fighter planes and books detailing every conceivable weapons system and their theatre of operation. I memorised payloads, thrust-to-weight ratios and the minutiae of flight. One hundred per cent nerd alert.

Repeated high scores on the Star Wars Arcade game proved to me that my acceptance into the RAF was a mere formality. 'Waive the vetting process, fellas, send this one straight up to splash Migs.'

Mum recommended I go for an eye test just to be sure.

I perched on a leather stool and after considerable winding it was high enough for me to view the testing screen. I stared at a sequence of glowing shapes inside a hooded computer, listening to the optician's breathing as he tapped his keyboard. His swivel chair clattered across the floor and he whispered a string of impatient instructions.

The test was over after a few minutes. My stomach tightened with a flush of excitement. I had taken the first step on a greater path.

'How did I do?'

The optician glanced briefly in my direction. 'They wouldn't even let you load the bombs, son, let alone fly one.'

If he had only known how close his crown jewels were to extinction, he might have shown some respect. In Han Solo's vernacular, I had jumped out of warp speed straight into an asteroid belt. My hopes and dreams evaporated. I was grounded.

I hated being told what I couldn't do, but it was a powerful tonic. The harder they push you down, the harder you come back up, overcome and overwhelm. Mind you, there was no overcoming my eyesight.

Mum tried to console me by suggesting other possible careers – the forestry commission perhaps? I sat in my room for hours surrounded by pictures of machines that I would never fly.

My competitive instinct discovered another outlet for my emotions. My introduction to swimming was not exactly of my own volition, but it was the best thing that could have happened.

The Collins family moved to California when I was five; my father had been hired to turn around a haulage firm. My parents took me to the local swimming club. The coach was a tanned surfer dude with sun-bleached locks and a ripped torso. I shivered at the side of the pool, looked at the other kids pounding lengths, and decided against it.

Dad had a temper that was even quicker than his wit and I went to great lengths to avoid it.

'Ben, get in.' He didn't look pleased.

'No,' I replied anxiously.

He went for the grab and I dived for cover. I managed to hook my arm through a sun-lounger, which came with me as Dad lassoed my kicking legs and pulled them towards him. I knew I was safe as long as I could hold on to that lounger. Dad upped the ante. He picked up the lounger with me attached and threw the job lot into the pool. I was in at the deep end and it was a case of sink or swim or come up with an alternative cliché.

I was furious and puny and grew angrier still as Dad looked down at me, failing to restrain his laughter. I set off at a rate of knots to the other end of the pool. Reluctantly, I discovered I was quite a fast swimmer.

After my turbulent initiation, I enjoyed training with the club and began competing. The whole family turned out for my first appearance at a regional gala and my grandma wished me good luck. 'Go and win all your races,' she told me. To my astonishment, I did. Winning felt good; it gave me a sense of purpose.

The Ojai Valley swim team punched well above its regional weight and I was soon competing at Junior Olympic standard. Our coach wrote training exercises on a blackboard during our daily sessions and I learnt never to read too far down. If the top read '600m', that was all that

mattered, even if the next line read '1,000m through crocodile infested swamp'. Focusing on anything but the present only made life harder.

The techniques were challenging, sliding your arms in a controlled arc around your body to propel yourself through the water. Mastery over breathing was essential and it developed the cardio-vascular system. The controlled intake and release of air was calming and a vital element for keeping the body platform stable and fast.

I was good but I tended to get carried away trying to go too fast, spinning my arms through the water like a windmill.

The explosive nature of the races was all-consuming.

The word 'can't' was banned by our coach, but regardless how hard I trained with him or how much I attacked the water, I felt unable to produce true excellence. Without that goal, swimming became a hobby rather than my sport. But it remained an invaluable introduction to the art of mental and physical conditioning that would prove essential in racing, and beyond.

3

WINNING

I wanted to be inspired by something I could excel at, consumed with a passion to succeed. I caught the first glimpse of the path I wanted to choose on my eighteenth birthday.

My father's exceptional gift was a trial in a single-seat racing car at the Silverstone Grand Prix circuit. I had only been driving for a few months – around the country lanes in my mother's L-plated 4x4, with her riding shotgun. Mum hit me so often with her handbag that she broke the handle. Apparently I 'left no margin for error'.

Dad had been raving about his experiences of racing; he'd just started competing himself. After a tooth-jarring trip across the snaking stretches of the Cotswolds with him working the wheel, we arrived at the circuit gates.

The moment we pulled off the road, the tarmac inside became more generous. Grandstands grew skywards in preparation for a big event and the unusual barrier walls were painted in blue and white blocks. I caught glimpses of the track from behind the grass banks. The bare breadth of bitumen with no road markings was unlike anything I had ever seen.

I climbed into one of my old man's racing suits and tied on what looked like blue ballet shoes. A man gave a briefing to a group of us that involved plenty of crashing and potential death. We were using the high-speed Grand Prix circuit and had to show it due consideration.

The racing car was nothing much to look at. It lacked Formula 1 wings and hardly made a sound as the mechanics fired it up, but every component had an essential purpose. Business-like wheels carrying 'slick' tyres with no tread on them were attached to bony steel suspension arms bolted to a slender steel frame tub, at the front of which sat the nose, honed like the tip of a rocket. The bodywork was trim and crafted purely for speed.

Standing off to one side, I raised my right leg over a sidepod containing the cooling system, and into the cockpit. I rested one arm on the highest point of the car, just 30 inches from the ground, then pulled in the other leg. Standing on the moulded seat, I gripped the sides and slid my feet forwards.

The rev counter, speedo, oil and water temperature gauges were hidden behind the small black steering wheel, along with numerous mysterious buttons. The stainless steel gear stick to the right was the size of a generous thumb. It shifted with a delicate 'thunk' from one gear to the next.

My feet touched the pedals jammed closely together ahead of me. The brake was solid as a brick, the throttle stiff until you applied pressure, when it responded precisely to tiny movements. The steering felt heavy with no power assistance, only the strength I applied to it transferring energy to the front wheels which I could see turning ahead of me.

I tightened the belts and they jammed me into the seat, connecting me to the car. The hard seat grated at the bones in my shoulders. Everything was so alien, yet I knew it then. I was home.

The instructor deftly turned a red lever a quarter turn clockwise, flicked a pair of switches and an orange light glowed; the car was alive. 'Put your right foot down a quarter of an inch.'

I responded.

He pressed a black button and a high-pitched squeal was followed by the rhythmic churn of the engine. It sparked into life and beat an eager pace, rumbling faster than any car I had ever heard. The sound alone was enough to splash adrenalin through my veins. I was at the edge of the unknown. The responsive throttle, the direct steering, the beating engine, the slick gearbox … All were built with a single purpose: speed.

My first laps were shonky; I missed gears and adjusted to the precision of the controls. Once I built up some speed the steering became intense

and darty. When I ran over a bump the floor actually hit my backside, I was sitting that close to the ground. The sense of speed in a straight was pale by comparison to the corners.

The belts dug into my shoulders as I sped through the turns like a cruise missile, albeit a largely unguided one. I pushed the envelope a little further with every lap.

I overcooked it several times and spun at Copse, the fastest corner. The wall was close to the track and I sensed danger until the car miraculously pointed itself in the right direction. I pushed on.

The session ended in a flash, a million years too early. I reluctantly pulled into the pits and spotted Dad in the distance next to one of the Ray Ban-toting instructors. In spite of numerous No Smoking signs, he had a Marlboro 100 glued to his bottom lip and was clapping his four-fingered hand. He'd lost the little digit rescuing a horse.

My times equalled the track record for the car. Ray Ban man was telling my dad he should really get me into a race. The old man was clearly sold on this plan all along. We had to convince my mother, but I figured another trip around the country lanes should do the trick.

From that moment on, my sole ambition, my obsession was to race. The life I lost as a pilot was reincarnated as a racing driver. Every day from then until this morning my eyes opened to the same living dream. I wanted to be a Formula 1 champion. Nothing else mattered.

The traditional route to Formula 1, or to any top category in motor sport, was to compete in go-karts from the third trimester. I'd grown up competing in pretty much every other way, as a swimmer, on skis and getting out of scrapes at school. I had the killer instinct to win, but no experience of motor racing, and it was a major disadvantage. Not that I saw it that way.

I duly obtained a racing licence at Silverstone and found myself looking down at aggressive short people. Karting, with its performance so closely linked to weight, had weeded out the big ones.

I joined the bottom rung of the racing ladder: Formula First. It was derided as a championship for nutters and the scene of too many crashes. It was the cheapest form of single-seater racing and the best way to go about winning my way to Formula 1. Piece of cake.

The other drivers wore colourful helmet designs and important looking racing overalls plastered with sponsors. Dad suggested I start out with something simple based on the Union Jack. In the end I opted for

an all-black race suit, black gloves, black boots and a black Simpson Bandit helmet with a black-tinted visor ...

From the first day I began testing the car, every waking thought revolved around a single subject: driving fast. With no prior racing experience, I learnt the trade by word of mouth, from books about great drivers like Ayrton Senna and Gilles Villeneuve, magazine articles and television. Mostly, I learned the hard way by just doing it. And shit happened.

One bit of training saved my life many times over. I attended a skid control course, which had nothing to do with brown underpants. The instructor, Brian Svenson, was a former wrestler known as 'The Nature Boy'. He had no neck but gave plenty of it as he talked me through his Ford Mondeo, fitted with a rig that could lift the front or rear wheels off the ground to make them slide.

Every time I turned the steering, the rear would spin sideways as if it was on ice. My hands flayed at the wheel like a chimpanzee working the till at McDonald's. Fingernails went flying, the horn was beeping, and before I knew what had happened we were sailing backwards.

Brian pressed a button on the control panel in his lap and calmly pulled the handbrake. The car came to a rest in a cloud of burnt rubber and I relaxed.

'Oversteer, *right!*' he barked.

'OK. What does that mean?'

'Well in that case it means the fooking car spun around, yeah. You lost the back end, so it feels like the car is turning too much. Over. Steer.' His words sank in.

'When it 'appens, feed the steerin' into the slide as fast as you can. None o' that DSA shuffling bollocks. You've quick reactions, just spin that wheel across a bit further.'

'OK, Brian.'

Off we went again. My psychotic instructor pressed more buttons as we approached a tunnel of orange cones with an inflatable obstacle at the far end. I turned the steering left to dodge the obstacle and nothing happened, so I turned more.

'Stop turning,' ordered Nature Boy.

'Sod that.' I turned more. Nothing.

Whumpf.

'Shit.'

'You can say that again.'

'What happened then, Brian?'

'*Understeer,* right. When you turn nothin' happens. The car goes straight on, yeah?'

'What should I do?'

'Not much you can do, but turning more only makes it worse. Just get the speed off then the grip comes back.'

We upped the speed to 60. After several gut-wrenching 360-degree spins, Nature Boy taught me to flick my head around like a ballerina to see where I was going and control it. It was incredible. We would enter a corner at pace and the car would start rotating. Wherever I looked, my hands would follow and the car pointed back in the right direction.

I started to complete lap after lap of the circuit, drifting from one gate through to the next. I forgot I was even carrying a passenger until the sound of Nature Boy clapping brought me back to my senses. I realised that Brian could no longer unseat me.

'Excellent. You've got it. When's your first race?'

'Next week, at Brands Hatch.'

'What you driving?'

'Formula First, at the Festival.'

'Oh Christ,' he said, biting his top lip. '*Good luck.* Just try and remember what I've taught ya. If you can tell your mechanic what the car's really doing, you'll go far.'

Formula First was a series for 'beginners'. The grid for my first event boasted a karting world champion, two national champions and race winners from the previous season. Most had been racing karts since they swapped nappies for Nomex. After several days of learning to drive the car at labyrinthine circuits like Oulton Park, I arrived at Brands for my first motor race.

Brands Hatch being a former Grand Prix circuit, even I had heard of this place. Formula First was supporting the Formula Ford Festival that was host to over a hundred of the best aspiring drivers in the world.

I approached my first qualifying session with the intention of re-enacting my best driving at every corner. As an inexperienced driver, just re-creating a way of driving through a corner time after time was a big challenge. It was key to posting consistent lap times. To the surprise of everyone in the championship, I qualified third on the grid.

After a short lunch break it was time for the race. I stumbled out of the Kentagon Restaurant with a bellyful of nerves and beef casserole. I was immediately accosted by a race official with a breathalyser.

I breathed gingerly into the machine. 'Do you actually catch anyone drunk on race day?'

'Five so far.'

I didn't even drink, but I was apprehensive.

'You're all clear.'

I hurried to the pits and climbed into the car. My young mechanic straddled the top cover and heaved down on the shoulder straps with all his weight, strawberry-faced with the exertion.

After confirming that I could still breathe, he shot me a knowing smile that said, 'One lamb, ready for slaughter.'

'Good luck,' he said.

I gave him a gobsmacked thumbs up. My heart rate was off the Richter scale. Wave upon wave of adrenalin hardened my veins. The back of my throat swelled, my mouth dried and the left side of my face tingled. *What the hell am I doing?* I was so tired. I hadn't slept the night before and would rather have griddled my testicles on the exhaust than drive at that particular moment.

Get a grip, I thought, I'm here to get to F1. Problem was, so were the other lads.

Sweat on the pad of my left foot made my toes slip inside my boots as I depressed the clutch and nudged the gear-stick left and forward. Every movement I made felt strained and heavy.

Moving into the pit lane, I joined the two long columns of the dummy grid. After what felt like an eternity (no more than five minutes) we were waved out of the pit lane under a green flag. More adrenalin, and now I needed to piss.

The copious advice I'd been given swirled around in my head. 'Lay some rubber on the start line for extra traction', 'Warm the tyres up', 'Anticipate the start lights', 'Go when the red goes out, don't wait for the green', 'Don't look in your mirrors'. After one short lap we formed up on the grid. I searched the start line gantry for the lights.

A white board with 'five seconds' written on it suddenly appeared from behind the gantry. Acid flooded my stomach.

Three seconds later the red lights sparked up. I knew that sometime between three and eight seconds after that they would switch to green.

The engines in front of me began revving. The driver alongside started chasing the throttle – on, off, on, off, louder and louder. Adrenalin dumped painfully into my chest and my heart slowed into a hard, raging thump. The force of the beats was so strong I had to drop my chin and open my mouth to catch a breath. I winced; my eyes glazed over. GREEN.

I bolted off the start line, then the wheels spun wildly. Another car instantly appeared to my right, then two others powered up to my left as we approached the first corner. I was jammed right in the middle.

My thumping heart slowed, crashing against my ribs with the weight of a sledgehammer. For a moment I thought the damn thing might actually stop.

I swallowed hard, gulped for air and edged into the fast sweeping right-hander at Paddock Hill. I was at the centre of a swarm of jostling machines, so close you could have covered ten of us with a blanket. Somehow my body carried on the business of driving and breathing.

The pack screamed through the dip at the bottom of the hill. The car in front bottomed out in the compression, shooting a shower of sparks at my helmet. I followed the four leaders into the tight right at Druids, narrowly avoiding the one immediately in front as he jammed on his brakes earlier than I expected.

Gears changed on auto-pilot, iron-clenched fists dragged the steering from one direction to another. We blasted through the fast Graham Hill left-hander line astern, like a rollercoaster without rails.

Wheel to wheel, nose to tail, we hammered along the short straight at nearly 100mph. As we sped into the Surtees Esses I was so close to the guy in front I couldn't see the raised kerb past his rear wheels. My jaw clamped shut.

I somehow braked for the final corner, the right called Clearways. I went in too fast and lost control of the front wheels. I knew I'd lose a position if I couldn't accelerate on to the straight. I forced the throttle to try and drive out of the mistake. The car was already past the limit and the rear snapped sideways. Already off line for the corner, I slid off the edge of the track into the gravel trap and towards the welcoming tyre barrier.

As the wall approached I pushed harder on the accelerator, peppering onlookers with stones from my spinning wheels but maintaining enough speed to get back on to the circuit. Having lost just one position, I

rejoined the pack and we buzzed down the pit straight to complete the first lap. I was exhausted.

During the eleven laps that followed spectators were agonised and baffled by the sight of me driving defiantly on the racing line as my competitors drove for the inside, time and again, in a bid to overtake me.

My father choked his way through two packets of Marlboro in the space of twenty minutes, lighting each fresh fag from the last. Every time I came round he was shouting at the top of his voice, 'Defend, defend, DEFEND YOUR LIIIINE!!!'

I heard nothing over the din of the engine. I was busy driving as fast as I could. Moving off line to defend meant driving slower and that didn't compute. I stayed persistently wide, braked as late as I dared and aimed at the apex of the corners like a missile.

I was oblivious to most of my near misses, but Dad had a bird's eye view as the other vultures pecked at my heels. Our wheels were interlocking at over 100mph and a single touch would have easily catapulted me into the air.

By some miracle, I finished unscathed having conceded a handful of positions. One of the spectators was a journalist called Charles Bradley, who had observed my antics from Clearways corner. A shard of flying gravel had cut his cheek, but he still gave me my first mention in *Motorsport News*: 'Ben is frighteningly fast ...'

I was intoxicated. I'd lived more in twenty minutes than in the rest of my life put together. The time that passed between races was just that, time passing. I dreamt racing, day and night. All my aspirations now centred on becoming the best driver in the world. After a couple more races, I managed to lead one, but was harpooned out of contention by the second-placed car – yet again I'd failed to defend the corner. But the taste of potential victory was firmly entrenched. I decided I should win every time from then on. In blinkered pursuit of that goal, I discovered ever more inventive ways to have enormous accidents, from silly shunts to full-blown hospitalisation.

On the Brands GP loop, I tried to outmanoeuvre two drivers by speeding around the outside of both into the super-fast Hawthorn right-hander. The guy on the inside squeezed the one to his left who did likewise and shoved mc on to the grass at 120.

I hit the Armco with such force that my head would have hit my knees had the dashboard not intervened. We never found the front left wheel,

but the whole front right corner went into orbit and landed on the straight in front of my team-mate. On the second bounce it took the sidepod clean off another car, then bounded into the trees.

I finally came to rest a few hundred metres down the track, regained consciousness and slowly opened my eyes. I was coated with bright green algae that inhabited the gravel trap. Like Bill Murray in *Ghostbusters*, I'd been slimed. The car now resembled a bathtub, a bare chassis with a single wheel loosely attached by some brake cable. My dense cranium had even broken the steering wheel.

Over time, I broke every component of the car from the drive shafts to the suspension, gearbox, engine, chassis, everything. I once tried to find a little extra power in a drag race to the chequered flag. I pushed harder on the accelerator, which broke the solid cast metal throttle stop and ripped the throttle cable out of the carburettor.

After I wrote off my third chassis, it was clear that the 'balls out' strategy needed fine-tuning. During qualifying at Lydden Hill I was on the limit through a fast right when I had to lift off to avoid a spinning car. Seconds later, I was spiralling through the air and sitting in a bathtub again.

Dad sprinted to my side, absolutely livid. Not only was he funding this enterprise, but it would have been his neck on the block if I'd been converted into a limbless corpse. I couldn't make the race, so I climbed into his car for a very long, silent drive home.

I knew he was pissed from the way he was twiddling his sideburns. After half an hour he said, 'What the fuck were you doing waving your arms around like that anyway? You could have lost an arm.'

'I was just ducking …'

He shot me an incredulous look.

'I've just had to buy that car you trashed. If they can't bend it straight, your season's over.'

It was my much needed wake-up call. It seemed I had an answer for every catastrophe, but no sense to avoid one. I had to preserve the car, only risking it in measured bursts when absolutely necessary.

A part-time job in a warehouse packing cheddar cheeses the size of breeze-blocks provided plenty of opportunity to analyse past events. I spent the rest of my time hanging out with my newly acquired girlfriend and practising essential driving skills in her Ford Fiesta. Georgie was a bit special in more ways than one. She could do a handbrake turn *and* spin the wheels at the same time. It was love at first sight.

I figured out that even if I was the best driver on a given day, I would never win every race because there were too many circumstances beyond my control. My problem was, I'd been forcing it. Every race had a natural order, a structure I had to respect and learn to predict. Once I accepted that, the frequency of my visits to the podium exceeded those to the infirmary.

I was totally focused on learning the craft. My body began reacting like an alarm clock, 'going off' weeks in advance of a big race. I prepared my logistics ahead of time, drove the track a million times in my head.

My naïve concept of sportsmanship took a hammering at Castle Combe. I learnt the ropes the hard way from my 'team-mate', a Formula First veteran who led the championship. He had a nose like a beak that found its way into my side of the garage whenever anything worthwhile was going on. Then it was all smiles, which front rollbar was I running, what tyre pressure worked best and so pleased to meet you, Mr Potential Sponsor, here's my card.

Later the same day I was leading him through a very fast corner on the last lap. He poked his nose up my inside but I held strong on the outside. He couldn't get through, and it felt like he steered into me and punted me off.

I slid across the grass like a demented lawnmower and rejoined to finish fifth, just behind him. A crimson haze descended over me, but I managed to resist the temptation to T-bone him on the way into the pit lane, drag him from the car and use my helmet on him as a baseball bat.

The next race was at Cadwell Park, the best track in Britain, with more pitch and fall in its curves than Pamela Anderson. I had terminal understeer in qualifying and ended up running behind my 'mate' in third place, but I had my evil eye on him. I drove the wheels off my machine and discovered the power of controlled aggression. The car bent to my will and unleashed a furious pace. The closer I got to my old pal, the more mistakes he made. We approached a section called 'The Mountain' where an S bend climbed a steep gorge and before I had the pleasure of dispatching his ass personally, he spun off the circuit. Good karma.

Motor sport was dog eat dog, which went against the grain after five years making friends for life in the process of surviving boarding school. Popularity in racing lasted as long as you were competitive, and people were prepared to go to any lengths to remain so. I found one driver

stealing my engine one night; another team sabotaged my suspension. But there were always a few rays of sunshine.

The final race of the year was at Snetterton in Norfolk, which had been a Flying Fortress base in the Second World War. Two giant straights connected two lurid high-speed corners and a couple of slow ones. I managed to get the team's senior mechanic on to my car. Colin was a grey-haired Lancastrian who'd won the championship with my team-mate. He had eyes like Master Yoda and talked me through what to do if and when I was in a position to actually win.

'Around this track the *last* thing you want to do is lead the final lap. Whoever is in second will draft past the leader on the back straight unless you slow down, so don't get stuck out in front or … *Jeezus Chriist*!'

Colin's gaze suddenly disappeared some way over my shoulder. 'Look at 'er, she's *gorgeous*!'

Still grappling with his advice, I looked to up to see the blonde bomb-shell swinging down the pit lane. Glimpses of her perfectly sculpted figure appeared from beneath a leather bomber jacket as she swished back her hair and beamed in our direction.

'That's my girlfriend, Georgie.'

'You must be *jokin'*!'

He had a point. I couldn't quite believe it myself.

I'd met her when we were seventeen and she took my breath away. I fell in love with her on Day One – she has one of those smiles that make you feel like the six million dollar man. My mates and I were all horrid little oiks who spent our whole time playing rugby and pouring buckets of water on to girls' heads as they walked beneath our windows, so I didn't give much for my chances. But a few months ago I'd somehow summoned the balls to invite her to a racing dinner – a very glamorous affair (not) at Brands Hatch's onsite hotel – where she won a tyre trolley in the raffle. She seemed to enjoy watching my car come back with fewer wheels with each successive contest. I can't think why; she was far too attractive and kind to be with me. When she entered a room my mouth filled with tar, reducing my vocab to Neanderthal grunting. Yet here she was looking lovely and looking at me, but …

'What do you mean – slow down to win?'

'Rule number one: to finish first, you must first finish, right? With these cars you sit two car lengths behind the ones in front to catch their

slipstream and draft past 'em on the straights. If you get one on yer tail, back off into the corner so he can't get a run on ya.'

I shared my newly acquired wisdom with Georgie over lunch. She was riveted. 'So does that mean you won't crash in this one?'

'I hope so,' I sighed.

The race that followed was a drafting masterclass. I became embroiled in a four-way scrap for second place whilst the leader ran away. Against every instinct, I backed off through a flat-out bend to put some space between me and the three cars in front. I braked slightly early for the next corner, Sear, then smashed the accelerator.

I hauled up behind the guy in front as he zigged left to overtake the other two running line astern. I stayed put and felt the suction of the two-car draft propelling me down the straight.

Whilst the relative speeds of the other three cars hardly changed, mine doubled. I pelted past all three in one move. I was fully clear as I approached the Esses corner and was so excited I nearly forgot to brake.

The leader was too far ahead to catch but I summoned the fury I found at Cadwell and strained every bit of speed out of my black bullet. I closed in on the final lap but not enough to pass, until he made a mistake at the final bend. I powered out of the chicane and we raced to the line. I won it by one tenth of a second.

Crossing the line first meant *the world* to me. And I'd learnt some key truths about the sport. Had I forced my overtaking moves early on, I would have crashed. Had I not driven flat out through every corner of every lap, I would have lost the crucial tenth of a second needed to win. It was a delicate balance, knowing when to risk everything and when to hold back. Luck had been a factor, but at least I had started making my own.

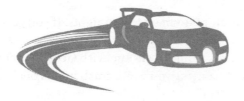

4

SNAKES & LADDERS

My second season produced a 100 per cent finishing record. A string of podiums and race wins put me into the lead of the Vauxhall Junior Championship, battling with talented pilots like Marc Hynes and Justin Wilson, two of the most genuine blokes in the sport. Marc was sponsored by Nestlé Ice Creams and looked a bit like one himself: a tall teenage vanilla speckled with hundreds and thousands. Justin was on his meteoric rise to Formula 1, somehow squeezing six foot four of northern sinew into a soapbox racer every weekend to post stupendously fast lap times.

I dropped cheese packing in favour of studying for a law degree, which absorbed nearly all my time when I wasn't racing. Turning into a very focused, self-centred daredevil meant my relationship with Georgie suffered. She gently bounced me into touch, and I was so hell bent on my career that I refused to acknowledge that my heart was, in fact, irretrievably broken.

My luck on track dried up around that time and I lost the championship to Mr Hynes, finishing alongside Wilson. But it was enough to get me noticed by the crack outfit run by Paul Stewart, Sir Jackie Stewart's son. Paul Stewart Racing was known for one thing in every category they competed in: winning.

PSR ran a team in the next rung up the racing ladder called Formula Vauxhall Lotus. The cars ran on fat slick tyres with Formula 1 style wings that shoved the rubber into the tarmac and a 2-litre engine that propelled the car through corners at over 145mph. Sexy piece of kit.

The first test was at Donington Park, a grey circuit in the Midlands. Its sequence of fast, flowing turns was made famous by Ayrton Senna's gutsy overtaking moves on the opening lap of the 1993 Grand Prix. I watched it more times than I can count.

I scanned the colourful articulated trucks lining the old brick pit lane and found the polished blue and white of PSR at their head. The team were always decked out in matching blue clothing and had a systematic approach to everything they did. The mechanics were like young doctors, and their work area looked like a spotless surgery. I prayed no dirt fell from my shoes as they clacked across the pristine plastic flooring.

Graham, or 'GT', the team manager, was a young guy with an endearing smile that belied his ruthless inner ambition. Underneath the rosy-cheeked veneer was a head shrinker who probed the depths of a driver's every performance via the onboard data logging system and by asking difficult questions.

'Did you notice we put another hole of front wing on, and you ran a heavier fuel load? How many laps do you think these tyres have done? Do you think a stiffer rear rollbar would help you through the fast corners if we drop the ride height and adjust the camber for the low speed? Why did you change your line into Turn One after lunch?'

Graham used onboard computers that logged the car's information and driver inputs. They were recorded so accurately that you could analyse every movement of the steering, brakes and throttle to develop the perfect style, which further deepened the mental dimension.

The Lotus accelerated from 0 to 60mph in three seconds and took me by surprise at first. The scenery went flying by and the engine was bumping off the rev limiter, demanding the next gear. Something clicked in my brain that day, because I never sensed speed the same way after that. Once I got used to it, nothing ever *felt* fast again.

The blind crests of Donington's Craner Curves were not for the faint-hearted as the sharp descent doubled your acceleration through a long left. In a machine like the Lotus with more relative grunt than grip, you hung your balls over the wing mirrors to take Craners flat, then wrestled the chassis across to the left in time to put your affairs in order for the equally hairy off-camber right known as 'Old Hairpin'. With tyres

stretched to the limit, a tiny error of timing was punished by a rapid departure from the black stuff.

I prepared for a new tyre run to see what time I could set. GT squatted next to me and rested his arm on the sidepod. If I could just impress him enough, Jackie Stewart's staircase of talent could lead me all the way to F1. After a silence, GT gave me a warm smile. At last I was winning him over. Then he casually said, 'We've just been watching Wilson at the Old Hairpin. He's flying, head and shoulders braver than anyone else there.'

The words cut me to the bone. I'd have preferred him to have called me a raging poof.

The winter air was crisp, ripe for the engine to produce its best power. After a mega run out of the first corner I took Craners flat out with a squeak of understeer from the new tyres, without compromising my line for the Old Hairpin.

The engine bounced off the limiter in top gear, I dabbed the brake and guided my missile right, carrying an extra 5 mph. It went in so fast the front wheel floated over a blurred apex kerb. I held on, ran wide and mullered the big exit kerbing. Dust spewed up and I knew the lap was already miles faster than anything the others had managed. I wanted to monster their times.

I left my braking super late into the next corner, a fast cresting right, at just over 140. The brake pedal hit the floor. I pumped again. Nothing. I was travelling 60mph too fast to make it. I was leaving the circuit. By the third touch of the brakes I was skipping across the grass, spinning sideways through the gravel trap, then airborne for the remainder of my journey. I stonked into the barriers with the rear left wheel first. It ripped off the suspension, shattered the gearbox casing and whipped the nose into the wall, shattering the front wing. What a ride!

My body took the impact well. I withdrew my hands from the wheel before it spun violently through 180 degrees, which would have broken my wrists had I clung on.

I explained what happened to Graham, who never looked up from his computer when I walked back in. 'Did you kerb it at the Old Hairpin?' he asked matter-of-factly as he frowned at my speed graphs.

'Big time.'

'Sounds like pad knock-off then.'

'What's that?'

The mechanics tutted behind me as they unbolted tangled remains of bodywork from the chassis and half the gravel trap unloaded on to their operating theatre.

'Sometimes when you hit the kerbs, it knocks the pads away from the discs. You have to pump the brake pedal back up to get them working again.' He waved a hand up and down for emphasis.

Well, wasn't I the moron? That kind of general knowledge would have been more useful at the start of the day, but that was how it worked with racing. You either figured it out, or got spat out.

Graham sucked his teeth with interest as he calculated my split time, acknowledging it would have put me fastest by a considerable margin. Then he looked me in the eye to ask if my neck was OK. Seemed he was warming to me after all.

The structure of the Winter Series consisted of two heats that qualified the drivers for the final at Donington – 'winner takes all'.

Graham taught me that there were no friends in a race and to 'kill the car' in the warm-up lap. The difference this made to the temperature and performance of the tyres and brakes over the first lap was significant and helped launch me into the lead of the qualifying heat.

I found myself battling with a Japanese regular from the series who was pressuring me with every trick in the book. He was tapping my rear wheel to unsettle my car into the corners, then driving into the back of me in the straights. The rev counter buzzed higher as the rear wheels left the ground. The gloves came off.

I waited until he was right up my chuff and jammed on the brakes so hard his front wing went under my gearbox and lifted me into the air. All our shenanigans were closing the field up behind us.

He got a run on me down the pit straight, pulled alongside and we banged wheels as we ran neck and neck towards the first corner. The third-gear right required a severe brake to avoid the sea of sandy gravel beyond. He stayed on the outside, ballsy to say the least.

I would sooner have driven off a cliff than be outbraked. I wasn't backing down. Neither was he, so our futures merged. His front wheel caught my rear and I flew over his sidepod. We rotated around one

another in *Matrix*-style slow motion, and gave the pursuing pack nowhere to go but straight into us. I was T-boned and as the spinning car flew overhead its rear wheel caught my helmet.

As the dust settled in the gravel trap I thought to myself, *Not again*. I never felt any fear when I raced, so I had to figure out a method for avoiding dumb accidents with people. I quickly rubbed the tyre marks off my helmet – otherwise the marshals would have insisted I bought another one – and trudged out of the gravel.

Graham was not amused, calling me a rock ape. The combined qualifying results put me in twelfth for the final race on Sunday. Overtaking opportunities in down-force cars were notoriously few, so my chances of winning were slim.

On the day of the final I arrived at the circuit early, determined on a positive result. Sir Jackie had already inspected the team ahead of his sponsors and guests, which included members of from the Royal Family. Pandemonium reigned and there were red faces everywhere. The race truck was being lifted into the air on stilts in order to rotate the wheels until their Goodyear logos all faced twelve o'clock. The floor was being washed and a gearbox moved.

Roland, the number one mechanic, was putting the finishing touches to my car's new undertray. I brought him some tea and he surprised me with a smile.

'You guys must hate me,' I said.

'Nah, mate. You're out there to win. We don't care how many times you smash it to bits – we'll rebuild it.'

It made all the difference having him onside. Roland increased the angle of attack of the dive plane on the front wing by raising it and screwing the bolt into its new hole. 'Adding a hole of wing' meant I could steer better behind the jet wash of the other racers. He asked what I thought of our chances. I told him I thought we could win.

The team's PR lady summoned me to the corporate hospitality unit with my team-mate, reigning Irish Formula Ford Champion Tim Mullen. We arrived on the team's golf buggy at a marquee the size of a football pitch for Jackie to introduce us to the sponsors.

Three hundred pairs of eyes turned in our direction from across the silver service. Tim's rusty red suit had seen five innings too many, and my scrunched black number was more bin man than Batman. Then Sir Jackie appeared, the triple Formula 1 World Champion, former Olympic

clay pigeon wizard and one of the most meticulous and successful drivers of all time.

Decked out in immaculate tartan trousers with creases that could slice roast beef, a beautifully cut tweed jacket and a bonnie cap, Jackie had the presence of a laird. He gave us both the once over and his beady eyes fell on me like a hawk. I sensed there might be warmth behind them if you were in reach of the podium.

The PR told him our starting positions. 'Tim is seventh and Ben is twelfth after a shunt in the second heat.' I wished she hadn't.

'Looks like you have some work to do today, lads.'

Och aye, that we did.

Jackie picked up the microphone and delivered a perfectly manicured talk about the team and the format of the day. We were excused.

I knew I had to impress him if I wanted to stay with PSR, and that meant really delivering in the final. I had the overtaking opportunities mapped out in my mind, the perfect start and the fastest laps. Scripts rarely survived first contact with the enemy, but preparing for success improved your odds.

I strapped in and sat on the grid with nothing left to consider except: 'patience, measured bursts'. Jackie made his extended walk down the grid, chatted with Graham for a bit before turning to me. 'Just remember, lad, it's what you have up here [pointing to my head], not down there [pointing to my balls] that wins races. The difference between the exceptionally brave and the plain stupid is a fine line.'

I listened carefully to the great man's advice, but something told me that I would definitely need my balls for this one.

The personnel cleared the grid – bar Roland, who held the jump battery. You fell in love with that last man the way a patient loves his nurse. Before going solo into the unknown, he was your final contact with the world. He signalled a thumbs up and cut the umbilical.

I stared at the pack of racers ahead. The green flag sent us off for the warm-up lap. Cars wove from side to side; one or two accelerated past their closest competitors and nearly collided. Everyone had eaten their Shredded Wheat that morning; no prisoners would be taken in the main event.

The formation closed up at the final chicane. I jumped on and off the throttle and brakes to ensure they were hot as hell. I found my pair of solitary black lines on the grid. *You guys are going down …*

First gear, revs to 5,400, the clutch bit.

The bright yellow five-second board rose over the gantry. Engines began pulsing. I crept forward an inch.

Red lights came on, then straight off; release, I was gone.

Everyone else froze, I powered off the line, instantly passing two crawlers and sliding past a third as I made the dreaded gear-change through the dogleg from first to second that could put you into a false neutral, with the race passing you by.

The drivers criss-crossed, searching for track position on the dash to the first corner. A queue stacked up on the inside, so I lunged for the outside to pass two on the brakes, hanging on as we squeezed over the jagged exit kerbs. I emerged wheel to wheel with another driver as we accelerated towards Craners. I had the inside line but on cold tyres the odds were even. He lifted first and I surged past. Sixth place already and closing on fifth.

We snaked through the back section of Donington and towards the chicane behind the pits where Jackie was hosting his VIPs. I wasn't lined up close enough to have a pop at the guy in front until he hesitated and braked early. I accepted the invitation and zapped past. I rode the inside kerbs and slithered sideways on to the straight, adjusting my sights to the view of just four cars ahead.

My Japanese friend in his silver bullet was pushing hard behind the lead group. I gave him a few close-ups in his mirrors to let him know he was next on my menu but it was hard following through the fast turns; you lost the air over the front wing and understeered wide. Running wide compounded the loss of grip because you ended up on the dirty section of track that was rarely driven on, typically covered in 'marbles' – chunks of rubber of various sizes that had the same effect as stepping on a banana skin.

After a trouser-ripping 130mph moment on the marbles, I remembered … *patience*. The opponent's turn in was heavy-handed and would lead to a mistake if I waited. We nosed over the rise on to the back straight at Coppice, I cut the apex, kept the front wing in clean air and got a run on him.

We drag-raced to the chicane. I pulled alongside, inches apart, and forced his hand. He braked desperately late, compromised his entry line and struggled to accelerate away. I sailed past into the next corner, the very place where we'd built sandcastles a day earlier. That left nine laps to pass two more and catch the leader.

With the race at full pelt, overtaking became harder, as drivers picked their optimum lines and dug in, but I held an advantage under braking. The front group were racing hard for position, trying to force a way past. It was winner takes all.

I lined up on Justin Wilson in third place. I got a run on him at Old Hairpin and gave him enough trouble through McLeans to pass him on the way out.

I chased down second into Redgate and found that my tighter line into the corner was yielding a couple of tenths a lap. The cornering mantra was always 'slow in, fast out'; taking a wider entry maximised your speed down the straight. But when the car allowed it, you could drive 'fast in, fast out'. It bagged me second place.

I saw Marc Hynes in the distance. Mr Whippy had managed to steer clear of the carnage I caused in the heat and was chasing down another championship. I was faster, but catching him with only a handful of laps to go was a tall order.

I set fastest lap after fastest lap until I finally got to sit on his gearbox. He was sluggish through Old Hairpin. I aced it. I powered up his right side, around the flat-out kink towards McLeans. With time running out, Marc put me on the grass.

I needed tarmac to round the kink at 120. As I went sideways my life should have flashed before me, but I was treated to a close-up of his Nestlé Ice Creams livery instead. I kept enough throttle trimming the lawn to lose only five car lengths. He had to defend at the chicane. I could taste victory as we rushed to complete the penultimate lap.

As I prepared to knobble Marc with the scissor shuffle, we were red flagged. A big accident behind us meant the race was being stopped. The jammy dodger took another title win ahead of me in second and Justin in third.

GT appeared, positively beaming. 'If you can drive like that every time you'll piss it next season. Incredible race; Jackie thought it was fantastic.'

A dream ticket was at the tips of my fingers. With the benefit of their vast experience I would have a clear shot at winning the main title …

But it was not to be. The feedback – via GT – was that I was 'too old'. PSR wanted to take on Justin. Halfway though the next season I made the jump to Formula 3 National Series instead.

★ ★ ★

The Formula 3 car was made of beautiful carbon fibre. Everything from the steering wheel to the gear lever were proper bits of kit. It had sophisticated push rod suspension like a Formula 1 car, with four-way adjustable dampers and a range of critical settings for tuning them.

It reacted to infinitesimal inputs from the driver. Visualising a perfect lap in your mind's eye was the only way to make the tiny adjustments needed to shave off the thousandths of a second on every corner that constituted the difference between pole and the rest.

Everything ran on a knife edge in Formula 3. It was the birthing pool for F1 talents, from Mansell to Schumacher and the great Ayrton Senna.

I won most of the remaining races from pole position, with fastest laps and a couple of lap records. It was time to move up to the International Formula 3 series and duke it out with the big boys.

In 1997 I took the seat vacated by Juan Pablo Montoya at Fortec. They were running Mitsubishi engines which had monstered the field in '96. The team manager reckoned that with me and Brian Smith (an Argentinian!) we should win the championship hands down.

Unfortunately the new spec Mitsubishi was a dud. Brian, Darren Turner, Warren Hughes (who ran Mitsubishi) and I only scored a handful of podiums between us.

It was time to prepare for the British Grand Prix support race at Silverstone. As always my old man was on hand, Marlboro in one hand and stopwatch in the other. He marked my split times through the different sectors and told me where I needed to improve.

He was so charming and gregarious, but he set the bar pretty high. I loved him to bits, but there were times when it wasn't that easy being his only son – or one of his workmates. They dubbed him 'Bionic Bill' because his idea of downtime was to stop working between midnight and five in the morning.

Having a poor engine meant that driving balls-out through the corners became *de rigueur*. I drove back to the pits after the kind of lap I could only repeat twice without crashing and sat down with David Hayle, my engineer, aka 'Mole'. Sweat dripped off my finger as we moved the cursor along the analysis screen. Formula 3 was all about perfectionism and absolute focus on one thing. Once that attitude became ingrained, it never left.

Mole lowered his specs and gave me a penetrating look. 'Do you need a few minutes to gather your thoughts, mate?'

I shook my head. 'Let's get it sorted before the next session.'

I recognised Dad's cough a mile away. 'Mark Webber's eating you alive coming out of Luffield …'

I was still glued to the monitor. 'We know.' I gritted my teeth, 'We've got power understeer in slow corners.'

'Why haven't you done something about it then? You look dog slow.'

My heart pounded and I leapt to my feet. 'Well go and smoke your fags at Maggots then.' We were standing eye to eye. 'I'm *pissing* on Webber through there.'

No one talked to him that way. His blood was boiling; my temples were pulsing. Silence. Dad tweaked his sideburn between finger and thumb. We would never come close to blows, but my money would have been on him if we had.

'Give it the beans at the weekend, son.' And with that, he left.

A couple of days later I did some media work with Uri Geller. It turned out that he was a car nut, a hazardous hobby for someone that warped metal just by touching it. I met him at his mansion on the Thames. He had a 1976 Cadillac that was covered in 5,000 bent spoons. He was a lovely guy and made absolutely superb coffee.

Uri didn't just bend spoons; he somehow managed to draw a shape that I had only pictured in my mind's eye: a broken arrow with a cross in its tail. He was full of common sense about sport psychology and was fascinated by my sponsor-finding challenges and my search for a competitive ride to propel me to F1. He conjured up an image I've recalled many times since, whenever I've felt frustrated: 'Each of us resides inside a bottle that is being carried by the current of a powerful river: fate. The shore is too far away to reach, but we can rock the bottle by running at the sides and though our efforts are small by comparison to the current we can influence our direction: perseverance.'

I believed in reaching the shore.

I rang Mum ahead of the race. After witnessing my first season she never attended in person.

'Hey, Mum, I met Uri Geller today.'

'You've upset him, you know?'

'You mean Dad? I know. All he does is criticise …'

'He's very proud. He probably didn't tell you, but he said he watched you all day at some fast corner called Maggie; said that you were the bravest …'

I swallowed hard. I was such an arsehole.

'We need more than bravery with this bucket. Maybe Uri can bend the pistons. Is Dad coming to the race?'

'I shouldn't think so. He's cross.' She sighed. 'You're both too *alike*.'

Uri arrived in the Grand Prix paddock as we were celebrating my team-mate's birthday a few hours before the start of the race. Brian's dad asked him to bend the knife we used to cut the cake, then rubbed it on the exposed part of the race car's exhaust system for luck. Uri left for the grandstand, setting off a chorus of car alarms in his wake.

The race got under way. Brian and I did our best to impress the Formula 1 teams in attendance, but he started to lose power and limped back to the pits. Joe Bremner, his number one mechanic, was first on the scene.

'What the bloody hell's gone on here?'

The exhaust had neither bent nor cracked; it had completely disintegrated – but only where Uri's knife had touched it. I don't buy into hocus-pocus, but none of the mechanics had ever seen anything like it before.

We didn't see the fabled forkbender again after that.

I spent a couple of years bouncing around America and Europe, maturing my skills alongside some truly great drivers like Scott Dixon and Takuma Sato. Scott went on to become the king of Indycar Racing. When I partnered him in Indy Lights he was one wild Kiwi who partied himself horizontal. He could also turn on the steely-eyed resolve in a heartbeat when it counted.

I also partnered Honda's Formula 1 protégé Takuma Sato, a wily, wiry, utterly fearless Japanese. We won races in International F3 and I came second in the Marlboro Masters World Series round at Zandvoort. Taku outqualified me in the dry, but in testing at Spa in Belgium I was comfortably faster in the wet. My car was so good that I was the only driver taking the infamous Eau Rouge corner flat out. As the race itself got under way, the waterlogged track was quickly obscured by a dense mist of spray. Taku pulled into the lead and was first to come

within sight of the teams as he blatted down the pit straight, towards Eau Rouge …

Boyyo, Taku's sublime race engineer, was perched on the pit wall. He dropped his lap chart, hastily grasped his radio and whimpered 'No Taku, don't …'

The rain was much heavier than it had been during the test. Taku made it past the first painted kerb with his foot welded to the floor, ran into a pool of water, aquaplaned and spun 180 degrees, straight into the tyre wall. It was pure 24-carat balls, and I absolutely loved him for that.

My performances were enough to gain some interest from a couple of Formula 1 teams and I investigated an opportunity to become the test driver for Arrows. This was the break I'd been longing for since Day One. I didn't have a manager, so Dad came to the meeting to impart some common business sense to the discussion.

We had a chat with a couple of nice chaps from their commercial team. We guzzled tea and biscuits in the boardroom until it was time to bring out the brass tacks. The test drive was mine for a very reasonable £1.5 million.

I tried not to choke on my tea and wondered what they charged per gulp. I was appalled at my sheer ignorance of the industry and the level of finance shaping these decisions. The sponsors who had supported me so far would turn tail and head for the hills.

But I had a back-up plan. It worked for Michael Schumacher; maybe it would work for me.

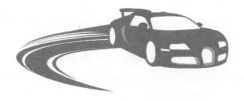

5

LE MANS 24

Two million roadside spectators watched the 1903 race from Paris to Bordeaux. Two hundred and seventy-five drivers slammed their cumbersome rides of metal and wood up and down dale for the glory of a face full of dust, in what was dubbed the 'race of death' after numerous fatalities along its 351-mile stretch.

Road racing was shut down, but their mission to measure the advancement of design through competition survived.

The Automobile Club de l'Ouest responded by creating a closed Grand Prix circuit at Le Mans in 1906, and the twenty-four hour course along the main roads to Mulsanne and back via Arnage in 1923.

The route from Arnage was later altered to take in the fearsome Porsche curves, a sequence of fast encounters where the outcome of each bend determined the fate of the one following. A last-ditch heave on the brakes at the Ford chicanes led onto the pit straight for a glancing moment at the pit board before engaging on a lap where 85 per cent of the journey would be spent on full throttle or braking because your life depended on it.

I travelled to Le Mans in 1997, to pre-qualify a 600bhp turbo-charged Porsche GT2 for the 65th outing of the endurance classic. By lunchtime the car was ready and I was blasting over the kerbs of Dunlop chicane, under the bridge and down to the Esses where you cornered at a seemingly impossible speed, veered left, then shimmied right over a blind rise.

Tertre Rouge was no mere dalliance. The ancient flowing right had to be taken balls to the wall in fourth gear to v-max the motor on the 4-mile Mulsanne straight. The Porsche 456s of the Eighties stretched their legs to 253mph here before the chicanes were put in. I settled for a humble 194, dispatching the chicanes with a twitter from the abs, hurling in and chasing away again, hanging on to the bouncing tail. I was still learning the place as I went; at 8.5 miles per lap it took over ten minutes just to run three laps. Then I noticed black smoke billowing over the treetops.

I kept on it as far as Mulsanne corner, the slowest point on the circuit, with a curved braking point that welcomed the brave and the good to overcook it and wind up at a roundabout full of locals taking photos and gnawing French sticks. Been there, done that, worn the onions.

The Porsche bucked from the hard lip of the blue and yellow apex kerb and stopped just in time to keep me on the black. From a virtual standstill I nuked the gas, spooled up the turbo and began the long charge to a top speed of 202 on the approach to Indianapolis, the fastest road race corner in the world. But that smoke was too much to be a BBQ. My heart wasn't in it any more. I coasted and turned right at Arnage towards the Porsche Curves.

There was smoke everywhere, mostly from the trees where a raging ball of fire was being tackled by the marshals. A few bits of torn bodywork lay on the grass along with something that didn't belong there and I wished I hadn't seen – the shocking remains of a helmet belonging to a young French knight called Sebastian Enjolras, who had been killed at high speed moments earlier.

Our entry was withdrawn before the race and it would be four years before I could return to continue the journey.

There was never a straight line in my career. I was given a drive at Donington in an ageing Le Mans prototype, the highest category above GT. The car I wanted to be in was the Ascari piloted by South African Werner Lupberger, a silver arrow with vents like shark gills, a razor-sharp nose and plenty of sponsors on the livery. It was reliable, fast and sexy. My machine was dayglo orange dotted with black rectangles that neatly camouflaged the tank tape holding together the bodywork.

Werner was on pole. As he led the field in this round of the FIA World Sportscar Championship, his engine cut out. My misfiring heap was barely mobile at the time and promptly died at the same corner, so I walked back to the pits with him.

Werner was as brown as a berry, with hair like a hedgehog and a thick Afrikaner accent. He looked exceptionally fit. In the course of conversation he mentioned that Ascari was running a series of shoot-out tests to find him a team-mate. He suggested I go for it.

The team was owned by Klaas Zwart, a Dutch engineering genius who made a billion from the oil industry. Klaas was bald and tanned and never sat still.

'There's twenty guys on the phone right now, F1 drivers some of them, and none of them can match Werner's pace in the Ascari. Tell me why I want you in my team ...'

I told him I would win races, that I was the man to push Werner, that no one else would work harder. Klaas took me at my word and arranged an evaluation test. Next stop, Barcelona.

Even at 7am the heat was making its presence felt. Ascari's number one mechanic, Spencer, looked me over with unsmiling eyes. His work area was spotless, every spanner, every component just so. We made a fitted foam seat and I asked about adjusting the pedals.

'That's how Werner drives it. Should be good enough for you.'

The Circuit de Catalunya had some brutally fast corners that went on for ever. The other turns flowed from one to the next, giving little respite. I watched Werner exit the fast corner on to the pit straight at 130mph. Within 300 metres of him stamping his foot to the floor, it was licking along at 180 and generating nearly 4G in the corners. He brought it into the pits and the belts over his chest rose and fell as he drew breath. He stripped to the waist, revealing muscles as shredded as Rocky Balboa's, then chewed into his drinks bottle like a butcher's dog.

I climbed aboard, tightened the straps until I could barely move and scanned the array of switches and LED lights that lined the dashboard. I began firing the engine and heard the most beautiful bark of V10 power. The Ascari LMP's Judd F1 engine churned out 650bhp on a Lola chassis. With no power steering it demanded hand-to-hand combat.

Werner chilled out and enjoyed the show as I spent my first laps hitting the rev limiter. The Ascari accelerated so fast that you had to pull through the gears on the sequential box as fast as your arm could snatch the lever.

The power would spin the wheels in fourth gear on a dry track, so you didn't switch off for a second. The wind at 180 blasted through the open cockpit and tried to rip your head off.

Braking from high speed using the giant F1-style carbon disc brakes involved standing on the pedal. I applied twice my body weight in pushing force to activate the down-force grip. After twenty laps I lost all feeling in my right foot.

The faster I dived into the corners, the more the wings gripped and the heavier it steered. It was like going ten rounds in the boxing ring and I was hanging off the ropes. My arms were jacked full of lactic acid and the temptation to ease up on the wheel was immense, but that meant slowing down or ending up in the wall. I loved this beast.

When I returned to the pits, our race engineer appeared and stepped casually in front of the car with his clipboard. Brian was wiry and had a moustache like Dick Dastardly. 'How was that, then?'

There was no disguising the effort I'd put in. My chest was heaving and I was sweating bullets. 'This car … is awesome … the best thing I've ever driven.'

Werner asked me how I found the steering by comparison to Formula 3.

'F3 was a piece of piss.'

'Yessus, man,' he grinned. 'Wait till you try it on new tyres; that makes it even heavier.'

At the end of the day Brian gave his verdict on my performance. Werner's time charts were metronomic, mine weren't, but I was the first driver they'd tested who could match his pace on old tyres. The seat was mine. I was signed by a works team.

To max the speed of a Le Mans car for four hours at a time required a supreme level of strength and endurance. It meant starting a completely new physical training regime.

I spent four hours a day in the gym, pushing tonnes of weights in a variety of unpleasant ways – attaching them to my head, running with them and pushing repetitions until I could barely lift a pencil. Then I'd run or swim for hours to build stamina.

Back in the days of leather helmets and goggles, an endurance race was a different kettle of fish. When Duncan Hamilton won Le Mans in 1953,

he was so drunk that the team offered him coffee during the pit stops to keep him going. He refused, accepting only brandy.

These days Le Mans was a twenty-four-hour sprint. The cars withstood thousands of gear-shifts, millions of piston revolutions and constant forces on every component. You couldn't afford to break them, but you couldn't afford to slow down either. You took turns with your team-mates to thrash the living hell out of it. We drove every lap like a qualifier. The physical and mental commitment to maintaining that performance was absolute, making it the purest all-round challenge in motor racing.

The eclectic mix of experienced amateurs and professionals raced an equally diverse range of machinery, from brawny Ferrari and Porsche GTs that resembled road cars to the 700 horsepower flying saucers loosely called 'prototypes' – basically Formula 1 cars wearing pretty dresses.

Audi's prototype was the one to beat. Their mechanical reliability was matched by outright pace. A gearbox change used to take a couple of hours in the old days. Now when Audi blew one, they bolted on another, complete with suspension joints, in just four minutes.

In 2001 the rain was torrential for nineteen hours of the twenty-four, and the swarm of cars skated along the straights like skipping stones.

From midnight until four in the morning I hammered around an eight-mile track, avoiding an accident every time I put the power down.

On my first visit to Le Mans I was lucky to even make the graveyard shift, following a disastrous run in the daytime. The crew had whipped off the wheels and banged a fresh set of tyres on to the red-hot discs whilst I stayed in the car. As the fuel hose slammed home and started pumping, I felt cold liquid fill the seat of my pants.

I thumbed the radio button. 'I think I've got fuel running down my neck.'

A look at the fuel rig revealed nothing out of the ordinary, but my backside was swimming in icy liquid.

There was no time for debate. Besides, I couldn't believe it myself. I drove away and my skin began to tingle at first, then started burning. This wasn't imaginary. I was forced to pit again. Werner was in the crew bus attending to the blisters on his hands and caught the first glimpse of my burning buttocks.

'Vok, you all right, man? That's one hot botty.'

Hours later it was my turn to drive again. Raindrops the size of golf balls created eruptions in the standing water. A journalist saw me waiting my turn in the garage and said, 'You must be absolutely dreading this. It's your first time here, isn't it?'

'I can't wait to get out there,' I said, jogging on the spot. 'This is what it's all about.'

He probably wrote me off as cannon fodder.

The team manager was Ian Dawson, who cut his teeth at Lotus Formula 1 team back in the days of Colin Chapman. He still had the retro moustache to prove it. Ian appeared at my side, lifted one of his radio cans and yelled into the front of my helmet. 'It's absolutely torrential out there. Harri's just done three complete 360 spins down the straight at 160 miles an hour. He's coming in this lap. We're bloody lucky to still have a car. We're running seventeenth. There's plenty of time. Just take it easy.'

The intensity in his voice spoke volumes. I was holding the baby.

An empty space in front of the garage was surrounded by the Ascari boys. Fireproof masks covered their faces, but I could see Don the mad Kiwi itching his nose with the wheel gun, big Dave on the fuel hose flicking his ankle to loosen off, Spencer with the other gun bouncing on his quads to warm up.

At any moment the space would be filled and I would have twenty seconds to climb in, strap up and switch on.

Every one of the boys had a critical job to do and they shared the pressure of the moment. The fuel man had to ram the hose home in a single clean movement. It sounded easy, but it wasn't. If he got it wrong he could barbecue every member of the team.

The mechanics on the pneumatic guns had practised the drill over and over again, so they could get clear as fast as possible without cross-threading a wheel nut. If any one of us made the slightest cock-up, it would cost seconds of hard-fought track position.

The car appeared, larger than life and shedding a heap of water. Harri Toivonen fought the belts off and leapt out. I barged past him and took his place. The seat felt wet and warm as my suit absorbed the water.

Harri lifted his visor and helped me with my belts. His face was red, eyes bulging, chest heaving. I pulled up both thumbs to let him know I was in OK and could finish the job myself.

The Ascari dropped on to the deck; the signal was given. My hands were poised over the ignition and start buttons and I cranked the motor. It was already in first gear. A touch on the throttle provoked a lightning howl. The Kraken was fully awake. I slipped the clutch and pulled away into the night.

I was soaked to the skin within seconds. Goblets of water fell out of the sky, whirring towards me at warp speed. As I slid under the Dunlop bridge my visor picked up the blurred lights of the Ferris wheel and intermittent bursts of flash photography. Only die-hard fans stayed out in this.

I sped on, my headlamps carving a 50-metre tunnel through the darkness. I accelerated away from Tertre Rouge in third gear and hammered down the Mulsanne straight, scanning for other cars, searching for puddles. The glistening surface ahead gave nothing away.

I had no idea where Harri had run into trouble. If I made the same mistake I might not be so lucky. I approached the first chicane, scanning sideways along the Armco barriers for something to reference: the marshal's post, the tree, the gap in the wall, anything that wouldn't move, for use as a braking point.

I turned right a little for the chicane, then regretted it and straightened again as the car aquaplaned. My stomach tightened as the wheels lost contact with the road; I resisted the temptation to over-correct the steering or brake harder and waited for the car to 'land'. The engine note returned, telling me the worst was over.

I accelerated cautiously out the other side and back on to the straight, short-shifted into fifth gear and everything went deathly quiet.

The car hit a river of water on the left side of the track at a speed of 150mph. All four wheels lost contact with the tarmac and I travelled 100 metres in freefall. The rear of the Ascari yawed to the right, verging on a fatal high-speed spin, crossed to the right side of the track and ran fast towards the grass. Once there I had another four metres before engaging with the Armco barrier. The odds favoured a hit more than a skim. Broken suspension at the very least.

Drastic action was required.

I stopped correcting the slide and centred the steering in a supreme effort to keep off the grass. As the wheels brushed the white line bordering the circuit the puddles retreated and the car straightened up. The Mulsanne straight had two chicanes to prevent speeds exceeding

250mph. The Rain God had bequeathed it a third but I now knew where it was – and how to drive it.

I motored on, savouring the guilty pleasure of a close shave. No need to tell the team about that one. Sixth gear was redundant because you couldn't hold the throttle down long enough in a straight line to engage it, unless I could locate the rest of the puddles. I chuntered along in fifth gear and counted the seconds between the big puddles, forming a mental map of the sections of track where it was safe to go faster next time round.

The first lap confirmed that Mulsanne was the worst affected straight and I began adjusting my lines accordingly. I remained cautious, but the car was revelling in the conditions. It was giving so much feedback through the tyres.

The team were quiet on the radio and there was no chance of seeing the pit board. I was alone, but contentedly busy in the mad world of Le Mans at night in a monsoon. I developed a rhythm and took my chances, passing one car after another, straining every rod in my retinas as I searched for a hint of tail-light or a familiar silhouette in the clouds of spray that cloaked every one of them.

The racer ahead might be a prototype as fast as the one I was driving or a GT car travelling at 100mph. The driver might be on the pace and in the zone, or half asleep, or gently urinating himself in response to the conditions.

The first he would know of my existence would be when his cockpit rocked from the blast of my jetwash as I passed his front wheels. Riskier still was tracking down another prototype caught behind one or even two of the slower GTs.

Every sensible bone in my body urged caution. But too much caution and I could be caught in their web for eternity. It was best to take a risk, splash past them and move on. I moved to overtake one guy just as he summoned the courage to hump the car ahead of him, which I couldn't see. He swung towards me and elbowed me on to the grass at the exit of the curves. I gathered it up and outbraked him at the following chicane as two GTs collided with each other. It was carnage.

I took my chances, like everyone else. The laps flew by, an additional puddle formed on Mulsanne and I figured a cute route through it without lifting. Before I realised it, an hour had passed. The low fuel light on the dash plinked on. I flicked a toggle to engage the reserve tank for the trip back to the pits.

I drove the in lap hard, not forgetting the pit lane might be flooded too. Earlier in the day I'd watched another driver skidding a damaged GT into the gravel pit at the pit entrance. He'd tried to push it out, but was forced to abandon it by the marshals, only metres away from his pit crew who were powerless to help him.

I snaked through the barriers, slowed and engaged the speed limiter. The Ascari's engine popping and banging like a machinegun, I found our pit amidst the jungle of hoses, boards and crews of other teams.

'I don't need tyres. These ones feel great; can we just check them?'

Spencer dived under the wheel arches with his torch and gave a thumbs up seconds later. With a perfectionist like Spencer you never had to second-guess the verdict.

The atmosphere vibrated with tension. Ian looked even more stressed than usual. Perhaps I needed to start pushing harder out there.

'How are we doing? Is everything OK?'

Before Ian could answer, Klaas leaned over the cockpit. '*Slow the hell down.* You're the fastest bloody car on the circuit. Take it easy out there, for *Chrissake*.'

Brian emerged from his warren of computers and calmly announced over the radio: 'You're in fourth place. You've unlapped the leaders, so you're now on the lead lap.'

Unlapped the leaders. We were in the big league. No time to contemplate. A hiss and a thud dropped me to the deck; another roar and I was gone. Team Ascari's Le Mans hopes rested solely on Car 20.

I wanted to get back into the thick of it, check the puddles were still where I remembered and pick up the rhythm.

After about forty minutes a yellow glow started pulsing in the gloom at the edge of the circuit. You never took the warning beacons lightly at Le Mans. I closed up on another racer and rode shotgun until we caught the safety car.

We joined the group bunched behind it, braking hard to avoid a concertina. I just hoped the guys coming up behind me would do the same. Some people swerved around to keep their tyres warm – pretty pointless on wets, worse if you spun on a puddle at 30mph.

I wanted to get past the pack quickly at the re-start and escape their muddle. It beat hanging around to be wiped out by another banzai racer coming from behind.

As we passed the floodlights I recognised former F1 driver Mark Blundell in an MG prototype just ahead. He might help clear a path.

I listened carefully for the all clear. 'Safety car is in, green, green, *go, go, go* ...'

We slithered on to the pit straight, past a near stationary Porsche GT. I had really good drive and stayed welded to Blundell's tail-lights, hoping to see where the hell he was going in the spray. I pulled out of the jetwash, flew past Blundell and outbraked two more GTs into the first corner.

Back into the groove. The rain kept stair-rodding down. The puddles swelled and then withdrew. Every lap was different. I kept updating my mental map, sliding through mayhem and living the dream. We were closing in on the leading Audis.

The Ascari filled me with confidence in the rain, but the guys on board the Bentley coupé, with its enclosed roof, weren't feeling the love. Their windscreen was so fogged up that when Guy Smith was driving he couldn't see through it. The rain forced eleven retirements and a whole lot of walking wounded.

At 4am it eased up a bit. After four hours in the hot seat I was nearing the end of my stint, running the Ascari hard along Mulsanne, when something knocked the wind out of it. The engine misfired; the beast lost speed. I flicked on the reserve tank. No change. The engine was dying.

I was a long way from the pits. The Ascari managed a few more fits and starts, finally cutting all drive at Indianapolis. I pulled up at the Armco, radioed the team and got to work. If I could just remember what Spencer had taught me and Werner during our invaluable engineering induction, I was saved. I reached for the emergency toolkit with Spencer's words ringing in my ears. 'If you end up using this toolkit you're probably fucked. Just do yer best.'

I tore off the electrical tape, picked up the mini flashlight and checked all the fuses were pushed in. They were. I switched ECUs, the engine's brain, plugged the new one into the mother board and flicked the ignition back on to reboot. No dice. I got back on the radio. 'The new ECU isn't working. Any ideas?'

'Wait a minute.' Then, after a long pause, 'We're coming out to you. *Stay right there.*'

Where was I meant to go ...?

There must be something I could do. I looked across to the giant plasma screen on the other side of the track and saw a small Japanese

driver having similar problems. He was staring down at his car with his helmet on and speaking to his team on a tiny mobile phone. After a minute he started gesticulating wildly, hurled the phone into the tarmac and stamped on it twenty times with both feet. Bad reception can really get you down.

Men in orange suits wanted me out of the car, but if I walked too far away it would be classed as 'abandonment' and could eliminate us from the race. Ian and Spencer turned up but couldn't find the fault.

As a last-ditch effort I put the car in first gear and bunny-hopped it 20 metres using the kick from the starter motor. This really upset the French marshals, who chased after me shaking their fists until the battery ran out of juice. Our race was over.

It was gut-wrenching. We came back to a warm reception in the pits.

They had done an incredible job, especially Brian. His beady eyes had disappeared into his skull. Guys like him never slept and he was still reviewing telemetry screens long after everyone else had cleared off. He dragged me into his data den. 'One of your lap times was ten seconds faster than anybody else on the circuit. TEN! Bloody brilliant. Looks like the sodding fuel pump packed in. Some tossing little wire that burned out, a fifty pence component, I bet.'

Hearing that we had paced faster than anyone for nearly four hours numbed some of the disappointment, but nothing compared to actually finishing the race.

The Audis continued their faultless run to victory the following day. Our crew fell asleep around the pit. Sleep was hard to come by. When my eyelids eventually closed, the dotted white lines of Mulsanne were still whipping through my retinas at 200mph.

6

DAYTONA ENDURANCE

After the dust settled from Le Mans, I started talking to some of the large manufacturer teams about driving opportunities for the following year. I was duly informed by one representative that they were 'talking to big names from Formula 1'. Ben was only a three-letter word, so she had me there.

Fortunately Ascari kept me for the following season for a programme that included two of the most prestigious sportscar races in the world: the Rolex 24 Hours of Daytona followed by the 12 Hours of Sebring.

I decided it was time to take the plunge and leave my day job. In between races, I had been working as a brand manager for Scalextric, which included a cosy five-hour daily commute on top of training. It was fun coming up with ideas for toys. I broke new ground by creating the first Bart Simpson Scalextric set, although I got into a little trouble for developing super-sticky magnets that made the model cars travel faster than light. My friends loved it too, dubbing me the 'smallest racing driver in the world' and referring to my backside as a hollow extrusion.

Well, this toy racer was off to Daytona, the birthplace of NASCAR. In the 1950s moonshine runners flocked from the southern counties to race the long flats of Daytona Beach; the best drivers of the Prohibition era had honed their skills outrunning the police on country roads. Here they belted along the beachfront avenue and blasted sand into the faces of spectators. People liked that, so in 1957 race promoter Bill France built the biggest, fastest Speedway the world had ever seen.

The 2.5-mile tri oval with its 31-degree banking was colossal. Even grizzly racers were shocked by the scale of the 'Big D' and the sprawling edifice of its surrounding grandstands. 'There wasn't a man there who wasn't scared to death of the place,' Lee Petty once said. The whitewashed wall that encased the Speedway was ever ready to punish the over-zealous.

An infield road course had been constructed inside the oval for sport-scar racing, and that's where we came in. My prototype rattled so quickly through the banking at Turn One that for the first few laps my eyeballs couldn't keep up with the sweeping sheet of asphalt. It was dizzyingly fast; a 180mph turn, tighter than a jet fighter could pull.

Racing a prototype in Europe through a packed field of GT cars had taught me plenty of cut and thrust. The difference at Daytona was the sheer volume of slower traffic in the tight infield section. I now realised how Batman felt driving the streets of Gotham after igniting the after-burners on a Monday morning. If you gave any quarter, the cars you wanted to muscle past sensed hesitation and only made it harder to get by.

Getting past a prototype of equal pace was more challenging. I closed on one at 170. I couldn't recognise his helmet but his car's body language looked edgy. The banking amplified the suspension compression from tons of down-force and the bellies of both our machines slammed the deck at every bump. My aero went light in his dead air and I hung on to the steering pretty tight while the whole world wobbled around me.

We were bearing down on a pair of GTs running line astern. I had a good slingshot from their slipstream, moved one lane higher towards the wall and overtook. The prototype didn't see me coming and swung out with me alongside.

The banking was beginning to flatten out for the straight, so this was not a good time to change direction. The only space left for me on the track was the high side, which was covered in sand and marbles, so that's where I went. The steering instantly went light as the slick tyres lost contact with asphalt, scrabbled with the dirt and pointed me at the wall. A microsecond later, the rear lost traction. As the camber fell away I had to get out of the throttle and tap some brake to nudge the front away from the wall.

I passed the prototype with a front wheel locked, pitched sideways so close to the wall I thought it would shave the rear wing endplate. It may have looked ugly but I made it stick.

I cruised the pit lane later to find the guy I overtook and maybe share a laugh. There he was, overalls tied at the waist, wearing a baseball cap with big aviator shades drooping off the end of his nose. His neck was frail for a racing driver, but not for a 77-year-old. His voice sounded familiar as he chatted to his mechanic, then Butch Cassidy's clear blue eyes saw me coming. I froze. Paul Newman, star of the silver screen for more than half a century, racer of old and charitable angel who parachuted millions of dollars into worthy causes, was the coolest dude I ever saw. And that's exactly how I left him. He had enough people bothering him for a piece of his time.

Werner was on spectacular form and stuck the Ascari Judd on pole position. He spent the afternoon flexing his muscles under the Florida sunshine and cooking the 'brai' so that 'none of you Engleesh burn my meat'.

My duty at Daytona was to develop an experimental turbo-charged engine in the sister Ascari. The words 'experimental' and 'endurance' made poor bedfellows. Not only was the engine gutless and expensive, but parts of the rear wing kept falling off.

During the race I had to watch my mirrors to keep an eye on things. After the third pit stop to repair the wing we realised that the entire wing post was being shaken loose by the deafening harmonics of the engine. It was deemed too dangerous to continue, so that was the end of that. Maybe one day we would finish an enduro event.

The twelve-hour race at Sebring was half the duration of Daytona 24 but twice as exhausting. Mars had a more temperate climate than Florida in March. And the Martians themselves were pretty conservative by comparison to the 150,000 fans who camped at the track during America's spring break. The usual petrolheads were joined by tens of thousands of college kids who partied hard. The police brought an armoured tank to keep them under control.

Swarms of them descended from the nearby beaches for a look at some fast noisy things. Tanned babes in scant bikinis toting dollar fifty plastic necklaces exchanged them at every opportunity for bodily fluids or a

flash of flesh. The race fans built their own bars, converted school buses into multi-storey viewing galleries and invented my favourite gadget of all time. A 200 horsepower engine beneath the cushions enabled the devoted fan to admire the racing from the comfort of his own motorised sofa from a variety of vantage points around the infield.

The heat built up to 90 degrees with 100 per cent humidity. All the effort of physical training was worth every bead of sweat when you set about the track. It was as rough as hell. The surface was a bumpy patchwork of different materials and there were some fast, challenging corners with minimal run-off. You had to chase the heavy steering for every second as the grip came and went. The constant jarring wreaked havoc on the vehicle's drive train, and the tyres shredded from all the wheelspin and hard braking. We ran the hardest compound tyre Dunlop could supply us.

Avoiding dehydration was a constant battle. The vital fluids in the car's drink system tended to boil by the time it reached your mouth and scald your lips. You thought you were warm whilst driving, but when you pulled up at the end of a stint the rush of air would stop and you found yourself in the asphyxiation chamber. I sprinted from the car, pulled up my fireproof leggings and stood in a bucket of ice water, looking like John Cleese in his *Monty Python* days.

One of our truckies was dating a local hussy with an altogether scientific approach to surviving the weather. Red leathery skin and greasy brown hair was her defence against the sun, and she arrived every morning with an icy slab of Budweiser beer. From then until dusk, when she emptied the last can, not a single drop of water passed her hirsute lips, and her vocabulary was, like, whatever. 'See ya'll in the mornin', boys, *baaaaaaarp*.' A real southern belle.

I was partnered with Justin Wilson, who had just won the Formula 3000 Championship. It was great having him on board, in no small part because he was happy with my only standing order: 'No pissing in the seat.' This feral habit was pioneered by many notable drivers including Nelson Piquet, who apparently used to wet his pants at the end of a Formula 1 race and leave the gift for his mechanics.

As team leader in my car I drew the lucky straw to run double stints when our third driver was injured in the pit lane. That meant running flat out for just over two hours between fuelling and driver changes. The combination of the continuous high G forces and the way the car was

always twitching tested driver and machine to the brink of failure, making Sebring a rite of passage. Even the track started melting part way through the race, so we had to run behind a safety car whilst emergency repairs were made.

Performance-wise we were right on the pace, having ditched the Turbo for the magnificent Judd. The Audis were running away on their grippy Michelin tyres, which at the time gave them several seconds a lap over our Dunlops. Our hard compound came to life when it mixed with the softer rubber on the track, which meant our pace quickened as the race went on. We began catching the leaders. Justin and I took turns putting the hammer down, competing with each other until we crossed the line in fifth place. At last, we had a finish!

Werner placed behind us in the sister car; beating him meant we had done something right. He had attacked Sebring with his customary gusto and kept us primed throughout the weekend with energy drinks.

At one point Werner's co-driver made an impromptu pit stop in the night and caught everyone off guard. Afrika-Bo was snoring away in the coach when Ian Dawson burst in and dragged him to his feet. Werner grabbed his helmet, leapt into the car and drove off. His helmet was still fitted with a fully tinted daytime visor, so he couldn't see a thing. Without floodlights, his task was as dangerous as a bush baby asking a hyena for a shoulder rub. He somehow managed to drive an hour-long stint within three tenths of our pace.

We packed our bags for Europe and geared up for Le Mans. I set about an extensive tyre-testing programme with Dunlop, and Klaas threw every resource at the project to give us a credible shot at winning the 24-hour classic this time round.

The new Ascari KZ1 supercar was on display to the crowds after years of development; this was the road car our racing project set out to promote. With all the lessons learnt from the previous year, everyone was confident of a result.

I partnered Werner and he started the race. The 60 cars filed on to the start/finish straight, and when they dropped the hammer my hair stood on end. The atmosphere was buzzing, doubly so because the 2002 World Cup was going on and the English fans opposite our pit were updating us

on the England vs Denmark game using their own scoreboard. They went berserk as each of England's three goals hit the back of the net.

Werner was whipping through the forest towards Indianapolis corner at 220mph. He lifted to turn right and the rear suspension collapsed. The rear hit the floor, lost aero grip and sent him into a horrific spin. He flew across the gravel, back on to the track and cracked into the wall at over 100 times the force of gravity.

Spencer was the first of our crew on the scene. 'Luckily Werner's head took most of the impact,' he said later. 'And there was nuffink in there to damage.'

The car was toast but Werner spent several minutes trying to get the engine going in spite of pleas from the officials. He only gave up when Spencer assured him the car was actually in two pieces.

Regardless of how the suspension fault occurred, my gut feeling was that the Ascari project was at an end. It couldn't carry on without a major sponsor. We'd needed that Le Mans result. Come July, I was looking for a job.

I phoned every team in the book for a drive, in every series from Le Mans to Formula 1 to NASCAR. One call paid off in September just a few days before the inaugural Indycar race in the UK. I'd been bugging the life out of the organisers for a drive, and at the last minute the Series Director rang and asked what I was doing that weekend.

'Coming to Rockingham to watch the Champ Car race.'

'Well, bring your helmet and overalls, there's a drive for you in the support race.'

Rockingham's newly formed programme was based on NASCAR, America's most popular racing series. One in three Americans was a fan; viewing audiences were enormous and the sponsorship and advertising revenues ran into billions of dollars. The stadiums, cars and fan base were all vast.

The formula for success was simple: they raced stock cars based on America's three most popular sedans that were virtually identical in performance and available to anyone. These agricultural machines were built of tube steel, with clunking metal gear-shifters straight off a Massey Ferguson and snarling V8 motors. The circuits were mostly ovals where you only steered left. The cars were set up with most of their wheels

pointing that way – so much so that you had to steer right just to drive one in a straight line.

Much to the amusement of the Americans, the UK series was called 'Ascar', prompting the enduring question: 'You race Ass-Car?' The packed grid boasted top British drivers like World Rally Champion Colin McRae, Touring Car Champion Jason Plato, some F1 testers and competitors from the USA.

They raced wheel to wheel at Rockingham's 1.5-mile Speedway at continuous speeds of up to 180mph. Rockingham was purpose built in an industrial backwater near Corby, Northants, a town famous for ... not very much. The stadium rose out of the ground like a modern Colosseum amidst a sea of tarmac parking for thousands of spectators. It was American-style BIG, with packed grandstands just metres back from the action. The track was wide enough to fit six cars side by side with gentle banking to assist the flow of speed through the four corners.

Europeans largely regarded oval racing as boring, having only seen it on television. When you attended a live race, you realised the droning pack of cars were largely out of control. It was a thrilling high-speed spectacle. The question wasn't whether they would crash, but when and how hard.

My car was owned by Mark Proctor, a Goliath of a Yorkshireman who also competed in the series. It was his spare, and looked like many of its vital components had been cannibalised. I sat inside its spacious cabin behind a steering wheel big enough for a bus and rearranged some electrical wiring that dangled from the roof. I resolved not to judge a book by its cover. The old girl might have it where it counts.

She didn't.

After missing the test session with an engine problem, I got to grips with my first stock car in the open qualifying session and discovered why NASCAR racers described understeer as 'push'. Whenever I went hard into a corner, the apex repelled the car as if it were the like pole of another magnet. I qualified two places from last and contemplated hanging myself from the wiring that had come loose again.

In the parc fermé before the race, a sports agent saw me leaning over my car at the tail end of the pre-formed grid. I tried hiding but he caught me.

'I see you're going well then!'

I smiled through clenched teeth. 'I won't be here long.'

At the rolling start, the cars sped into the first corner in side-by-side formation and slithered into the turn as they lost down-force in the hole they cut through the air. The volume of air being pushed in all directions was enough to barge neighbouring cars aside and affect their handling.

I felt the changing air pressures immediately in my inner ear. By nosing inside the car in front you could use the air buffeting from your bonnet to kick out his tail; by running outside you could suck away his air and make him 'push'. To exacerbate your opponent's handling problems, you sat in the same position for a few laps until his tyres burnt out.

My dog of a car floated like a butterfly in the wake of dirty air behind the other racers and stuck to the track like a squashed toad. In 'clean air' it was rubbish, so I had to leapfrog from one victim to the next without delay. The drivers made it hard. When people moved over on me I stuck my nose into their side and pushed back; they called it 'rubbing'. I had a few close encounters with the wall, and at 160mph it puckered up your ass cheeks tighter than a lobster's en route to the boiling pot.

This style of physical racing really suited me and before I knew it the race was over. Having started eighteenth, I finished on the podium in third.

If I was lucky, my performance might secure a drive for the following season. The prize for winning the Championship was a test in American NASCAR.

I still spent hours, days, months on the phone calling teams and looking for sponsors. Nothing. I offered advertising agencies the marketing opportunity of a lifetime to back the first British NASCAR Champion. I hit the Yellow Pages and talked the hind leg off alcohol firms, factories and pizza chains. Even as I did it my objectives felt increasingly shallow when I considered the host of causes around the globe that money could be more fruitfully spent on.

After another day of having the phone slammed down on me, the manager of a local automotive company gave me some air-time.

'The last racing driver who asked me for sponsorship was Damon Hill,' he said. He was nibbling the bait; time to reel him in.

'Of course,' I enthused. 'And he went on to win the World Championship.'

'Yeah,' he chuckled. 'The answer's the same now as it was then. *No.*'

Perhaps publicity would help attract sponsorship. I thumbed the Rolodex and spoke to every men's magazine editor in the galaxy, then the TV executives. I did a screen test with Channel 4, had an interview with *Fifth Gear* and drove a Ford Focus for some bloke at Dunsfold. Nothing had come of it.

I maintained a punishing physical training regime in the expectation that everything would work out for the best. It was like flogging a dead horse. I wondered how long I could hold out in hope of a drive without a job to support me. After seven months of climbing the walls, I knew the answer.

By March 2003 all the serious championship drives were gone, and in motor racing you were quickly forgotten. I had dedicated my life to racing, subjugated everything else that mattered and proved that I had the right stuff, but it didn't matter.

Without a sense of purpose I had no zest for life and felt I hardly recognised my reflection in the mirror. I couldn't bear sitting around watching life pass me by. It was time for a new direction.

I used to read about the lives of British soldiers like General de la Billière, Sir Ranulph Fiennes and Andy McNab, and I drew inspiration from their daring adventures. Even the titles of their books struck a chord: *Looking for Trouble, Living Dangerously* and *Immediate Action*. The more I read, the more I understood that military service had more to do with protecting life than taking it.

After school I'd passed the Regular Commissions Board to attend Sandhurst and become an army officer. I took part in an exercise that simulated warfare in built-up areas, with the Royal Irish Regiment and Marine Commandos being attacked by Paratroopers.

In the midst of the smoke, gunfire and camouflage paint, someone mistook me for a serving officer and handed me an assault rifle, so I made myself useful. There were bouts of furious activity and aggression, diving through windows, crashing down staircases and constantly coming under fire as the enemy came at us from all sides. Amidst the confusion, my fellow soldiers looked after one another like brothers. Covered in grime and sweat, they remained alert, orderly and intelligent. I admired their self-discipline and sharp humour, but above all the gleam in their eyes.

I rang the recruiting office of an elite Army Reserve Regiment, an Airborne Unit that recruited civilians, and left a message that I wanted to join. Unlike most of the calls I made that month, these guys actually rang back.

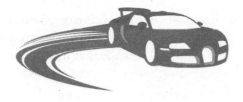

7

THE NEW STIG

Finally I heard back from Andy Wilman. It seemed that I did have a future with *Top Gear*, but I was to speak to no one about it. My first tasking was something called a 'powertest'. I packed my gear and made my way to the airfield.

I pulled up a few hundred metres short of the security gate and ran a mental checklist: No names, no personal info … No unnecessary introductions … Look the part, act the part.

I pulled a black balaclava over my melon and admired the view in the head mirror. *Yep, you look like a terrorist.*

The security guard approached me more cautiously this time, noting the registration plates in case these were his final steps on mother earth. I wound down the window and hailed him.

'Morning. I'm with *Top Gear*.'

He broke into a relieved smile, waved me through and returned to his cheese and pickle.

I drove on to the concrete staging area. Tripods and cameras and black travel boxes full of kit were strewn everywhere, and the place was seething with camera crew. I had no idea what any of them were doing, but they seemed very busy doing it.

Several had noticed the suicide bomber who had just drawn up beside them. I was bringing unnecessary attention to myself, so I climbed out and made my way as anonymously as possible towards the toxic cabin.

I loitered near the cardboard cut-out of John Prescott, waiting for some sign of Andy Wilman. Under his leadership, *Top Gear* had been through a successful revamp following its demise in the Nineties, but it remained essentially a car review programme. As I joined in the second year of the new format, it was as popular as ever, with over two million viewers. You'd think they could have spent a few quid doing up the place. It was the pits.

After five minutes there were signs of movement down the dim corridor. A young guy with a Tintin hairdo and Elvis sunglasses appeared, chatting to a skinny nerd in an Adidas shell suit. They walked straight past.

'Hi,' I said.

'*Whooooooaaa*,' Tintin shrieked, leaping through the air as if someone had just plugged him into the National Grid.

Back on the ground, he started to laugh.

'You must be Ben.' He waved a hand. 'I'm Jim Wiseman. You scared the living shit out of me. Nice balaclava, though. Bet it comes in handy on a cold day robbing banks.'

'Very. Should I just wait here?'

'Yeah, I think that's best for now. We'll find you a room later. It's great to have you on board, welcome to the A team!'

'Thanks. Am I actually on board?'

'You're kidding, right? Hasn't Andy told you?'

'No, other than turn up today and not tell anyone. I sent him the rushes he wanted and hoped I did some good times the other day.'

'That's so typical. I think you equalled Perry's best time on your second lap, and your best lap was over a second faster. Wilman was straight on the phone to the office and was like, "Boys, we've got a new Stig …"'

The Stig was the show's faceless racing driver who tested everything from exotic supercars to family saloons around *Top Gear*'s track, setting fast lap times to gauge their performance. Dressed in black and hidden behind a blackout helmet, he looked like Darth Vader's racing twin.

The vital component of The Stig's aura was anonymity. No one ever saw his face, knew his name or heard him speak. When Perry McCarthy, the chattiest racing driver on the planet, revealed that he was the driver behind the mask after Series 2, his days were numbered. Shortly after I took over, I observed the fate awaiting me if I ever broke that rule.

Black Stig, or rather someone dressed like him, was filmed being strapped into a Jaguar XJS to attempt a speed record aboard the aircraft-carrier HMS *Invincible*. A dummy Stig was then sent screaming down the launch pad, aided by the pressurised steam catapult used for launching Sea Harriers.

Stig 'missed his braking point'. Car and driver crashed into the North Sea, never to be seen again …

With him out of the way, it was my turn in the sandpit. But I knew that a character born of the media would inevitably die by it; that a single slip-up would lead to the catapult. Black Stig lasted a year on the show; maybe I could hold out for two. Carpe Diem. If it only lasted a day, I was determined to make it a good one.

I vowed to take The Stig in the White Suit to a new level of secrecy and hold out for as long as possible. I made my own rules: never park in the same place twice, never talk to anyone outside the 'circle' and keep a balaclava on until I was eight miles clear of the location, and certain that no one was following.

My golden rule was never to appear in the white suit without my helmet on. Conjecture was nothing without proof, and nothing short of photographic, tangible evidence could prove who I was. I sterilised my gear, left every trace of Ben Collins – my phone, my wallet and so on – locked in the car, then hid the keys. When the *Sunday Times* raided my changing room and sifted through my gear, the only information they gleaned was that The Stig wore size 10 shoes.

At work I hid behind a mask. At home I lied to everyone, including my friends and family, about what I was doing.

To me, The Stig epitomised the ultimate quest: no challenge too great, no speed too fast. He had to look cool and have attitude, so I ditched the crappy racing overalls the BBC gave me and acquired some Alpinestars gear and a Simpson helmet.

Apart from unparalleled skill behind the wheel, The Stig was rumoured to have paranormal abilities and webbed buttocks, to urinate petrol and be top of the CIA's Most Wanted list. There was only one possible hitch: I had never been a tame racing driver.

* * *

After forty minutes the balaclava began to itch like hell. The only place to give my head a break was the mothballed room Jim Wiseman had shown me where the test pilots used to change for pre-flight. It was more like a jail cell.

Paint flaked off the damp, yellow-stained walls; the red-painted concrete floor had survived an earthquake and the windows were too high to see out of. It was furnished minimally – with a rump-numbing, standard locker-room issue wooden bench. My only company was a plump beetle that I named Reg. He usually made an appearance mid-morning and scrambled across the pock-marked floor.

I waited there for hours on end, to be summoned to go ballistic on the track in whatever vehicle was lined up for filming. Food was brought to me and eaten in solitary confinement. In between eating and driving, two of my favourite pursuits, I busied myself reading books or doing press-ups. I pestered racing teams on the phone and drifted off into the recesses of my brain. It was like *The Shawshank Redemption*, minus the shower scene.

Only Andy Wilman, Wiseman and a couple of the producers knew who I was. I was just a voice behind a mask. Even the presenters were in the dark. When I coached the celebrity guests, none of them knew my name. They never saw my face. My helmet always stayed on with the visor shut.

It didn't take long to slip into my new routine.

It would begin with a knock at the door. The world turned Polaroid as I pulled on my helmet. The familiar scent of its resin bond filled my nostrils and the wadding pressed against my cheeks. I paced down the hall and on to the airfield to receive instructions from the director. People stopped in their tracks and stared at me like I was E.T.

The director swept his curly locks behind his ears and extended his hands, framing a square with his thumbs and forefingers as he breathlessly visualised the scene he was looking for.

'What we would like you to do, if you can, Stig, is pull away *really* fast. And *spin* the wheels. Can you do that?'

The cameraman, a North Face advocate with white blond hair, crouched like a rabbit six inches from a Porsche 911's rear wheel, evidently focused on the hub. 'Hi, I'm Ben Joiner,' he said. 'Am I all right here?'

I nodded. I was hardly being asked to skim the barriers at Daytona.

I red-lined the Porker, flipped the clutch and vanished in a haze of smoke.

The radio crackled. 'Cut, cut, cut … Wonderful. Let's do that again, but this time look at the camera first and *then* go!'

We did it again. And again. And again. Filming took … time.

I began to get my head around the compromise between fast driving and spectacular driving for TV. Sometimes it overlapped – a fast lap could be as exciting to behold on the screen as on the stopwatch, but that was rare.

I studied the edit inside a minivan with James, a dour young Brummie who received the footage hot from the track, tapped a whirlwind of inputs on to his hieroglyphic keyboard, and deftly dissected it into a meaningful sequence for broadcast.

To enhance the viewing experience – and to keep my new friend James at bay – I threw in some wheelspins and lashings of lurid cornering to complement the more sedate looking but faster driving shots.

The Porsche was down to set a time, but it was pissing with rain and the track was flooding in the straights. Just completing a 140mph lap without spinning on to the turf had been an accomplishment.

Andy Wilman wandered down and collared me. 'Can't you *do* something?'

'What did you have in mind? A good time is out of the question. The car aquaplanes from second right up to fifth on the straights.'

'The old Black Stig was a dab hand round this place, y'know. *Amazing* car control in the wet. Just *do* something. Something … interesting.'

Andy could already push my buttons like a jukebox.

As if by magic, the eight-year-old in my brain had a great idea. The Follow Through corner was named when Andy designed the layout of the *Top Gear* track with Lotus test driver Gavan Kershaw from Naaaarwich (which some people know as Norwich). 'The cars will be going bloody fast through this bit,' Gavan explained. 'You wouldn't want to go off, that's for sure.'

Andy is rumoured to have got quite excited at that point. 'You mean if you went off you'd shit yourself and follow through?'

I asked Jim Wiseman to reposition the Follow Through cameraman. I'd decided not to share my plan with him. If things went wrong, I could always blame the weather.

I pounded the Porker around the lap as per normal. As I exited the Hammerhead chicane the adrenalin began boosting. As every gear-change propelled me closer to the money shot, I started to wonder if this was such a good idea.

The rain slashed across the windscreen, I turned right into the Follow Through and buried the throttle. The Porker fired several warning signals but I was able to straighten up and point it towards the gap between the tyre wall and the verge. The pools of water were so dense they were picking the whole car up and aiming it in a load of different directions. For my plan to work, that was precisely what I needed.

Forty feet to go.

I passed my previous braking point and kept it lit, steered straight, leant left and handed over control to the Rain God.

The water lifted all four tyres off the tarmac and the steering went ghostly light. I passed through the tyre wall at a rude angle at just under 120mph. There wasn't a sound as the car pinged into its first 360-degree spin.

I stayed on my original line of travel, which was good news. It gave me 300 feet of runway to sort things out before I ran into the landing lights. To cap this manoeuvre in style I needed to end up facing in the right direction.

Once I was going fully backwards on the second gyration, I straight-ened the steering, then turned it gently right to swing the front around. I was still shipping at around 100, so I had to manhandle out of the manoeuvre with some hard opposite lock to catch the rear for the last time.

Gotcha.

I skirted the gutter bordering the runway and peddled round the final corners to cross the finish.

I pulled alongside Jim for a debrief.

'*Fucking hell.* Are you all right?'

'Sure. How did it look?'

Jim rolled his eyes. 'I don't know if it's better or worse that you did that intentionally …' He contacted the main camera unit on his radio. 'Biff, did you get that?'

'Uuh … Oh … Yeah … We got it.'

'Iain, what about you?'

'YYYAAAAAAAAAP (enormous burp). Got it.'

'What've you got, Jim?' Andy quizzed.

'The mother of all spins. Stiggy's changing his underpants as we speak. So am I, for that matter.'

'Good work. Get ready for the celeb, he'll be here in fifteen.'

With that, a black van was dispatched to collect the camera tapes and run them across to James. I went off to get some lunch.

The *Top Gear* catering unit consisted of a double-decker bus and mobile trailer. When the schedule was tight I grabbed my own scoff. Each chef greeted me with the same startled look as I bowled up like a white-suited Oliver Twist. They checked my wristband periodically to ensure I had a meal ticket. Can't be too careful.

'How do you eat it?' the chef asked.

'I snort it through a straw. What's for pudding?'

'Something squidgy.'

Depending on the guest, I might get a briefing beforehand. With my limited knowledge of TV personalities I needed all the help I could get.

Wilman took me under his wing and talked me through it.

'Right, Stiggy. Today we've got Martin Kemp driving the reasonably priced car.'

'OK.'

'Do you watch *EastEnders*?'

'I've seen it, yes. Is he the bald one?'

Andy shot a bemused look towards the heavens. 'No. He's the baddie. Everyone hates him; well, not the public but in the show. He used to be in Spandau Ballet. Can you teach him some good moves out there so he sets a fast time?'

'Absolutely, assuming it dries.'

It didn't. The track stayed as slick as Kemp's hairdo and he spun so far off the track during practice that he nearly collected a $6m helicopter.

I handed Martin over to the presenters, who went about filming their pieces with him in front of the studio audience. My job was done, yet the night was still young. I never hung around after studio days for a beer or a chat. It was decidedly antisocial of me, but I really did have somewhere else to be.

8

GREEN FATIGUE

We gathered around the Directing Staff Instructor, a decorated NCO who bore the angry scar of a shrapnel wound in his neck, a legacy of the Balkans conflict. Plissken was a stocky northerner whose boyish looks belied his frontline experience, and he spoke on rapid fire.

The reasons for us being there were many, though none good enough at this stage to merit more than veiled contempt from the real Men in Green. The Army Reserves may have been part time, but the Airborne ethos was all-consuming.

In modern times British airborne forces have become renowned for rapid insertion into theatres of operation around the globe, after fifty years of successful deployment in everything from jungle warfare and counter terrorism to the deserts of the Middle East. A free-thinking force with a will to overcome any obstruction.

Recruits had to develop the mental and physical resilience to cope with the most challenging scenarios. By the time we were 'wasting' Plissken's oxygen, swingeing physical tests had halved our number. The course itself took place mainly in Wales and involved arduous uphill work in the Brecon Beacons, a stunning range of heather-clad peaks notorious for their inclement and unpredictable weather. As primarily weekend warriors, it took the best part of a year before we were deemed worthy of further training.

Passing required a high level of navigational skill and physical stamina. The chances of making it through were one in twenty, which cheered me no end. They were considerably more favourable than the odds of becoming an F1 driver, and no one asked you to hand over £1.5 million for the privilege.

Slick weapon handling drills were critical to staying on the course. We disassembled, re-assembled, loaded, made ready and constantly karate chopped the sliding bolt action of the SA80 assault rifle, aka the 'piece of shite'. Safe handling and consummate knowledge of every component of the weapon system was vital. With our woollen hats pulled down over our eyes, we learnt to strip it blindfolded.

'We're not here to fail you lads. We're here to teach you to survive. I don't give two shits whether any of you make it or not. Quite honestly we don't need a single fucking one of you. If you want to be here, that's down to you.' Plissken paused to let his message sink in. 'Jones, where's your head cover?'

'I left it in the block, Staff.'

'Fucking spastic. Use my one.'

'*You!*' A boot thumped my own. 'What size rag do you use to clean this weapon?'

'Forty-five by forty-five, Staff,' I answered.

'Correct. Forty *fucking* five by forty *fucking* five, and if any of you dickheads try and shove anything else down the barrel you'll be paying for it with the armourer.'

His footsteps receded. I slipped the bolt carrier assembly back inside my rifle and fumbled for the recoil rod. A twanging spring suggested a fellow recruit had just got that part badly wrong.

'Lord Jesus Christ, what 'ave you done?' Plissken moaned.

'Sorry, Staff …'

'You will be, son. Start with fifty press-ups, the lot of ya.'

Men had died on the Welsh mountains while undertaking arduous recruit training. Training was relentless, punctuated by intermittent, brutal exercise called 'fizz' – sprint here, carry a man there – reducing us to gasping wretches within seconds. Lessons were never repeated. You learnt them or you failed.

Between work commitments I exercised every day in every way. Every escalator became a step machine, every run a beasting. I swam, surfed, cycled and climbed at ten tenths.

I was training in Snowdonia when my phone rang. It was the best kind of blast from the past. I told Georgie I was living in London but currently training in Snowdonia. Yes, I'd love to see her. Next week would be fantastic … I had goose bumps, and for once they had nothing to do with the harsh weather. I practically sprinted across the hillside.

The next few days took years. I wondered how much she'd have changed, and how much I had. It had been ten years.

We met in a dimly lit restaurant in town, and after the molasses had melted in my mouth it was just like old times. Her smile was as intoxicating as ever and for two hours nothing else in the world mattered. The difference this time round was I realised how much more interested I was in *her* life, *her* choices, *her* hopes. She had travelled the world, excelled in every kind of water sport and remained passionate about art. Work came second. And me? I suddenly realised I'd developed a potentially terminal case of tunnel vision – but, thankfully, she was still patient, and the wine was strong.

9

LIVE AT EARL'S COURT

I arrived at the imposing gates of Earl's Court exhibition centre in London. By now I was warming to the concept of just turning up at places with no idea what to expect. I pulled out my kitbag and wandered into the building. A raucous howl reverberated through the walls, followed by the shriek of tortured rubber. My kind of music.

My eyes adjusted to the darkness. Blackout curtains separated the hive of nocturnal backstage activity from the bright kaleidoscopic lights on stage. Row upon row of priceless supercars, new and vintage, were lined up so close it made you wince just looking at them.

Someone appeared at my side and eyed my carry-all. 'You 'ere to drive that Jag, then?'

I eyeballed him silently.

'It's all right, I know you're working for Andy. I'm Paul, the stage manager.'

'Ah, thanks …'

'We're in the middle of rehearsals at the moment. The first show's tonight. Go and 'ave a look if you like.' He pointed towards the stage.

A line of Le Mans cars waited their turn in the spotlight, escorted by some female racing drivers. The curtain whipped back as a familiar voice boomed through the PA system: '… and you see that's what we love about Le Mans: it's basically *men* trying to kill themselves at 200mph. But now it's even better. There's *girls* …' The voice was growing hoarse.

There was no mistaking this guy. One hand held the mic, the other wafted around in the air as he strode back and forth, pointing occasionally and cocking his head in exaggerated thought. The abundance of pubic curls gathering snow at the summit of this monster confirmed it was none other than Jeremy Clarkson, as much a household name to me as Maggie Thatcher, Heinz Baked Beans and Colonel Gaddafi.

Racer Girl Number 1 duly introduced herself, treating the empty auditorium to a sizeable slice of her life history, thanking her wonderful sponsors, the amazing team, her dynamite engine and was in full stride until—

'No, no, no … Get off. *GET OFF*. We don't want to hear all that bloody nonsense.' Racer Girl's Colgate smile evaporated. 'The people coming here tonight haven't paid thirty quid to listen to a sodding commercial! Off you go.'

The cars moved sheepishly offstage. Mobile phones buzzed, agents were bleated to. 'Who does he think he is, talking to me like that?'

This was the rehearsal for the MPH Show, now billed as *Top Gear Live*, a heady mixture of supercars, mega-stunts and talking heads in front of an audience of 4,000 petrolheads. Andy had just told me he wanted some 'precision driving, real close shave stuff'.

Paul explained that I would be driving head to head against Tiff Needell for a timed run around a 'figure 8 course' in a supercharged 600 horsepower Jaguar XKR. Tiff was a former *Top Gear* presenter who moved on to host a rival programme called *Fifth Gear*. Known as 'stiff needle' to the lady fans, he was the snake-hipped king of burning rubber and had thrashed more supercars than I could dream of. He'd driven in Formula 1 back in the Eighties and famously biffed Nigel Mansell into the wall during a Touring Car race.

I only had one shot at practice before the show went live, so I suited up and waited behind the curtains. With the visor down I could barely see my own feet in the dimmed stage lighting and could hear little better. Tiff peered at me through his pair of squints, knocked on the helmet and shouted, 'Is that Perry in there?'

I shook my head.

Tiff hopped in the Jag and drifted sensationally sideways around the figure 8, one-handed, whilst giving a running commentary in a voice that resembled a parrot on amphetamines.

The talking heads on stage blabbed away. Paul appeared at my side and, at some unknown cue, tapped my shoulder and hissed, 'STIG … *Go!*'

I ambled out into the arena and felt a rush of nerves. There suddenly seemed to be a lot of people watching. I had raced in front of 100,000 people, but this was far more personal. I felt like Hamlet. I walked the long walk to the Jag, sank into it and searched in pitch darkness for the ignition key. By the time I got the engine running the silence on stage was deafening.

'Yes, come on you, *go!*' Clarkson urged helpfully.

I dropped the hammer and the barbaric supercharged motor belted me forward. Dim lighting shone over two circular platforms that marked out the figure 8 course. I could only guess at the distance to the black curtains concealing the concrete perimeter.

I used a short oval technique, braked on the diagonal and waited for the front tyres to stop skidding across the slick metal panels. Then I turned hard and accelerated. The automatic box spun the wheels into a high gear towards the next platform.

I was playing blindfold baseball in a china shop, convinced I would slam into something at any moment and look a complete numpty. I only saw the platforms moments before missing them. With great relief I completed the figure 8 without hitting anything and exited the arena. As soon as I parked I analysed the run and worked out how to drive it faster.

Wilman arrived and directed me towards a nearby motor home. I snuck inside to get changed, then sat down to read a magazine. The door swung open. A curly mop brushed the ceiling, swiftly pursued by a pair of gigantic eyebrows. Judging by Jeremy's surprise, I'd trespassed on his sofa.

Andy appeared from behind him and introduced us. We chatted for a moment, then Jeremy made to go. Never shy of having the last word, he turned on the threshold and said, 'When you do the Jag next time, can you try not to drive it like a homosexual?'

Do I punch him or just give him a slap? I thought. 'Don't behave like your father …' Mum's words jangled inside my head for a few crucial seconds and Jeremy vanished.

A few hours later it was show time. Clarkson's comment had replaced my first-night nerves with a petulant colic. Tiff took the helm and

delivered a stunning display. The rear of the Jag slewed sideways and swept up the curtains covering the barriers, so close was he to striking the wall.

Tiff completed his performance and someone shouted, 'Go!' I assumed that meant me.

I strode across the arena, clocking Tiff's time on the giant digital read-out: 34.5. I slid under the steering wheel and cranked the key. My body shuddered as the V8 came to life.

The view ahead was worse than before. The camera flashes from the audience flared across my visor and blurred the platforms I had to navigate around.

The only way out was through. I decked the throttle and followed my earlier line with a series of jerky, uncertain movements, keeping my foot down for as long as possible, with no sense of the far wall and too angry to care. I caught sight of the platform a bit late and braked, skidded on to the dirty outer floor and nearly ran straight into the wall. Some grip came back to the front, and she just turned.

To score the best lap time I had to repeat the process on the other half of the 8 by braking as late as possible. I wanted to beat Tiff's time so much that my chest was heaving.

I wove between the platforms and lost myself in a sudden shaft of light. I instinctively added steering to compensate. My vision cleared. *Iceberg … dead ahead …* I swerved and braked to avoid it. Back on the gas, I slid the Jag around and finished the lap.

Eyes bulging, nostrils flaring, I demanded the time.

Jeremy guffawed to the crowd. 'The Stig's lap – it's not very spectacular … but it's *FASTER* – a 34.1!'

Yes. Stick *that* in your pipe, big boy.

I was beginning to understand Jeremy's World. Behind his brusque façade was a man working tirelessly and fastidiously to put on a good show, a man who wanted everyone pulling in the same direction. There was logic behind his madness, an unpasteurised honesty, and people either loved him or hated him for it. It was this politically incorrect fresh air that had attracted me to *Top Gear* in the first place, not an obsession with cars. I was glad I hadn't smacked him.

10

ROCKINGHAM

Someone representing the Ministry of Defence left a message saying I had a drive – the Army 'Stealth car' – in the European Ascar Series, starting that weekend. Maybe my fortunes were on the up.

I arrived at Rockingham for the first race as the morning sun fought its way over the grandstands. The pink skyline blossomed and the sun poured into the concrete bowl of the modern-day Colosseum. The warped reflections of thirty race cars glinted on the mirrored glass of the hospitality suites above the pit straight as the crews readied their machines. A 200-foot timing tower reached for the sky, ready to display the competitors' ranking.

The camouflage stickers were still being applied to Car 84, but my name was over the door and that was a good sign. The team, Ray Mallock Engineering (RML), were proven winners in everything they did. Their attention to detail left nothing to chance.

I climbed aboard and connected the window net. At the centre of the big wheel was a leather pad like a huge slab of liquorice, in case you wrapped your teeth around it during a head-on shunt. The joints of the chassis tubes were well soldered and you could eat your breakfast off the freshly painted interior. Even the oil smelt fresh.

I gradually built up speed on track. NASCARs ran on the edge the whole time, and one slip on a patch of oil could deposit you backwards into the concrete fence. Turn One, with its gentle banked radius, was at the end of the pit straight after the main grandstands and taken almost flat out. Two was trickier as the track dropped and veered sharply away, hiding the apex until you had already committed your soul at the entry. It was flat out for the brave. Three was easy flat, and Four required some brake, some wheel wrangling, then a heavy right foot to please the crowd. The car was superbly balanced and steered beautifully through the turns. I was fifth fastest in practice with plenty in reserve.

The field lined up to set two flying laps, one at a time, for qualifying. The tower displayed each time to the crowd, cranking up the drama.

I went out third and stayed in the car whilst Vince, my wiry mechanic, stood on the pit wall to observe how the first two got on. He suddenly ducked, as though a shot had been fired at him.

He came over sucking air through his teeth. 'That looked expensive. He's gone in hard at Two.'

I didn't want to hear that. In my mind's eye, I'd already taken Two completely flat. But if someone was in the wall there it meant the corner was already a bitch, and now there was debris …

After a delay, the next victim went out. Vince rotated his index finger to signal 'start engine'. I would be joining the track as soon as the other car recorded its time. My heart thumped as I listened to the roar of the V8 flying past. As it reached peak revs on the pit straight, the crisp note of the motor bounced back off the grandstands. It didn't come round a second time.

'Turn Two again. Nasty,' Vince said.

This was getting ridiculous. Phil Barker, the team manager, decided to have a word. Phil was a racing stalwart who tuned his team to run as efficiently as a Swiss watch. He saw me coming a mile away.

Phil came to the front of my car and brought his radio mic round to his perfectly planed silver moustache.

'Two cars in the wall at Two, Ben. Doesn't take a rocket scientist to realise there's something wrong down there. Remember, this is the first weekend and there's two races tomorrow. If you smash the car up, you've only got yourself to blame. All right?'

'Understood. Thanks, Phil.'

My first lap out of the pits showed me there was nothing to fear on the track but fear itself. I felt the tyres come in and stick like glue. Here was

an opportunity to assert dominance over the rest of the competition right from the start.

I backed off early for Four, then jammed the accelerator to the floor. I kept a stiff hold of the steering as the front end crept towards the wall. It ran to within an inch of touching and I kept it there down the length of the straight to benefit from the low air pressure, picking up a tiny amount of additional speed. With the throttle wide open, I cranked the steering wheel into One as late as possible, trailing off the throttle all the way down to the white line of the apex, with my left foot hovering over the brake. As soon as the tyres hooked up, I squeezed the gas back on towards Two.

You could tell yourself a corner was flat out all day long until you actually came to do it. Even the slightest lift affected your speed and there was never any going back. Turn in too early and the car would exit early into the wall. Turn too late and it wouldn't turn enough and I'd have to back off. On new tyres you had to believe the grip was there. Knowing that two cars had just greased themselves on the wall made the throttle pedal weigh a ton, but no guts, no glory. *Make it have it.*

I took a late line but turned sharply to make up for it. The fresh rubber soaked up the strain; it speared in, flat out. I cut the inside white line and howled up to the wall without kissing. Three was easy flat by comparison, a gentle float but you had to hang on. The extra speed from Two carried me all the way to the last corner. The engine bumped off the rev limiter as it reached top speed. That was new.

I squeezed the brake with my left foot for Four and accelerated at the same time – you never released the throttle completely on a fast oval because the axle was angled – then blasted across the finish line. My number went to the top of the tower and we set a new track record. After the other 24 cars completed their laps, it confirmed we had pole position.

From pole I led the race until the pit-stop window, which happened to fall on a safety car for another crash. We'd planned to come in at the end of the three-lap window, but you usually pitted on a safety car because it saved track time.

Well, we opted to stay out and as I led the field past the pit entrance, I looked in my rear-view mirror and saw every man-jack filing into the pits. I completed a lonely lap behind the safety car as it dawned on me,

the team, the crowd and the commentators that the race leader had just committed suicide.

I finally dived into the pits. The crew leapt over the wall, dressed head to toe in Army DPM clothing. Vince slammed his hydraulic gun into the front left like a demented Kwik-Fit Fitter and sparks from the wheel nuts ricocheted off his goggles. His hand was raised first, I red-lined, seconds later the jack man dumped me onto the ground and I gassed it away. I emerged from the pits dead last.

With less than half the race left to run there was hardly time to overtake twenty-four cars. But rather than focus on what I couldn't do, I had to adjust to the situation. The win was gone. I had to launch a clear-headed counter-attack.

My spotter, big Doug, was up in the clouds, at the highest point in the grandstands. He talked to me all the time, acting like radar to position me around other cars. A good spotter was worth his weight in gold, which made Doug more valuable than the national treasury.

'Sorry about the screw-up, Ben. The boys are gutted.'

'Don't worry. Let's see how many we can take down before the end.'

I was itching for the green flag to drop. With just over twenty laps to run, the signal was given.

I was still cornering at the tail end of the snake when the leaders passed the start gantry on the pit straight. I flat-footed the throttle in second gear, the V8 squirmed as the power raged through the rear tyres and I clunked the enormous shift across to third, instantly pulling alongside my first victim. We drag-raced to the first corner; I took that flat and raced the next guy into Three. I was coming through no matter what.

I kept the pressure on and went inside, outside and underneath one car after another, loving the stability of my machine more with every pass. Doug was on overdrive. 'Car inside, car outside, he's on your rear quarter, hold your line, you're clear, he's having a look, c-c-clear.'

Coming up on a pack was like running through a crowded street; their movements were unpredictable and you had to read their body language. These cars were so unstable at high speeds that a slight knock could put everyone in the wall, so it was a delicate exercise of positioning, slip-streaming and cutting through. In the end we placed fourth.

I started the second race in fourth position, took the lead and lost it again in the pits. For some reason we lost eight places during the tyre change. I couldn't catch the leader and finished second, which was

enough to leave the first weekend as the championship leader. In spite of the performance, racing economics reared their ugly head. I was told there wasn't enough funding to continue the season. Just as well I had a full-time part-time occupation.

11

HARD ROUTINE

As we moved off the muddy track it began raining. With an hour of light left, we made camp under our ponchos in a steep copse on the outskirts of the base. One of our comrades was struggling to undo the top flap of his bergen. When he succeeded, food, compass, dry kit and no end of other junk flew out across the wet ground. I tried to help organise the poor bugger before anyone saw.

'Don't waste your time on that waste of space,' someone growled from over my shoulder.

'What do you mean?'

'The guy's hopeless. You're really better off leaving him to it. You'll have enough to worry about.' The wrinkles in his forehead creased as he smiled.

Geoff had been a regular soldier in the Eighties and served in the Regiment for several years. Now he was going through the system a second time. My Boy Scout instinct to help others at all times was too firmly entrenched to follow his cold advice. I finished sorting the guy out and returned to my poncho, which had sprung a leak in my absence.

The oilskin coat spread out to form a simple shelter. Geoff deftly inverted the hood, bent it back on itself, hooked the para-cord around the neck and tied it off to the nearest tree, instantly making it taut and waterproof. I thanked him and he retreated to his spot. We both watched the continuing difficulty my hapless comrade was having with his wash kit.

Geoff didn't really strike me as a seasoned soldier. He was tall and lean, but seemed more like a geography teacher. He had floppy dark hair, a refined posture and spoke thoughtfully. He accepted his surroundings and they accepted him. The contrast with me couldn't have been greater. I pictured a Drill Sergeant behind every bush, poised to leap out and hold a knife to my throat for having shit admin.

There were over a hundred of us out there that night, and I doubt anyone slept too well in his wank chariot, as the sleeping bags were known. We had no idea what to expect or when to expect it.

Reveille was at 0430, with breakfast in bed followed by 'PT'. I surgically removed the roots of a tree from my back and broke into a carton of army issue compo rations to whistle up some culinary delights over a hexamine stove. After a lengthy cooking process, I succeeded in turning my aluminium pan black and a bag of Lancashire hotpot lukewarm. I eyed Geoff's roaring mini gas stove enviously and he handed me some boiled dregs for my brew. Some people made pigs of themselves and gorged on food, which seemed short-sighted. I hurriedly stowed my kit into the limited space inside my bergen and reported for parade.

We formed up on the track and were notified of the course's first casualty. The recruit was led away to receive stitches to his hand following a vicious attack by a tin of mystery meat. A few guys started warming up, for what I had no idea. My stomach churned. The tension was too much for one boy, who doubled over and spewed his breakfast across the Land Rover tracks, prompting a chorus of jeers.

'Fucking crap hat,' spat one, an insult that covered the whole of the armed forces bar the Paras.

The DS breezed past the steaming puke and handed out two sets of scales for weighing our packs. Each bergen had to weigh exactly 40 pounds. We opened our water bottles to prove they were full. A nondescript man in plain clothes appeared beside me.

'Have you been on the course before?'

'No sir, this is my first time.'

'What is your profession?'

'I'm in marketing.'

'How old are you?'

'Twenty-eight.'

He nodded and walked away.

The DS barked, 'Three ranks.'

We lined up accordingly.

'When we get to camp we'll march through in formation, not like we're on some countryside bimble. Keep your traps shut and your shit in order. Let's see if you ladies can at least look like soldiers.'

We slowed through camp and marched along the frosty tarmac road in an orderly fashion. As we reached the exit gate a young girl jogged up to ask in a thick Welsh accent who we were and where we were going. God knows what on earth she was doing hanging around an army barracks at five o'clock in the morning.

Someone muttered something about orienteering.

'Well, watch out there, lads,' she chirruped. ''Cos them boys at the front aren't from this base and they're 'ard as fuck.'

The DS marched us briskly out of the gate then back into double time.

The hundred or so trainees came from different stations from around the country. Mine was from London and boasted an eclectic mix of tinkers, tailors, former soldiers and sailors as well as a few bankers and other forms of 'rank civvie' like me. Most had some former military experience. A few had failed the course once already and were taking it again.

One chap boasted that he had been a member of Portuguese Special Forces, another the Foreign Legion. The experienced guys were the least interested in the rest of the 'gangfuck', as one recruit called Bernie referred to our collective. Bernie had dark hair, legs like tree trunks and a boring day job judging by the way he tore off his suit before every training night.

The shared frustrations, fatigue and pain of PT made it an aggressive form of group therapy. It instilled a selfish kind of camaraderie. This phase was primarily about survival. As much as you coaxed your comrades along, you could only help those that helped themselves or you risked sharing their fate.

As the run wore on, sweat poured down my face and back. My shirt bunched beneath my bergen and rubbed the skin off my spine. The blisters forming on the heel of my right foot were a welcome distraction.

The formation broke ranks as we darted up a dirt track leading on to a range. The DS rounded on us and screamed, 'Sprint up that fuckin' hill, every one of you.'

We scrambled across deep gullies where heavy rainfall had washed away the soil. Many fell back and some closed to the front. I opted for the

latter, falling over, pumping burning thighs until the lead in them prevented any more bravado.

We endured another forty minutes of hacking, grunting and moaning. We'd been running for nearly one and a half hours with no sign of looping back to where we had started. The DS turned us on to another tarmac road. A line of green trucks appeared to hover in the distance.

A few guys pulled out their water bottles as we reached the edge of the parking area. But the DS didn't stop. He went straight up another hill. It was a sickener, a test of character to see who would quit and who would keep running on empty.

The bulk of the group carried on going before finally being ordered to stop and jog back to the transports. The ones that stopped short were never seen again.

One of the support staff bobbed up to me. 'Collins, you need to see the OC next week about your medical. Looks like you failed your hearing test yesterday.'

That was *bad news*. I would have to come up with a plan. In the meantime, we all had jobs to get back to. We loaded our gear on to the wagons and braced ourselves, our battered knees bent at 90 degrees, for the five-hour journey back to London.

After a successful raid on Burger King we started looking forward to the week ahead. Flashman, one of the few officer recruits, was planning a speed-dating extravaganza with forty 'hand-picked honeys' in a Soho nightclub. His chiselled jaw, naturally manicured eyebrows, brown hair and blue eyes made him quite the Army pin-up.

I declined Flash's opportunity of a lifetime because I already had plans, starting with a date with Georgie that night. I spruced up for the occasion, farmed the harvest of crud out of my ears and then we hit the town. Naturally I took the lucky lady out for dinner, went back to hers and – so she claims – kept her up all night.

Apparently I passed out as soon as my head hit the pillow, snored like a congested rhino and played out every step of a recurring nightmare that my legs would seize up on the hills. Casanova, eat your heart out.

12

TORTOISE OR THE HARE

My next assignment with *Top Gear* involved turning my back on Le Mans in favour of what was probably the slowest motor race in the world – the Citroën 2CV 24-hour race at Snetterton.

Thirty horsepower gently encouraged the vehicle to a whopping top speed of 65mph, at which I drove for the entire lap. If you wanted to stop you posted a letter to the brakes and asked, politely, if they didn't mind slowing the car down. I only lifted off the accelerator once, briefly, for the tight chicane on to the pit straight. Negotiating corners required a level of driver response you expected from a lemur during winter hibernation.

This unlikely event was billed as The Stig's debut appearance in a motor race in June 2003. By the time I reached the circuit, the plan had changed. I had to muster another set of racing overalls to compete as Ben Collins.

I walked into the garage to find that 'The Stig' was emblazoned in vinyl on the side panel of the Deux Chevaux alongside the names of my team-mates. The first of these was Anthony, a 'Racing Reverend', who had earned his stripes by winning the '*Top Gear* challenge for the Fastest Faith'. The other co-driver was a *Top Gear* presenter called Richard.

'Who are *you* then?' the team manager asked me.

'I'm Ben,' I said. Then, before the penny dropped all the way, 'I'm replacing The Stig. He can't make it.'

Whilst the peace of the Loire valley was being broken by the crack and throb of V10s and V8s for Le Mans qualifying, I drowned my sorrows with a cup of tea. A fellow tea addict approached briskly in my direction, rubbing his hands together in expectation.

'Ah, *tea*!' he exclaimed.

'PG's finest.' I passed him a polystyrene cup.

I guessed this was the presenter. He looked familiar, had a confident chirp and a clutch of hippie bracelets. Some abrasions on his otherwise perfectly formed hands suggested a rugged lifestyle. He was bubbling about his tea but was clearly even more excited about the race.

We shook hands and Richard nodded like a stag offering its horns before locking. His hair was short back then, before the days of the shaggy-dog bouffant that would snap the knicker-elastic of female audiences across the UK.

'Have you done any racing before?' I asked.

'No, never. Well, I did an historic race in a Rover once.'

I grinned. 'Well it all helps …'

I talked Richard through the basics, showed him the track and where he might expect to jostle with other competitors. I explained how he could slipstream other cars and dive down the inside to pass them. He assured me that he had no interest in overtaking but appreciated the advice. He was 'just here to have a good time and soak up the experience'.

Within a few laps of his opening stint, Richard Hammond was dicing four abreast down the pit straight. He was clamped to this pack of racers like a junkyard dog for forty minutes until he stopped for a driver change. He emerged red-faced, beaming from ear to ear.

I raised an ironic eyebrow. 'Not interested in racing with anyone then, Richard? Just here for the craic, slow and sensible?'

'Well, sort of, you know …' he said a trifle sheepishly. 'That guy in the green car cut me up, I had to do something!'

'Of course. That must be why you scythed past three of them into the first corner and nearly ran into the turnip field.'

As for the Reverend, his Christian driving nearly resulted in a punch-up. A jumped-up, pumped-up little man with square shoulders appeared outside our garage and began remonstrating with him.

The Rev held out his palms as if he were delivering the Sunday sermon and politely explained that he'd only been trying to let him past, then apologised profusely if he had accidentally crossed him.

Mr Angry's abuse continued unabated. I found myself drifting across the garage along with a few kindred spirits, including Hammond.

A few curt insults were exchanged and I may have suggested the other driver try cornering on his roof sometime, whilst Hammond's stare became increasingly fixed and dilated. He looked like he was about to audition for a George Romero movie. 'You *really* should leave,' he rasped. '*Right now.*'

I liked Hammond; he was naughty.

Mr Angry scuttled off and I felt strangely proud to be included in his parting salvo, '*Top Gear* wankers …'

I had so far encountered two of the show's presenters. The one with mad hair would have to wait. I had some pressing concerns of my own to deal with.

You know that your hearing test isn't going well when you have to ask the doctor if it's started yet. He looked up at me from his panel of buttons and switches and then threw in a few loud beeps as if to say, 'Can you hear those, numbnuts?'

Some weeks later, I was facing the results with the officer in command of training.

The OC calmly laid down the law. 'You failed the test quite considerably. I gather it's something to do with your motor racing. The remainder of the course will be spent on the hills and we can't have you being run over by a Land Rover because you didn't hear it coming up behind you. You need to be signed off with a clean bill of health in order to continue.'

Driving noisy racing cars had damaged the hearing in my right ear at certain frequencies. There was no way I could pass the hearing test without cheating and I determined not to get binned unless I'd broken my neck. A hearing aid seemed like the best solution.

I procured a CIC (completely in canal) earpiece from a firm that supplied OAPs. It slipped deep inside my ear and avoided visible detection. The only trace was a tiny flesh-coloured stem that facilitated removal.

The drawback of the CIC model was that once the battery was engaged, it tended to emit a loud, high-pitched squawk as you inserted it into the ear. The kind of noise an Army doctor might notice.

I practised licking and quickly wedging it in with the battery door open so that I could keep my ear empty for inspection until the very last moment. I went for a medical at another, less suspecting regiment and duly passed.

The moment came to unveil my results before the official medical staff. I waited in line for my fate to be decided. I clung nervously to the hearing aid in case I was tested again, making sure not to drop the tiny battery. I accidentally closed the hatch.

'BWOOEEEEPP'.

A few heads turned as I reached for the thigh pocket of my DPM trousers and pretended to adjust a prohibited mobile phone. Cold sweat spread across my face. I was rescued by a pair of double doors slamming open to our left and a red-eyed, red-faced, red-haired recruit bursting into view.

Mungo was one of the strongest guys on the course and had just been sacked for some bullshit anomaly with his eyesight. His outrage was evident. Such was the delicate balance we all hung on by.

A young medical officer hopped along the line. 'Collins, you're here for a hearing test, right?'

'I passed it last week, sir. Here …' I handed him my hooky papers. He glanced at them and moved on.

After an agonising wait, a clerk came out of another door and ordered me into a room to be tested. My heart sank and my clammy fingers cradled the earpiece. As I stepped forward the young doctor reappeared. 'He's fine, he's already passed.'

He turned to walk away, then stopped and added, 'Even if you fucking bluffed it.'

It was better than a lottery win. I stared blankly ahead and pretended simply to take this news in my stride. My reward was the Fan Dance.

13

CHIN STRAP

'It pays to be a winner today, lads,' the corporal smirked.

Up until this point our training had consisted of tabbing long distances across the Welsh mountains within a designated timeframe. For one of the longer, harder routes, involving a double traverse of a killer peak, candidates were required to double their speed across the hills in a test of willpower, aggression and bloody-mindedness. It was pass or fail. The march was led by the staff, so assuming they didn't get lost, all you had to do was run.

Bernie was relishing the bleak forecast he'd seen on TV. 'Gonna be fucking epic. Weather warning says there's a force 8 gale this weekend.'

We enjoyed the rare pleasure of a night in a bed inside Barracks. It was a welcome indulgence, even though my pillow smelled like a group of piss-heads had wiped their asses with it. Even better, the following morning we had a cooked breakfast followed by the briefing.

'This is a basic test to see whether you have the physical stamina to pass this course. Anyone wearing a wristwatch will be sacked; you won't know the magic cut-off time, so you fucking push it all the way. If you notice that your legs are spinning and your bergen has overtaken you, that means you are falling over. Try not to let your bergen pass your body when you're running downhill. No doubt there will be a mass urination, so get your kit squared away and be ready to move at 0900.'

We stripped down to the bare basics: DPM trousers and Helly Hansen T-shirt under a Gore-Tex outer liner. Staying warm wouldn't be a problem.

Kojak was a bald regular Army veteran with a mysterious past, who met every challenge by ripping its face off. He had opted for a black knee-brace contraption that was fresh out of *Mad Max*. He dropped his trousers in front of everyone to reveal his retro Y-front skivvies before diving in with a fistful of Vaseline. He swallowed some super-sized Ibuprofens, clapped his hands together and yelled, 'Come on then, ladies, let's fuckin' do this.'

We were issued mini flares and lined up alphabetically, which meant I started near the front.

The training OC was a ginger whippet and led off like someone had just set off the hare from the starting gate. He must have been forty-odd, but was a mosquito on the hills. Dirck, the uber-keen South African, was glued to his shoulder, as always, but the furious pace was too much for me. My chest was wheezing and rattling 'like a whale giving birth to triplets' according to Ninja, our resident martial arts guru, as he sauntered past me. Next to overtake was Flash who puffed, 'Stick with the pack.'

I couldn't, and sank further back.

A DS with an unusually large head saw I needed some encouragement. 'Bloody hell, mate, this is just the start. In through yer nose, out through yer mouth. Not exactly match fit, are yer?'

I'd always struggled running uphill. It was utterly demoralising being unable to summon the energy to keep up. The Lord of War, a guy I disliked intensely, was the next to catch me up. He thought he was some kind of military genius, had a grade one haircut, frowned on those outside the club and blew his nose repeatedly into his sleeve.

Our speeds were matched the way trucks are when they block motorways by overtaking each other with an infinitesimally small speed differential.

I went to pass him on his right and he blocked me. I ushered him aside with my rifle and we traded a few blows, swapping places another five times on the way up the mountain. A bit of venom went a long way to helping us get within 40 metres of the lead group as fog descended on to the open ground.

The wind kicked up, driving the cold rain hard and sideways. Fog clagged in like pea soup, engulfing the leaders and the mass of blokes

behind, which meant we had no clue where we were going. The Lord of War turned right to follow the fence-line. I went straight over.

I checked my map on the run and fell through a bog right up to my tits. Bernie came to my rescue and dragged me out. We exchanged the same look. It said, 'Where the hell are we?' The DS at the last checkpoint had said to follow the fence-line, but we'd crossed two of the bastards since and lost sign of the footprints in the long grass.

We ran off in what turned out to be the right direction. Not everyone would be so lucky.

My beanie hat had swollen to the size of a turban, so I ditched it and jogged after Bernie, stuffing frozen chocolate into my mouth. The weather pounded in, the rain slashing so hard you had to make slits of your eyes to peer through. At the top of the hill we found a tent.

Laughing Corporal popped out with his arms outstretched like the messiah. 'All right there, lads, give us your numbers … crack on, boys, there's a brew at the bottom, get your skates on.'

We bounced off rocks, tripped over clumps of grass and shimmied in the wind under the weight of a bouncing bergen, jolting belt kit, tired legs struggling to control our trajectory. I slipped on the wet grass, my head snapped back against the top of my pack and I found myself sliding like an upended tortoise 25 metres down the hill.

We caught one of the DSs, an officer, and followed him down a steep slope to the top of a waterfall, whereupon he produced a map … Not a good sign. The turnaround checkpoint was just 200 metres below us. I could see it. But it was five times the distance on the conventional trail. The edge of the waterfall wasn't quite vertical and the trees either side looked like a possible route down …

'Don't even think about it,' Bernie rasped.

'Are you sure?'

'Fucking certain. We'll go back up the track.'

A grey-haired couple made their way past us, walking their dog. 'Good morning, boys.'

'Good morning,' we replied in choirboy unison.

Following Indiana Jones had cost us ten minutes we didn't have. We reached the bottom and charged along the tarmac road towards the 'twat wagon' parked in the layby, arriving in the nick of time. I necked my milkshake and used the hot tea to help me gobble clumps of concrete chocolate. Four swigs later it was time to saddle up for the return leg.

We headed straight back up the minging slope we had just come down, before curling round the mountain, back into the weather. You could lean 45 degrees into the wind without falling over. As the slope neared the vertical I dragged myself up by pulling on a barbed wire fence, leaning on my weapon, hands and knees, chin strap. I was flat dead. At long last the descent began, and I started to catch people again. I ran past Plissken's basha. He flicked the ash off a cigarette and shouted, 'Straight down the hill, son. Keep it up.'

For the first time, I felt I was going to make it. It made the back of my head tingle. We sprinted the last kilometre. My boot lost traction for one final spectacular face plant into the muddy track.

The finish was in sight and the lead group were cheering us in, with Kojak whipping up proceedings into a drag race with a guy who suddenly appeared behind me.

'*He's catchin' ya. C'mon, lads, he's catchin' ya!*'

I was the seventh man in.

The DS stared at me over his clipboard, unable to identify the bog man standing before him.

'It's Collins, Staff.'

His pencil ticked me off. A little over half our number made the cut-off point. Laughing Corporal described the cull as 'carnage'.

We shuffled towards our transports like a gang of rubbery-legged John Waynes. The pain in our bodies was far more bearable than the anguish of the guys who didn't make it; some were lost in the fog for hours, including my old chum and navigational genius the Lord of War.

I melted into my seat and turned on my mobile. A text from one of the *Top Gear* production assistants read, 'Naughty naughty mr stig, heard you were telling people who you were in a restaurant last night ...'

'*What?*' I said aloud. I must have missed the section of the Naafi with white tablecloths.

I angrily texted my reply. 'No I didn't, no I wasn't. Must be someone else.'

A couple of beeps heralded the reply. 'Watch out. remember what happened to the last stig ...'

The brutality of the march had reduced our group to a more manageable number. The survivors included a few surprises like Johnny, the silent but apparently deadly schoolteacher, Milo the IT technician and one born-again racing driver.

* * *

The RML team put their faith in me and kept my car on the track for the remainder of the Ascar season, in spite of the financial burden. It was a magical year. We led every race, winning most of them, with the help of soldiers from all regiments, some of them working on the pit wall. Colonel White, who was running the exercise, reckoned it was the most effective recruiting drive they'd ever employed.

We had a good lead going into the last race weekend of the season. The championship title was within our grasp, so it was time for a pep talk with Phil, the team manager.

'Now, I'm sure you're aware of this Texaco Trophy they've thrown into the mix for this weekend ...'

I certainly was. It was a special award for the driver who scored the most points over the final weekend.

'Well, you can forget all about that bollocks. You're here to become a champion and that's all you need to focus on. All you need to do is finish tenth in both races to win it.'

He was absolutely right. Settle for tenth. No brainer.

I took the TA car on to the track for practise and realised we had a gift. I'd been driving the wheels off it all season, running on the edge to be faster than the other drivers. This time, we held the advantage. And with Phil's new, faster wheel-change guns it meant we could keep the lead during our pit stops.

I parked the car on pole position, which raised one of Phil's eyebrows.

We absolutely romped both races. I knew that I was safer out of reach than stuck in the pack. The only time the others came close was during a safety car with a few of the really fast boys on my tail.

The one directly behind communicated via our spotters in the grandstands that since I needed to finish this race to win the championship, I'd better let him past, 'or else'.

It was a physical form of racing, so this didn't leave a lot to my imagination. I politely asked Doug to tell him to eff off. When the flag dropped I drove the fastest, most perfect laps I could. I pulled clear and sealed the championship by passing the chequered flag in first place.

I couldn't wait to get back to the pits and see the boys. I flung off the belts, clambered out of the car and bear-hugged every one of them. They'd run a faultless operation all season without a single mechanical failure.

Phil had given birth to kittens on the pit wall but did well to conceal it behind his Oakleys. He had one more race to run. 'Do whatever you like now, mate,' he beamed.

We'd saved my best tyres for the second half of the final race, which meant I struggled to hold the lead in the first half on the old cheddars. When the new rubber boots went on I had a light fuel load and nothing to lose, so I could really push the envelope. I went flat out through all of the first three corners, so fast that the engine was hitting the limiter just after Number Three. I'd always braked for Four but it felt so good I just lifted off the throttle and went in. It pushed me a little wide, but I cured it with some throttle and crossed the line with a new track record. I drove that way for four laps. It was total freedom.

We took a clean sweep: a maximum points score from two pole positions, two fastest laps and two race wins to claim the Texaco Trophy and the European Ascar title.

Even Mum had felt it was safe to attend, and some dust from the pit lane must have blown into her eye when I saw her afterwards. Dad had secreted multiple cases of champagne inside the team's hospitality unit, which he distributed liberally as he set about embracing the crew. In spite of his considerable experience of drinking the stuff he sank the first bottle a bit too quickly and it was fizzing out of his ears.

The awards ceremony took place a week later at the glorious Hilton hotel in Leicester. I dressed up like a penguin and laid off the booze being quaffed liberally by the rest of the team. The curtain slid back and we watched the season highlights with all the crashes, bashes and action. It was a proud moment receiving my award, but it was getting late and I was itching to hit the road.

I was beating a hasty exit when a hand clapped me on the back.

'Not so fast.'

Colonel White from the TA had become increasingly avuncular during the course of the season. He beamed at me. 'Bloody marvellous this year, lad. I'm so sorry we won't be joining you next season; our new civvie marketing wizard just doesn't get motor sport. Remember my offer, though; you're still young enough to enlist.'

* * *

I beat it away from the Hilton in the middle of the night and followed the now familiar route towards the Welsh quagmire. My headlights eventually picked out one of the DSs with a brew on the go. As I parked up, he flicked on a head torch and wandered over.

'How'd you get on then?'

'Good, Staff. I won.'

'Let's 'ave a look then.'

I handed him the crystal championship trophy and was rewarded with an appreciative expletive. Then, 'Well … better get changed and join the rest of the lads. Here's your weapon.'

The rain started chucking it down. I trudged through the mud and scraped my way into the shelter of the pine trees. An acrid stench began to strip the membranes off my nostrils as I curled up for the night on a bed of sheep droppings. Their erstwhile owners were clearly in dire need of medical attention. I heard a rustling sound nearby. One of the boys was moving off for a piss, hopefully not on the face of the last man in.

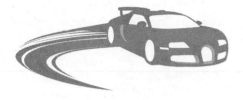

14

COWELL'S GOT TALENT

I made my way to Dunsfold a couple of days later and climbed gratefully into my silky white suit. Lieutenant Nick Arkle from the Royal Navy climbed into his olive green one. We were about to see if a flyboy driving a Harrier Jump Jet could beat The Stig in a Saab 9-5 Aero.

James May was looking eagerly across the airstrip from the shelter of the production office with a coffee in one hand and a scrunched yellow script in the other. I found James to be a thoughtful character, who looked like a motoring version of Doctor Who with his floppy hair and stripy jumpers. As I greeted him he turned and saluted. 'Good morning, sir. How do you fancy your chances?'

'Not great. But if he doesn't win he'll probably shoot me.'

He gave me an indulgent smile. 'Did you ever see the flying bedstead contraption they used to develop the Harrier back in the Fifties?'

'I think so. The one that looked like an insect?'

'Mmm. Marvellous technology, especially when you think that jets had only been around for a few years back then. Brave men tinkering with the extremities of physics.'

I knew a bit about Harrier pilots from growing up in America during the Falklands conflict. I had a poster detailing the fleet of ships that carried our troops and aircraft thousands of miles across the ocean to face an unlikely but determined enemy. As a kid in a foreign country I felt proud to be British, watching TV clips of Paras and Marines tabbing across the desolate, misty terrain, into the unknown. Ace pilots like Flight Lieutenant David Morgan became heroes to me as they flew dangerous missions to defend the fleet.

I never imagined that twenty years on I'd be racing against a Harrier pilot at the very airfield it was first flown and developed.

The Harrier weighed in with 21,000 pounds of jet thrust versus the Saab's 3-litre blancmange. I asked Nick how close to the ground he wanted to fly, just in case I needed to duck.

'Shouldn't be hanging around long, Stig. Once I get a few knots under my belt I'll be pulling angels.'

Slick and self-assured, Nick really looked the part. I could imagine him at the bar popping out lines from *Top Gun* to a melting audience. The fact that he was a good bloke only made it worse. .

We'd start alongside one another on the runway and blast off together. The Harrier would get in the air and follow the course of the lap – ish – whilst I blatted round the tarmac.

The Harrier started to get noisy even though the director still couldn't make up his mind whether Nick should start the race in the air or on the ground.

I looked across the Saab's modest felt interior and watched the Sea Harrier pull alongside me. It was a hot day and with no air conditioning the sweat was trickling from my helmet lining and stinging my eyes. The radio crackled. The director shouted instructions, one word at a time, over the screaming jet engines. 'RIGHT … STIIIG … THE … HARRIER … IS … GOING … TO … HOVER … OVER … THE … TOP … OF … THE … CAR … AND … WE … MIGHT … START … THE … RACE … OK?'

'OK.' With zero chance of being heard, I added a thumbs up.

A few moments later Nick cranked his engines and rose vertically some 40 feet. The noise inside the Saab was deafening.

The Harrier moved in my direction. The 1,000mph, 400°C exhaust announced its presence loud and clear. The right-hand side of the car lifted a little and wobbled. The director had his eyes closed and his high-visibility jacket around his ears. The crew shielded their eyes as plastic bags and other debris careered towards them, but kept their cameras pointed in our general direction.

I could hear nothing above the sound of the jet blast, so I would miss the start unless someone waved. Then Nick must have done something,

because the pressure seemed to double and the Saab sank into its suspension until the tyres topped out on the wheel arches. The wobbling stopped; there was a moment of peace, and then, all of a sudden, one side of the car flicked up.

There was no time to phone a friend for an expert opinion on the consequences of close-range thrust, but my backside told me that we were about to be inverted.

'TELL THE HARRIER TO GET LOST, NOW!' I shrieked, making the cut-throat signal with my hand for good measure.

Nick landed alongside for a restart. The Harrier held all the aces but I figured I could at least get one up on him off the line.

The director counted us down, using a high-tech starting system involving three fingers.

Nick went on 'Go', just after I left on 'One'.

The Saab held the lead for about 10 metres until Nick gave it the berries. In moments he was airborne and gone.

The old Saab lolled around in the corners and was in no hurry down the straights. To its credit, the pudding-like suspension made it entertaining to drive; the rear rolled and slid when I jammed it into the corners. I ran out of steering lock to stop it from spinning at the penultimate corner, and by the time I gathered it up and approached the finish line, I could already see a smug looking fighter jock hovering above it.

I crossed the line in 1 minute 37.9 seconds. It had taken Nick just 31.2 seconds to set the outright track record.

I gave it my best shot, but he refused to hand me the keys ...

With a few episodes under my belt I was getting used to *Top Gear*'s guerrilla filming and they were getting used to my unorthodox method of training the celebrities. My goal was to beat Jodie Kidd's celeb record of 1 minute 48.0, and that meant pushing people hard. I just needed a celeb who was willing to hang it out there.

On the morning of my fifth episode I was completing a vital experiment with a bald man in a toupé. He sat in the passenger seat whilst I hammered three cars up and down the runway to see which one was best at keeping his wig on. The syrup stood firm at 140mph in a Mercedes SL, so we had a winner.

Jim Wiseman was standing by the luxurious Suzuki Liana, awaiting the celebrity guest. He checked the footage coming through the clamshell recorder for the Suzuki's minicams. One was positioned right in the eye line of the driver, to pick up their reactions or pieces-to-camera.

Dennis, our minicam perfectionist, double-checked the exposure. There was no rain in sight but he was dressed in his all-in-one waterproof anorak, prepared as ever for the worst.

'Good picture, Dennis. Are these secure?' He nudged the clamps that held the cameras to the roll cage.

'When have I ever let you lot down?' Dennis moaned.

Simon Cowell strolled down the airfield towards us. He looked momentarily bemused by the cartoon scene of me dressed like a storm trooper alongside Tintin and Mutley, standing by a cheap rental car.

His smile broadened again as he rolled up his black shirtsleeves to shake hands with everyone, instantly sweeping his TV's Mr Nasty persona to one side. *Pop Idol* was already a huge hit, and every TV format and pop act he touched was turning to gold.

We fitted Simon out with a seriously unflattering helmet, an 'egg' as he called it, and climbed aboard the Liana.

I explained that the best way to drive the lap was with his hands firmly at 'a quarter to three' and his thumbs just over the steering wheel's T-bar. Most people thread the rim through their grip as they turn. Why? Because that was the rubbish we were all taught to pass our driving tests. I urged Simon to fix his, and cross them all the way over. He'd know immediately when he'd gone into a corner too fast. When your arms run out of lock, the tyres have long since run out of grip.

We'd leave braking until the last possible moment, I said, and in some corners it would feel like making an emergency stop. Simon remained expressionless, nodding occasionally and cocking his head to one side as he thought about it.

I drove a slow lap to pinpoint the corners. It was surprisingly easy to get lost in the featureless landscape.

'This time round I'll go flat out, so you can see it won't tip over.'

The speed didn't faze Simon whatsoever; he could have been signing another record deal in the Sony boardroom. I knew I could really push him.

He got into the driver's seat and wiggled the gearstick, which crunched in anticipation.

'You *really* have to hand it to Jeremy,' he said. 'What a piece of shit.'

I told him to rev it to three and a half thousand and just dump the clutch. 'Don't slip it like you would in Sainsbury's car park.' As if Simon hung out at Sainsbury's.

We sped off. After a single sighting lap, he began marrying every suggestion I made with small adjustments to his rather basic style.

Simon drove like my mum, with an upright posture and a stiff upper lip. He did shuffle the wheel through his hands to take the corners; the habit was clearly too ingrained for me to change it in the short time we had together. I focused his attention instead on taking a wide approach to the corners and gauging his speed by looking ahead.

What set him apart, made him truly sublime, was his ability to feel the level of grip the car was producing and to match that with precisely the right speed for each corner. He was a real natural.

When he cocked up, he would laugh or call himself a wanker. When the Liana pirouetted at warp 9 through clouds of dust and grass, he remained as calm as a Hindu cow and asked, 'What happened that time?' in a tone that was drier than Ghandi's flip-flop.

I explained the tiny adjustments he needed to make to his line into the corners, turning in later to give the tyres less work to do on a continuous arc, where to brake less and carry extra speed.

His improvement impressed him. After a few laps he said, 'You're really good. Who are you?'

Coming from a talent scout with the world at his feet to someone looking for a way ahead in it, there was only one logical answer. But I didn't give it. After nine laps of my backseat driving, I stayed silent for a lap and he didn't make a single error. Simon was ready to go solo.

Dennis rolled the in-car cameras and Jim politely asked Simon for 'plenty of chat'. I suggested he put in a banker lap first time round, nothing too crazy.

Every lap began from a standing start, which enabled us to chat to Simon and move cameras during the re-set. He set off to the shrill sound of spinning tyres and I followed his progress from the edge of the track.

Jim and I watched transfixed as the Liana crossed the line. Jim carefully angled his stopwatch in my direction in case any of Simon's people were peeking. It was within a second of the lap record.

Simon pulled up, his elbow on the window ledge, and asked what gear he was supposed to use in the second corner.

'Second.'

I asked him to brake later at the penultimate turn. The next lap was audibly faster; we could see him wrestle the steering. I got him to brake later, corner by corner, and he went faster every lap.

Simon took a cigarette and water break and asked how he was doing, but we couldn't let him know before his interview.

His eyebrows disappeared beneath his immaculately sculpted hairline. 'Do you seriously expect me to believe that?'

Yes we did.

We bolted him back into the five-point harness. I always found that the most uncomfortable part of my job; I never quite got used to reaching between a celebrity crotch and yanking a strap across their balls or breasts.

As Simon put in some more fabulous laps, Wilman turned up to check on things. Jim showed him his notepad.

'Bloody Nora.' Wilman gave a soft-shoe shuffle. '*Don't* tell him.'

Simon shared our enthusiasm, so we kept pushing him until he reached a plateau on around lap ten. I told him it was an excellent time that he probably wouldn't beat.

Andy then offered him a passenger ride in the Noble M12 supercar, so I wheeled it out.

The M12 was light as a feather. Its V6 motor was powered by twin turbochargers that took time to spool up before belching the machine forward with gigantic thrust. By selecting the right gears and keeping the turbo's pressure peaking, I could slide the car all the way up to 80mph. I was keen to register a reaction from Simon, so I gave it my best shot.

He remained as cool as a cucumber, arms folded and a serene smile on his face. Perhaps he knew something I didn't. I fired the car across the bump at the tyre wall corner at 135mph and, when his panel judge composure didn't flinch, I drove back to the pits to drop him off.

Wilman reappeared. 'Could you just give Simon a go now?'

Nightmare. Had I known that he'd be driving, I'd never have shown him the machine's full potential. He was too good a mimic.

I kept my belts loose so that I could reach the steering wheel from the passenger seat if I had to. Simon dumped the clutch, just like I'd taught him in the gutless Suzuki. The twin turbos went 'whooooshhhhh' and the car was tearing down the track at 100mph eight seconds later.

He started trying to copy the fast power slides I'd been doing. We were so close to losing it that I didn't dare distract him by speaking. We

approached the super-fast tyre wall corner. I told him to back off where I hadn't.

Simon took an apocalyptic amount of speed in and I knew we were going off big time.

The car spun at 120mph and I leapt across to fling the steering hard over into opposite lock. That sent us down the tarmac, bought a little time and shed some speed.

I was keen to avoid the grass because the car might roll. Once we started going backwards I yanked the handbrake and hollered at him to stand on the anchors. Cowell hit the pins and grinned. I think it meant we were even.

We'd come to a rest on the grass after narrowly missing two landing lights that could have ripped the bloody doors off.

'Now, really, what happened there?' Simon cackled with laughter.

'You went in too fast is what happened. Please, let's go back in so I can collect my P45.'

We bumbled back on to the track and returned the car to its owner. Simon had really enjoyed himself, which meant the crew did too. I'd never seen someone with no experience adapt so quickly to a supercar and wring its neck.

Jim pulled in his footage and I went to the Outside Broadcast truck. Brian Klein, the Studio Director, was sitting in front of a raft of TV screens and waving his hairy arms about. He was wearing a typically garish outfit that comprised a vertically striped T-shirt, knee-length white trousers and leather shoes.

Brian controlled the crowd via his production assistants. They scurried around the floor, moving any gargantuan men out of the way of camera and bringing forward the pretty girls, whilst juggling the three presenters to make sure they were saying the right things at the right time, cueing the pre-recorded footage and keeping an eye on the unedited stuff streaming in hot from the track. All these inputs were performed live to the assembled audience whilst being time coded for packaging into a one-hour show for broadcast four days later.

After a well-executed interview in which Jeremy opined that bus lanes should be banned and traffic wardens exiled, they ran Simon's lap. They stitched on some loony driving from his early runs, but the finishing time was what counted: 1.47.1, nearly a second faster than the track record. Simon double punched the air and Brian smiled at me, raising the

little black carpets above his eyes before he settled back to his control panel.

With Cowell at the top of the leaderboard, only one other marker needed setting straight. Black Stig held the *Top Gear* track record on a 1.23.7 power lap, courtesy of the mighty Lambo Murcielago. To beat that, I needed some serious kit.

Porsche kindly delivered an appropriate weapon with their Carrera GT, a quantum leap in design and performance from their standard line of midlife crisis cures. The GT was panned by limp-wristed critics because the ceramic clutch was too aggressive for pulling away at traffic lights, making it prone to stalling. Driven right, it launched like a scalded cat.

It had a belting 5.7-litre V10 lump in its core, fat tyres and enough front grip to strip the surface off the tarmac. The shrill V10 strafed the ears like a Le Manster. It drove like one too. The GT was light on aerodynamic grip, making it delicate and edgy in the corners but so rewarding once you learnt to apply less steering than normal. That knowledge came the hard way. I spun at least three times during practice. When you drove it on the limit the throttle response was so precise that if your foot moved slightly over a bump it would spin.

The interior wasn't Ferrari fancy but was no less beautiful, with carbon weave and subtle leather trim around a seat that came straight from the Starship *Enterprise*. The giant golfball gear knob was a lazy drop from the wheel, making it vitally accessible during gob-stopping bouts at the helm when the engine ran into the rev limiter mid-slide and a rapid upshift was required.

Jim Wiseman gave me some time to warm up the GT. I took it down the runway and killed the tyres, weaving left and right on full opposite lock, smashing the throttle and braking to a stop to red up the carbon brakes.

It was only ever me versus the track for a power lap. I treated it the same way as a qualifying session and summoned the great drivers I had raced with over the years, guys like Webber and Sato, who would fight me tooth and nail for every hundredth of a second. They may not have been at the track that day, but as Darth Vader aptly put it, I felt their presence.

There were some funny looks from the cameramen, and the deep voice of experience boomed over the radio: 'Not to be contentious – but are we actually gonna have a car left to film?'

'It's OK, Casper,' Jim replied. 'Stig's just warming up the tyres; stand by to shoot in a minute.'

Jim let me drop the hammer without delay. I sawed at the wheel throughout a frenzied lap and the GT popped the record by just over a second, giving me plenty to fold my arms about.

Casper and Ben worked their magic behind the cameras, with Iain May shooting from an elevated mobile platform, or 'cherry picker', which boasted a maximum speed of 4mph. Iain's thinning blond hair and hooded eyes gave him a distinctly mature look, but during the long pauses between takes he shifted its position with all the enthusiasm of a five-year-old on a Tonka Toy.

'Don't park it there yet, Iain,' Casper hissed. 'I'm on a big wide as he comes through the tyres so you'll be in frame. Let me get one more shot, then I'm going tight.'

Camera-talk was slowly sinking in. If Casper was shooting a 'wide' profile it meant I needed to keep it fully lit for a considerably longer distance than if it was a 'tight' close-up moment in one corner. It was fascinating to watch the film crew work together and to be giving them the confidence to creep nearer the action. As the trust grew on both sides, the crew employed their superb skills to define the whiplash-quick shooting style that *Top Gear* became known for.

Iain ended up lying in the gutter less than a foot from the track as I howled past his shoulder at max speed. Most cameramen would press record and walk away. *Top Gear* crews put their necks on the line and operated manually in order to pull focus and pan with the car.

The lairy cornering shots were achieved in much the same way. Jeremy and I would fly sideways into the corner with the crew rotating through different positions, a hair's breadth from our intended line of travel. The boys covered every angle within minutes. Having them so close to the gliding cars focused the mind as much as any motor race, and we never took our eyes off them.

We were expected to get it right first time, so I stopped asking for practice. 'Fine to practise, Stiggy,' became the refrain, 'but we'll just roll cameras anyway.'

The Spanish Yeti, Dan the cameraman, legging it across the track with a Steadicam stabilised mount attached to his torso, was the most unnerving sight of all. He sprinted to and fro, capturing tight gritty sweeps of the action, with his curly black mane flowing in his wake.

The end of my first series came up fast and I wondered if I'd be asked back for another. My hopes were buoyed when a contract arrived in the post, but it was retrospective and was followed by a pay cheque made out to 'The Stig Only'. I was sure the bank had already heard the one about Donald Duck, and unlike Batman I needed the money, so I straightened that one out sharpish with Accounts.

With no certainty if or when *Top Gear* would need me again, I pressed on with the Army.

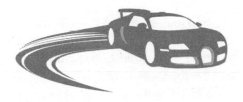

15

A WALK IN THE PARK

The ground froze overnight, and as the sun came up it cast a magic light across the frost-dusted valley. My ground mat had to be snapped and folded like cardboard. I started warming up my shoulders to prevent the shooting pains across my back and neck caused by the five-hour marches. The straps on my ancient bergen had lost their padding and cut into my shoulders like cheese wire. I pressed the store-man to exchange it for a newer one, but the SOB refused. The Chief Instructor just laughed.

We formed up for the morning brief in the middle of a cutting covered in loose shingle and stones from the quarry. The senior NCO emerged from his 'twat wagon', an ugly box-shaped Land Rover. He was in jovial mood.

'Mornin', gentlemen. Little surprise for you all today: owing to the fact that it's Christmas there's no march today, so you can all go back and get your 'eads down …'

Silence. We'd all been here before.

'No takers? OK then, suit yourselves.'

I was called across to the wagon to receive my first rendezvous point. I read the grid and found RV1 with the tip of my compass … on the farthest side of the map, bloody miles away. I looked at the instructor in disbelief.

'Having trouble motivating yourself this morning?'

'No, Staff,' I said, and jogged away.

Typically, the routes were no longer than 25 kilometres as the crow flies, with ascents in the region of one to two thousand feet. This monster tab looked at least 5k longer, and taking the wrong route could add an hour and result in a fail. I opted to go straight up the side of a sheer waterfall, reducing me to a snot-faced mop of sweat within metres of the start line.

I managed to scale the wall of the ravine and make it on to open ground, but things didn't get any easier. Every conceivable physical obstacle stood in my path. The correct procedure for river crossings was to strip naked, suit up with Gore-Tex and wade across, facing upstream. That seemed over the top for the stretch of water that now confronted me. It was 15 feet at most from bank to bank. I could clear half that in one bound.

I misjudged the depth, submerged and disappeared downstream, saturating every bit of my kit and sorely weighing myself down. I cursed my stupidity, but thanks to an earlier rushed barbed wire fence crossing that had nearly ripped off my family jewels, my crotchless trousers vented quickly.

I plodded through endless fields of 'babies' heads' – clumps of ankle-high bog-grass that rendered forward movement almost impossible – and braced myself for crossing Death Valley, so named for its double-dip profile and the fact that so many recruits had voluntarily withdrawn from the course after climbing it.

The incline was sheer at times, making the climb truly biblical: you had to dig in with your fingernails. It was three steps forward and four back, knowing all the while that every agony would be repeated on the second peak.

After Death Valley I put in a short cut through a range of felled trees. The layers of broken branches snagged every movement or gave way to shred the front of my shin.

An hour later the fog descended again and a few cairns appeared ahead that I couldn't place on the map. I had a 'dead stop' if I walked too far, because there were cliffs behind the RV I was looking for. A sensation of weightlessness would give me the first hint I'd walked too far. But where were the bloody cliffs? Eventually I saw one of the lads to my right amidst the sea of fog.

'Hey, do you know where the RV is?'

He was too engrossed in his map to reply. I checked mine and shouted again. After a while I realised I was shouting at a small tree. I finally made it to the last checkpoint and limped over to the woods we were using as a holding area to stick up my basha and get my head down.

An hour later I was woken by a five foot five pocket rocket with a voice like Cartman from *South Park*. 'Well, that was fucking emotional,' he puffed. His little legs had to spin like cartwheels to keep pace over the hills. I peeled back an eyelid as Cartman's bergen crashed into the deck.

'That was, like, thirty fucking K or something. And Jesus Christ, there was some fucking headcase on my route. I was up the side of Fan Y something or other and there's this guy crashing through, like, a million babies' heads and barbed wire fences below me. I was looking and thinking, mate, what the fuck are you doing?

'He gets to the fucking river, takes off his bergen and chucks his webbing across to the other side, puts his bergen back on and, like, jumps in.'

This story was beginning to sound awfully familiar.

'Then he disappears from sight and reappears about twenty metres down-stream. I seriously thought he was fucking dead.'

'Me too,' I said through the opening of my sleeping bag.

'Collins, man, where the fuck did you come from?!' Bernie was hanging on Cartman's every word, his racing spoon frozen over a steaming bag of sausage and beans.

'I knew I was in trouble when my feet didn't touch the river bed. My bergen weighed a bloody ton after that.'

He shook his head in bemusement. 'My job's fucking boring; that's why I'm doing this. But you, Collins, you're just a complete nutter.'

Kojak toked on his cigarette. 'I just love the Phys. It's the best bit of the course.' He really was mad.

The banter continued, with everyone swapping routes, mistakes, medications and personal agonies. The course was thinning down to a hard core of guys who were willing to tough it out to the end. As the marches became longer, harder and higher we dug deeper and our bodies adapted. Small courtesies like sharing rations and helping each other with admin were now common. But when it came to survival you were on your own. No one could carry you.

Our training course had been whittled down from over 100 candidates to just 23 that now faced the final hurdle. The final week consisted of seven days of hell, running the marathon of marathons.

In the evening briefing the Officer Commanding laid out the timings. He was careful to leave us in no doubt that some of us were hanging on by our fingernails.

I ate like a pig in preparation for that week, but the volume of stodge consumed at camp was on a new level, even by my standards. Speed was of the essence in order to spend more time sorting kit or sleeping, so I ate dessert whilst queuing for the main meal. Later, as we were having our bergens weighed at the starting point in Zulu Valley, we were ordered to line up and display our consumables. Scales varied, so it paid to pack heavy. If you came in underweight by so much as a biscuit, the penalty was severe.

'Where's your food for the day?' asked a coarse Scottish NCO with an Alsatian at his heel.

I produced the mulched banana milkshakes I was carrying in a pair of Nalgene bottles and took the tops off.

'Where's your proper food for the tab?'

'This is it, Staff. It's crushed bananas, nuts and carbohydrates.'

'What are you,' he said in disbelief, 'some sort of fucking fruitcake?'

He dispatched us one at a time into the sopping valley. The range we were running through was notably more boggy than the Black Mountains and my boot strategy stank. Lowa boots were taller than my usual Skarpas, which meant they should keep more water out. Once water got in, however, you carried the extra weight on your feet and the weight was multiplied by the leverage of your lifting legs. A wet boot also acted as a greenhouse to a blister. I doubled up with knee-high gaiters.

Within sight of the start line I managed to find a bog and slurped into it as far as my armpits. The Lowas acted like a sponge and quadrupled the weight of my feet for the rest of the tab.

Each day was as relentlessly knackering as the next. Eating, drinking, sleeping, pissing, tabbing. But as wearing as the whole process became, you had to admire the scale of the natural beauty in the National Park. We ran along the black, peat-like soil tracks through the wild heather, drawing in gusting bursts of fresh air, then up and around the horseshoe scarps of Fan y Big, with its straight drop into the green basin below. The layered sandstone ridges looked freshly carved by the hand of a giant.

First sense of speed, aged 4. Dad is out of shot and out of breath from pushing.

The serious pose.

Training in the pool, four hours a day, seven days a week.

Downtime, surfing in Costa Rica.

Celebrating Team Ascari's Le Mans Sportscar win with Werner Lupberger. On the right Jan Lammers and Jean-Marc Gounon on the left.

The RML Lola Honda on the way to a class victory in the Le Mans Series.

Le Mans pitstop in the rain at dusk.

Driving Red Bull's F1 car.

Racing a Jack Daniel's V8 supercar during Australia's 'Great Race' at Bathurst. Probably the wildest racing event in the world.

Army recruitment, Hugh Hefner style.

Dawn at Lakeland Speedway, testing in NASCAR with Red Bull.

The 'Stealth car'.

Leading in Indy Lights, with Indycar champ Scott Dixon alongside left.

Dropping the hammer in the big league, NASCAR Sprint Cup.

Tension ahead of a big race. Preparing to switch my brain for earplugs.

The Suzuki Liana took a hammering at the hands of the celebrities. Here it lost a front wheel and sent Lionel Richie off-roading.

Jay Kay, space cowboy and speed freak.

Hugh Grant asks for directions to Sunset Boulevard.

Mr Cool: Simon Cowell, shortly after he tried to kill me.

Jordan applies for a new post as Silicon Stig.

Tom Cruise after he smashed the lap record in the reasonably priced car.

Filming the US Top Gear with Jon Favreau. Our reasonably priced car was expensive, so the producers covered it with mud.

Dan De Castro.

Casper Leaver with
Iain May in the background.

'Give us a kiss, Jeremy.' Shooting at Willow Springs in California in the Ford GTX1.

Producer Alex Renton plays the pikey in Top Gear's Man and Van Challenge.

Jim Wiseman, KAPOW! Creative guru and one of the 'originals' who brought new Top Gear to the screen.

James May: white-van man.

Top Gear Couriers Ltd
Telex TG5684

Driving the pod car with Nicolas Cage.

Milesy smashes the beer truck through a police blockade outside the Bank of England.

Back at barracks news broke that the final lengthy march of the week was being brought forward, reducing our recovery time from the previous run. A little extra test of character was needed to thin out the recruits to a more manageable number.

Where previous 'walks' had taken five or six hours, the final march took over eighteen. And we carried nearly 80 pounds, all in. Heavier, harder, longer.

Everyone was mentally and physically shattered. Just walking to the shower block made your thighs burn.

As darkness fell, the orange street lighting crept through Seventies curtains into the partly vacated dormitory. I lay on top of my sleeping bag pretending to sleep, but running a checklist of all my equipment, worrying about spare shoelaces, food and the little I remembered of the route. A blue flash signalled a text message from a mate in London. 'Happy birthday big boy.' I'd forgotten about that. I was twenty-nine.

Zinc oxide tape was all that was holding the welts across my back together, so I left it on and strapped a new batch around my ankles and feet. We formed up to receive our final marching brief in an atmosphere of apprehension. People stumbled around using head torches and small pocket lights to seat themselves on their bergens in front of the four-tonners.

The DS opened proceedings with a total ban on head torches and walking in pairs or groups. 'If we catch any of you walking hand in hand like Mary fucking Poppins, you're binned.'

There was limited gossip en route to the start point except for Cartman, who was buzzing on a powerful cocktail of brufen, codeine and cough medicine. There was no stopping him now.

We arrived in the dark and scaled our equipment. I knelt by the headlights of the four-tonner, pounded some painkillers and tightened my shoelaces for the big off, with the barrel of my weapon on my foot and the butt on the ground.

'Whose *fucking* gat is that on the floor? Who is that with their fucking weapon on the floor?!'

My heart sank. It was no time to argue the toss. 'Collins, sir.'

'Go and get a Fucking Big Rock and bring it here.'

I grabbed an FBR, had it authenticated with a number so that it could be checked at any one of the checkpoints along the entire march, and added this vital piece of equipment to my bergen.

Within minutes of starting I was scaling a slippery, muddy slope in total darkness. I drank all my water within the first half-hour. I had nothing left – pathetic. The enormity of the task suddenly overwhelmed me. It seemed I had found my breaking point. I stopped.

Breathe. I imagined hearing Cartman and Flash talking rubbish, singing the stupid chart-topping milkshake song, telling me to get the fuck up. I made out a tiny patch of light on my immediate horizon: the peak of the first hill. I broke the crest and felt a little better.

The first checkpoint lay at the bottom of a small valley next to a reservoir. It was littered with guys sitting on their bergens. I realised the group had jacked it in.

Next came a goat track that snaked its way up and around two giant mountains. There was plenty of tripping over loose stones in the blackness of the night, but at least each trip was a step in the right direction. At the highest point the track was bordered by a sheer drop. A few guys ahead pinged on their head torches to speed their progress and I followed suit.

After a few minutes I looked behind me. For over a kilometre, sixty or so head torches bobbed the length of the path. It was a magnificent sight, like the fiery beacons along Hadrian's Wall.

The guilty pleasure of the head torch was short-lived. On the way back down the hill I made up some good time by running, but the further down the mountain we went, the more open the ground became. It felt exposed.

I cashed in my chips, switched off my light and slowed to a fast walk, once again at the mercy of the broken ground and babies' heads. Some guys ahead cracked on, lights ablaze.

I became aware of something moving from cover to my left. There was a rustling sound as black shapes sped across the long dry grass, followed by several thuds and the familiar sound of bergens slamming into the deck. The lights went out. I never knew what happened to the guys wearing them.

Dawn came and went. Legs pumped endlessly through the day. The peaks of the Beacons National Park were withering. Daylight brought a fresh perspective and extra energy. I ran along the flats and caught up

with Ninja at a queue for an RV point. Some boys lay poleaxed on one side whilst fluids were pumped intravenously into their arms. A more hopeful lad squeezed the saline bag and jogged on the spot to speed the process.

Ninja was hollow-eyed, shaking and confused, bordering on hypothermic. He was trying to get his Gore-Tex on but couldn't even pull the zip, so I squared him away and we plodded on.

Legs pumped endlessly through the day. Pen Y Fan, again, was withering. As dusk approached once more we walked down a tractor track across an open field. I was a zombie, rifle flailing at waist height, legs on autopilot. There was a gap in the hedgerow ahead. As my right foot made contact with the solid incline of a tarmac road my face turned left towards the hill, then I heard a sharp metallic thwack.

My bergen picked me up and spun me through 180 degrees into the hedge. I looked up to see the back of a square-framed steel trailer, laden with canoes, winging past at a rate of knots. The front of the trailer must have caught the outer pouch of my bergen.

I kept monging along, remembering Plissken's final words: 'You don't need to be superhuman, lads. You'll all make mistakes, but you push it to the end.'

We had to cover 10km in four hours to make the cut-off. More than enough time to cover the distance in normal circumstances, but I knew I was losing the plot. Stomach cramps gripped me every 30 seconds. My head was pounding and my legs were so swollen that every step made my eyes water. I couldn't eat anything except Jelly Babies, which were running out fast. One navigational error in the dark and we were done for.

'Come on, Benny, we've *got* to do this,' Ninja urged.

To be sure of reaching the end, it was time to start running. I closed my eyes, detached myself from reality and pounded up the incline. I heard a voice inside as every system in my body spoke with unanimous certainty: 'You are going to die.'

All the pain could go away in a millisecond; all I had to do was stop, rap, throw away the bergen and sleep. I was bouncing off the limit of my physical endurance.

A lyric by The Killers popped into my head and offered twisted solace: 'Smile like you mean it.' I shouted the words like a lunatic with each breath. We finally crested a rise, contoured a wood and descended the

ankle-smashing shingle of a dried riverbed. It was the hardest hour and a half of my life.

Moonlight bounced off the water of a reservoir ahead. The end was nigh and carried its own demons. Realising we would make it, my brain signalled its helpful endorphins to switch off. As far as the grey matter was concerned, the serotonin and dopamine had done their job. My legs returned to pillars of fire, the pit of my stomach tightened and gravity doubled.

I told Ninja to get lost. We couldn't finish as a pair anyway, and I didn't want to hold him up. I staggered the rest of the way, stopping for every third stomach cramp and dry retching the others on the move.

A golden head torch flickered in the distance. Voices ... An unforgettable sense of euphoria grew inside me and made the pain irrelevant.

It was acutely personal. No car had carried me to this place, nor had luck. The training officer took my name and number at the final checkpoint. No one asked to check my Fucking Big Rock.

I slumped on my bergen in a shit state. One of the DSs handed me a brew with some 'airborne smarties' to kill the pain. It was the best tea I had ever tasted, followed later by the best shower in the world and the kind of sleep that money can't buy. I never felt so alive.

We lost some strong guys during the final exercise. One had even fallen off a cliff, but managed to stagger into the next checkpoint, where he was withdrawn by the DS. Having passed one of the toughest military recruitment training courses in the world, the rest of us might have been forgiven for expecting some respite going into the continuation phase of our training, the skills-at-arms for soldiering in small tight-knit patrols.

Our new training staff introduced us to a Welsh cyborg by the name of Jones, a multiple Iron Man champion and uber-athlete. He had sunken eyes and the physique of a half-starved cage fighter. Alongside him was a stacked Geordie of an African persuasion on secondment from the Regular Army, there to impart the wisdom gained through his extensive and distinguished service. Geordie had encyclopaedic tattoos scrawled across his sizeable biceps and a penetrating glare that I tried hard to avoid.

Our new webbing, or fighting order, was far more advanced than the old belt kits, containing numerous pouches for carrying ammunition and survival equipment, but the trusty bergen lived on. When we were

ordered to drop bergens and prepare to move I thought we'd arrived at Butlins.

'You haven't met Ken yet, have you?' enquired a big Canadian bear who had joined our course.

'No, who's Ken?'

'Can you hear that noise?' asked Bear.

'No.'

'*Exactly*. He hasn't arrived yet. You'll know it when he does.'

'Right, stop yappin',' Jones mumbled. Then he ran off up a metallic road.

Jones ran the legs off us, legs that still remembered being reduced to jelly on that long final march across the hills. Then the DS dined out on our lack of performance, our unworthiness and so on. A raft of new and unpleasant physical exercises would cure our ills. About twenty-five of us moved into a field and began doing fireman's lifts, sit-ups, jumps, monkey crawls, endless press-ups, burpees, run, down, up, run, down, up.

A dangerous looking man appeared through a turnstile and strode towards us with clenched fists like he wanted to kick someone's head in. He was hairless, in his mid forties, wearing the disco jungle pattern uniform popular with Paratroopers. At this point I was clinging on to Flash's legs whilst he pedalled his arms across the ground for the final leg of a wheelbarrow race. We collapsed in an undignified heap a few metres short, then crossed the line first and heaved in the oxygen.

'Fackin' listen in, fellas,' the Para began.

Someone choked on their puke and Para's neck stretched like a meer-kat in search of the culprit.

'Fackin' pack it in when I'm talking, yeah? You lot better start *fackin' sparking*, right. Some of you are treading water. Well, your fackin' faces don't fit ...' and so forth.

This, I presumed, was Ken. We moved along to an innocent looking basin with a short sharp rise to a tree-lined hedgerow. At the foot was a pile of sandbags that needed shuttle sprinting to the top. After the third one, it was hard to look like you were trying when the grass was growing faster than you were moving. By the sixth, you were utterly bollocksed. Johnny fell out with chest pains. That made him a marked man in Ken's book.

Eventually our bodies could take no more. We were told we had a long way to go to be fit enough to handle the ranges; firing and manoeuvring

at pace in tight formations, firing live rounds. You've guessed it: if we couldn't handle it, we were out.

There was so much information to take in: medical training, tactics and, above all, contact drills for killing the enemy. We learned patrolling skills and spent all night putting them into practice. Then came the assault course.

'Speed, aggression and safety' was Ken's byword, though he never concerned himself much with the third item except on the ranges. We walked parts of the course and learnt the best way to handle the obstacles, before being taken to a section we hadn't yet seen. I resigned myself to the fact that my body no longer belonged to me and warmed up with the boys behind a shed. Jones took us to the starting point one at a time.

I turned the corner, put on my green helmet and lined up 30 metres away from a wall with a window four feet above the ground. The little incline before the window prevented any indication of what lay beyond.

Ken was eagerly looking on. 'Now don't fack about, Colin.'

Jones leered at me and tapped my shoulder. 'Go.'

I sprinted at the window and dived through head first. There was a sizeable drop, a rattle of body parts and a forward roll. Next came the cargo net. Another leap cleared the first eight feet of it as I punched my arm through and hooked in at the shoulder, climbed up and flipped over the top. This pleased Ken, who jogged alongside.

The next sprint was less fluid. This upset Ken.

More climbing, jumping, swinging and running led to a brick wall.

'Colin, get up that fackin' wall.'

I ran in, dug my foot into the mortar line and hopped up, getting a hand on to the top. A big pull, then the other arm, and over to the finish.

The next course was a team event and unsighted. I hooked up with the Bear, Johnny and a lad from another company. We attacked the course and its festering water obstacles before approaching the monkey bars, where Geordie was lurking with a mischievous smirk. It wasn't long before we found out why. When we were halfway across the bars, he whipped out a high-pressure hose and artfully switched his fire between our eyes, balls and fingertips.

We had a problem with our heavy Bear, who spent more time swimming the lagoon than on the bars overhead. I went back for him with

Johnny and we shoved him on top of the bars, where Geordie couldn't squirt him off.

'Ah, that's quick thinkin' there, fellas.'

We sprinted to the final obstacle. I vaulted up the high wall with Johnny, but we struggled to drag Bear over, so I climbed back down and shoved him over the top with his boot in my mouth. I was wrenched over as the last man, falling in a heap on the other side, where everybody else was already waiting.

I lifted my saturated helmet from over my eyes, got to my feet and collided with the training officer. 'Switch on, Collins. You need to work on your phys.'

An Officer and a Gentleman it wasn't …

I loved the Army. It had become the only constant in my career. Back at 'work' I had to try and capitalise on my championship title and get a NASCAR drive. When I wasn't training with the boys in green, I was back on the phone selling my soul to the marketing and advertising genii of Madison and Vine. I also had to earn some money and pitched endless ideas to *Top Gear*.

Winning the Texaco Trophy had opened the door with their UK marketing agent. Given that Texaco also sponsored a car in NASCAR's top category, it was a link worth forging. I struck a deal to drive for them in the UK, with the proviso that I would compete in a NASCAR support race at Charlotte at the end of the season.

I joined a new team with a tiny operating budget. As returning champion I had it all to lose. But I still had a lot to learn about NASCAR racing, so I figured it was a risk worth taking.

The team collected our car from a pool of spares held by the series organisation and put it together. Then we set about testing, and my first laps in it confirmed my worst fears. The back end shook around as awkwardly as a John Sergeant mambo on *Strictly Come Dancing*. I couldn't get anywhere near my own pace from the previous season and we ran out of adjustment on the car trying to fix it.

The first weekend was an exercise in mediocrity. We crossed the line in fifth and sixth positions. I met with one of the series organisers in his ivory tower at Rockingham and pleaded our case. Our car was incapable of winning; we needed to exchange it.

'You are the *last* person we would want winning the series again,' he explained as he rocked back on his leather chair. 'That's half the problem with Formula 1 these days, right, it's bloody boring watching the same person winning again and again.'

I knew it. This was all Schumacher's fault.

'Well, I assume that you want Texaco to stay in the series?' I bluffed. 'Basically if we can't have another car, I'm pulling out. And so will they.'

I had no authority to say that, but it paid off. We were granted a new car for the next race a few months later, one that could actually turn left. In the meantime the soldiering business became a full-time preoccupation.

After months of intensive training our assault rifles became extensions of our bodies. Contact drills, our immediate response to enemy fire, were honed from hundreds of rehearsals of choreographed moves designed to inflict maximum damage on the enemy.

We crept across the vast open plains of the firing range on the tips of our toes, rifle in the shoulder. Every sense was jacked; we could almost smell the targets before they appeared. The river to our left offered potential cover, as did the rising valley to the right.

The glimmer of a target – the weapon fired and the target dropped.

'Contact front.'

Our tiny group dealt out a murderous rate of fire. Live rounds pierced the air as we wove past one other, taking control of the ground. Fire and manoeuvre, all under the watchful eyes of our instructors, who were judging our performances.

'Baseline, break left,' Ninja shouted.

I lobbed a smoke grenade and we hurtled into the confines of the river one by one, pepper-potting along it, firing all the way. Sprint, down, fire, up, sprint, down, fire; lead turned into brass.

Burning legs pumped through the river towards my buddies as we broke away from contact. We were so close we were firing past each other's shoulders. I noticed a flash and heard an unusual noise, the hiss of a close round. Tread carefully.

Magazine changes became a bodily function. You felt the weapon lighten, anticipating the click at the end of the magazine,

diving into cover, automatically slapping home the next magazine, releasing the working parts, re-engaging – *Bang*. We were totally tuned in.

My rounds ricocheted off another target 200 metres away, but it still wouldn't fall. Ken pounced on my shoulder. 'Fack's sake, hit that fackin' target!'

I rounded on him. 'It's fucking broken, Staff!'

I switched to another and blatted it down.

All morning we leapt over obstacles, rolled through firing positions and sprinted from one objective to the next. We bombed up for the next assault, established security and analysed the situation. Sweat poured and hands shook from the adrenalin and the high lactate concentrations in our muscles. Ken was looking for the smallest error.

'Fackin' switch on. This is when we're looking at you, when you're *facked*. Right. Fackin' close in, lads.'

We huddled around Ken. Our steaming breath rose from the circle like a halo. He stared intently at each of us, one by one. I took a slug from my water bottle and hacked at the phlegm in my throat.

Ken was the devil to most of us but I admired his perfectionism, and not just the ability to swear several times in every sentence. His relentless abuse was timeless, whether it was lunchtime and someone wasn't loading rounds into a magazine fast enough, or 3am and someone wasn't in exactly the spot where they were supposed to be for an ambush. He cared, I suspected, because he had witnessed the consequences of getting it wrong.

'The next objective is in that fackin' wood up there. You fight through that position, yeah. Fackin' whatever it takes, lads. In Para Reg, right, we fix fackin' bayonets.'

We advanced to contact in sections, losing sight of the far right flank behind the tree line as we cleared the open ground.

There was a crescendo of loud bangs.

'CONTACT FRONT …'

'You, you, you and YOU – you're fackin' DEAD.'

Unlike the real thing, being 'killed' on the range wasn't all bad. I checked my safety and hit the deck. Johnny and Bernie started hauling me towards cover. The effort was carved across their faces.

'You two, pick up his fackin' bergen.'

'You're joking,' Bernie moaned, adding the dragging weight of my pack to my carcass. Out of sight of the DS I kicked my legs as much as I could to help propel my weight.

They dropped me and laid down more fire. People were opening up at the tree line from all sides. I leaned over to my right to get a better view of the advance as the group nearest me switched fire and the flanking section took the position. A searing hot pain entered my armpit, then wriggled quickly down my ribcage to the small of my back.

Being a hypochondriac, I thrust my hand inside my body armour to check for blood and quickly realised I hadn't been shot. After plenty of digging, I removed a pair of hot, flesh-stained shell cases that had fallen from Bernie's rifle. I looked back up to see Geordie and Jones laughing their asses off at me.

'STOP.'

Geordie gathered us round.

'So what have we learnt from this exercise, lads?'

'Should've joined the Air Corps,' Cartman said, catching his breath.

'Don't get shot, simple as that. Otherwise you're all fookared. Right, collect the brass, pack up and Foxtrot Oscar.'

We absorbed volumes of information on assault techniques, situational awareness, observation skills, reconnaissance, patrolling, signals, close-quarter combat, fieldcraft, routines, teamwork. It paid to listen and learn. You could be put on the spot at any moment.

'Collins, Johnny, you're with me in the gun group. The rest of you lads, get fackin' bombed up for the assault.'

I took the General Purpose Machinegun, Johnny took the Minimi. I carried enough belts of ammunition around my neck to film the entire *Rambo* series. We made a tactical approach to the fire support position overlooking the area where our brothers would be assaulting a range of bunkers and targets. 'Tactical' meant the hard way, the steep way, avoiding open ground and maintaining cover, dragging ourselves and our kit across rocks and fallen trees. Ken walked alongside and dished out his usual brand of encouragement.

The Gimpy could dish out up to a thousand 7.62-calibre rounds every minute, and Ken wanted Armageddon. That meant switching barrels regularly to prevent them overheating and I ran the drill in my head. Sometimes the barrel would get so hot that it glowed red and the passing rounds were visible from the outside.

Lying flat on my belly in the firing position, I set out my stall with spare barrel, oil and ammo. With the butt of the gun pressed into my

shoulder, I flipped open the top cover and splashed oil over the working parts like a drunk pissing over his shoes. I loaded a serpentine belt of live rounds mixed with ball and tracer, slapped down the cover, racked the cocking handle to make ready, clicked on the safety and sighted for 400 metres.

In seconds, the boys would sweep into view from the left of my arc of fire. My job was to suppress as many targets ahead of them as possible. Policing the exercise was just as intense for Ken as for us on the triggers.

I stared down the iron sights with both eyes open to take in the periphery, scanning for a target, watching for the assault group. A jammed round or a belt change had to be dealt with as fast as possible to maintain the rate of fire and support the attack. Everything was prepared. Shit. Apart from my earplugs ...

Movement, an obscured white object that wasn't there before ...

'Staff, target at 400 metres, centre of arc behind the bush, can I engage?'

'Crack on.'

I flicked off the safety and gave a short burst to gauge the fall of the rounds. Johnny followed suit. The crackle of fire slashed at what was left of my eardrums. The bush exploded as the tracer thudded into the bank just short of the target. I raised the barrel a hair, squeezed and the next burst tore through the target.

Firing in bursts didn't look as cool as the Rambo method: stripped to the waist and freshly lubed, legs apart, gun under one arm, hosing an infinite belt of rounds across the entire battlefield. The upside of stroking the trigger was the accuracy, which the 'spray and pray' method rarely achieved.

Smoke drifted across the area, signalling the arrival of the rifle group. 'Get the fackin' rounds down!' Ken chanted.

We poured fire into the forward positions at an increasing tempo as they moved towards them. I could make out Bernie and Flash dashing forward and dropping, signalling and firing.

Our fire intensified, decimating the position. The boys closed in, metres away from the falling shots, then just feet. If I aimed a quarter inch to the left the fire would split Bernie's head open like a cantaloupe. I gripped the weapon with all my strength, as if some imaginary force might draw the barrel towards him.

Ken left it to the last moment. 'GUN GROUP, switch fire to the right – bunker, 450 metres, rapid *FIRE*.'

I swivelled the Gimpy on its tripod until the sight met the target. BLAP, BLAP, click.

Ken was on me. 'Clear that stoppage!'

I cracked the top cover and racked the working parts, which jammed in protest. I pulled on the lever with all my strength. *Not now, you bastard, open …*

The bolt whipped back, I peeled off the belt and cleared the smouldering link obstructing the feed, slapped on a fresh belt … rack, engage …

The gun chewed through the belt like confetti; targets rose and fell. I must have gone through at least 350 rounds.

'BARREL CHANGE,' I shouted, putting Johnny on notice to hold the fort. I fired through the belt and sprung into action, dislodged the smoking barrel, attached the fresh one and carried on. The rifle group closed in again. Grenadiers took out the bunker as we went cyclic on the guns and blew it to smithereens.

The boys cleared through the final position and took off up a re-entrant, a small cutting that covered their movement. It was our turn to run.

Our charred fingers gathered up all the bits and bobs. Ken rushed us along, piling on the pressure. *Gun over the shoulder, start running.* The burning first gasps of air rushed through the backs of our throats. By the time we reached the blokes, Johnny was waddling like a pregnant duck. In between bursts of fire at an imaginary enemy, I cradled the Gimpy like a newborn baby, with arms jacked too full of lactic acid for my hands to hold it.

Geordie beasted us through fire positions all the way up the re-entrant. Everyone was ball-bagged. It felt like having bench pressed one too many and not even being able to get the bar back into the rack. Do you cry for help, or just slow down a little?

'I'm gonna start FACKIN' PUNCHING CUNTS. Fackin' *MOOOVE*,' Ken screeched.

A gnat's fart could have blown me over.

'Stop.'

I quietly puked some baked beans.

'Well done, lads,' Geordie said. 'Sometimes a breakaway like that goes on for hours. You stop pushin' and you die, it's that simple. Have a ten-minute break, sort yer shit out, everyone ready to leave in five minutes.'

We tabbed into the night and returned to our base in the woods. 'Stagging on' was never a popular part of field routine and involved fighting to stay conscious during the small hours to provide security for the patrol, whilst every fibre of your being begged for sleep. Sleep deprivation, the stress of constant evaluation, cold, hunger and arduous exercise made your eyes welt.

My head barely had time to sink into my gonk bag before I was thumped in the ribs by the sentry I was replacing. Wild horses wouldn't drag me out of bed at home when I was feeling this tired.

My face screwed up like a walnut. I double-checked there was a round in my weapon, peeled off the warm bag and re-attached my webbing. I slipped on my cold wet boots and stood like an old man. My smock was next to go on; the sweat from the day had had just enough time to freeze. I moved quietly and carefully through the jungle of para cord, camp paraphernalia and prone bodies.

I found Ninja drooped over his rifle, barely awake. I had to make sure we both remained alert until he was relieved. We scanned constantly for the 'enemy', but the only real fight on offer was with our eyelids.

The only way to stay awake was to have deep and meaningful conversations that would inspire enough cerebral activity to stay conscious.

'Jelly baby,' Ninja grunted.

'I'm out,' I replied.

I pushed a grubby hand into my smock pocket and carefully extracted a paper packet. I tipped half the coffee powder on to my tongue before passing the rest to him.

The stillness of night went unbroken for twenty minutes. Nothing pulsed in the green glow of our thermal imager. Skeletal branches broke up the low moonlit sky like cracks in a pane of glass.

Something caught my attention to our right. One, then two dark figures loomed into view 200 metres away, at the edge of our line of sight.

I kicked Ninja and signalled that we had company. As they came closer we could see more men trudging in line, fifteen at least. It was probably best to let them walk by, but what if it was a test by the DS to see if we were awake? The leading men pinged on their head torches and that clinched it.

I took up a firing position and, as the leader reached us, Ninja nodded and challenged them. 'Halt. Advance one and be recognised.'

I took a step forward from the trees and aimed at the point man's face. He froze as his torch beam told him the good news. It took a few seconds for him to clock the 40mm grenade launcher slung underneath the barrel of a foreign rifle. Unlike his SA80, ours were not fitted with adapters for firing blanks.

'Identify yourself!'

Point man's feet left the ground as he performed a jumping jack, thrusting his arms into the crucifix position, legs akimbo. *Not* the DS then.

He didn't know our password and began desperately pleading for someone called Stu to help him. In a real battle, these would have been his last words. Lieutenant Stu duly appeared and we decided to let his platoon of Royal Marines go this time.

16

PASS OR FAIL

The Army had a way of making you feel invincible. So I decided to run the London Marathon.

The cheering crowd and the folks wearing the daft hats with pointed ears for the Whizz Kidz charity I was running for made the whole experience unforgettable. With 5 kilometres to go, I was handed a Lucozade by a big hero of mine, Jonny Wilkinson. Under different circumstances we might have had more than two words to say to each other, but it was an honour just being alongside the World Cup rugby legend.

The ligament in my knee was less impressed with the whole performance. Back on the military ranges I had to sprint with a limp. On the weekend before the last hurdle of battle camp, the referred strain finally tore my Achilles tendon. The Army medic thought it might rupture and was threatening to withdraw me from the course when Geordie waded into the twat wagon. 'Let's not be too hasty with the prognooosis, docta.' They agreed to keep an eye on me, but if things got worse, it was game over.

There was better news at *Top Gear*: I was brought back for a second series. The second guest was Paul McKenna, the celebrity hypnotist and mind-bending wizard.

Paul's smooth baritone voice radiated the calm and control of a reflective mind. His eyebrows converged around his nose like a hawk as he listened to me explaining the laws of speed. I imagined that Paul, being a globally renowned expert in mind management, would just hypnotise the car into running smoothly around the circuit. He took a rather different approach.

From the moment we swapped seats and McKenna put his foot down, it was like watching Mr Hyde strangling charming Dr Jekyll. McKenna's facial expressions behind the wheel could inspire generations of Picasso impressionists.

Fists of iron clenched the wheel with such force that the blood drained from his knuckles. Every gear change was like a death-blow. The faster he cornered the more his face contorted with rage. When his mouth gaped open and his tongue started lashing his ivories, I began wondering if I had missed the giant Scorpion at Hammerhead. Paul was in a dark place.

I felt thoroughly unprofessional when he caught me laughing, but I explained that he needed to relax to drive fast. I coaxed Paul towards taking a gentler handle on the controls and he posted a very respectable time.

He later hypnotised Hammond into believing he was a baked potato that had forgotten how to drive, so I figured his mind magic might extend to fixing my Achilles. He kindly recommended a healer in North London. I'd maxed out on conventional medicine and therapeutic ultrasound, so happily steered myself in the direction of the witch doctor.

Apart from the occasional blast with *TG*, my whole life had become centred on passing the Army course, whatever it took. I prepared all my equipment for the final exercise and streamlined my webbing with fresh bungee cord that made it lighter, tighter and very Gucci darling. I loaded essential condiments such as Tabasco and olive oil to transform my 'rat packs' into the kind of pukka taste sensations that would make Jamie Oliver drool.

Lastly, Dr Collins's surgery was stocked with eight packs of synthetic ice to soothe my creaking Achilles tendon between beastings, enough oxide tape to mummify a giraffe, and elephantine doses of anti-inflammatories. For all the bravado, I was crapping myself about the prospect of failure. It would only take one misplaced step on a cold morning to put me out of action.

* * *

With my kit squared away I was ready for war, but before that I had to go and compete at Rockingham. I switched my head into racing mode. The team had been working around the clock to put the new car together. As I climbed in for the first time, Graham, the team manager, stood in front with his headcans on, arms folded. Graham was a grafter. His normally gentle face was taut and unsmiling.

'Radio check.'

'Good, yeah,' Graham replied.

'Don't worry, if it drives half as good as it looks they won't stand a chance.'

I got the impression he didn't necessarily agree.

I took her out for a spin and felt the grip hook the chassis into the track again. We were back in business.

I qualified on pole and we blitzed the first race of the day. Graham personally worked one of the pneumatic wheel guns to guarantee a lightning pit stop; the sparks flew off the spinning metal and he kept me in front of the pack until we crossed the line. He was so ecstatic when I came into the pits that he threw his radio on the floor and picked me up off the ground and grinned the winner's smile. It put us on pole for the second round later that afternoon and I planned on repeating the result.

I led the field into the rolling start and wove and slammed the throttle to get as much heat into the tyres as possible. As we approached the back straight I lined up to sweep through the final corner and allowed the other cars to form around me. Colin White's bright green machine pulled so close we nearly collided. A gesture of intent.

I sped up and found my engine's sweet spot in second gear as we approached the start, and the instant the flag twitched I buried the long throttle pedal. As we hurtled towards Turn One I narrowly held the advantage, committed my entry speed and opened a tiny gap. Colin held close inside.

I kept enough margin to be able to take a racing line through Two, with Colin darting inside in a futile harassing move, but my tyres just weren't gripping enough to shake him loose. The last thing I wanted was to concede the lead and get embroiled in a dogfight.

I forced the throttle wide open through Three and skidded towards the exit wall. Colin had a run on me. The back straight was four lanes wide and I was in lane four on the right-hand side. To have the lead going

into the final corner, I had to get left across the track into lane one. So did Colin.

As I covered across the track the green car went with me, then he pulled towards my inside. According to the rules I could block his move once, and only when he was fully behind. By the time I reached lane two, the green car was alongside my rear bumper in lane one. I had raced him hard; now I had to be fair and give him room. I stopped covering and let him pull alongside as we wound up to 175mph.

An almighty force rocked through the cabin as I was flung around into a spin. I instinctively jammed the brakes, took in a half breath and waited. As the car sped backwards it felt like I was falling. I stared through the windscreen at the pack of pursuers slowly blurring around me. Smoke blossomed from my tyres as the topside melted away and the canvas shredded and punctured. The wall rushed up behind me.

There was a moment of peace, then the concrete intervened. I shouted the air from my lungs on impact. My head ricocheted off the restraints and my knees walloped the steering column, then the chassis frame.

Pain flooded my body and bright spots of light burnt into my retinas, but I knew I was all right. In fact, I was livid. I wanted to see the film footage of what had happened.

The car was toast. It had pummelled the wall so hard that concrete dust enveloped the whole Texaco livery. The splayed wheel angles suggested the chassis was museum material.

I was sent to the medical facility for a once-over, but all I wanted to do was see Graham and apologise for killing his car. Things were hotting up outside the medical area. The opposition had protested to the officials about *my* driving and I was being summoned to the race stewards …

I stared, transfixed, at the footage. The camera had a bird's-eye view of me leading Colin through Three. We were hellish close. I gave him room; he pulled alongside my rear wheel and then … contact. To my eyes, he steered so hard into me that I never had a chance of saving it before I hit the wall. It was a total waste of a fine machine.

The main steward eyed me nervously through his square glasses and his hands were trembling as he turned off the video. Not a good sign. Obviously, I said, he'd seen the other driver spin me off. No.

In their view, my defensive line was dangerous driving. They were docking all my series points from the weekend, which made it impossible for me to win the championship.

The racing was over for the day and my mind had already shifted on to the ranges, with Ken on my shoulder. But first I directed a volley of profanity at the stewards that would have made him fackin' proud. Realising I wasn't improving matters, I headed for the land of the brave. In spite of the calamity, I was buzzing from the win.

By the time I reached the Army training area at one in the morning the tiredness that follows a hectic race weekend was kicking in, along with a hangover from my concussion. Geordie sympathetically fed me a brew before leading me down through an abandoned camp of box-like concrete buildings. He gave me a bearing towards my new digs.

Within a few hundred metres a squadron of mosquitoes was gorging on my blood. The bearing led me to their humid HQ, a swampy wood. I squidged through the dank undergrowth.

Johnny was on stag. 'Good race?'

'Won one and crashed one.'

'Welcome to Shangri-la. If the DS don't get you the mozzies will. Get some repellent on you asap.'

I set my alarm for 0530 and passed out.

I woke early and used the time to prepare for the Combat Fitness Test. I dug my fingers deep into my bloated tendon to get it mobilised, feeling the fibrous tissue scrape against its outer sheath. I warmed up my calf, stretched and cloaked my ankle with the zinc oxide tape. I added a Neoprene layer of synthetic rubber for good measure.

I breakfasted with drugs and hot chocolate and walked down to the assembly area with the boys in full combat gear, bergens and all. It felt like marching to the gallows, but I was ready to run on a stump if I had to.

The DSs disappeared in their vehicles to line the route, and Jones craned his head around for a final look at his prey before moving off.

'Prepare to double ... DOUBLE!'

The opening stretch was downhill, on tarmac. I kept movement in my right leg to a minimum by swinging it like a golf club. We crossed a stone bridge over a brook and began to climb.

The sweat started to work its way through our clothing, and by the time we reached the first peak our tightly packed unit was a steam-pumping locomotive in the morning air. Earlier in the course you might

have relished another recruit biting the dust, but not now. Everyone had been through hell to get this far. Tunnel vision had caused guys to break up with their girlfriends or lose their jobs. All that mattered was getting to the end.

My Achilles started to burn and I struggled with the pace. I focused on the others, the rhythm of the march, the distance to the guy in front, and dug deep to keep up.

We crashed along a dirt track and up a steep field. A few stray rocks tested our balance but not Jones, whose robotic legs churned it up at the front. His head and shoulders barely moved.

We took a road that led across an infinite patchwork of fields and I drew deep breaths, but started to slip back.

'C'mon, Benny,' Ninja puffed. 'C'mon, mate.' Everyone was hanging out of their arses.

The road kinked and curved and I pictured the ideal racing line to carry speed and power up the hill. It was a monster climb, clobbering the group down to a fast, thrusting walk.

In a lay-by up ahead a DS climbed from his Land Rover. The pressure was on. Forget tea and biscuits – it was Ken. He spotted my sorry carcass a mile away and started licking his lips.

I, dumb beast of burden; he, master.

'It hurts, yeah? *YEAH?*' he shouted.

'*Yes, Staff.*'

'You ain't got all fackin' day!' He jogged alongside. 'Right, you're gonna fackin' sprint and catch that group in front. NOW – *GO! Fackin' move, you cunt.*'

Bollocks to my leg – anything to get him off my back. After a gut-busting 250-metre sprint I caught the tail end of the main posse, but I couldn't live with them. I fought a lonely battle to complete the march without crippling myself in the process.

A decade or so later a radiant sight appeared on the horizon, more beautiful than what might lie at the end of any rainbow: a wagon.

Ken breathed, 'Fackin' good maan,' as I hobbled past. I swear he might even have smiled.

I was totally ball-bagged and almost the last man in, but crucially within the cut-off time.

We still had to complete a minefield of tests and acquire skills that were integral to the Unit to prove ourselves worthy of being counted

among them. Simulations of life at the front – and behind the lines – were as hardcore as the DSs could make them. Once they had seen enough, we settled into the final stages of the exercise.

Afterwards, we sat on a muddy grass bank and re-assembled the utter shambles of our kit. My trousers were torn through the knees, my boots had been cut off, my big toe had a section missing and something green was growing out of my hands. Our own mothers wouldn't have recognised us for the fur and grime on our faces. My bergen stank of shit. It was the best of times.

'Well done, fellas,' said the training officer. 'Transport will be here to collect you in forty-five minutes. Get some packed lunches over by the wagons.'

Then he tossed our berets at us like Frisbees. It was the proudest moment of my life.

A few minutes later my neglected mobile phone connected me to the world with a mixed bag of messages. During my absence the race organisers had banned me from the next race meeting, then reduced my 'suspended sentence' to starting the next event from the back of the grid.

17

HAPPY LANDINGS

In spite of my exotic nightlife, I hadn't missed a single episode of *Top Gear* and they had green-lit one of my mad ideas. A friend of mine was a shit-hot freestyle parachutist who reckoned he could land in a car if I held it steady at 50mph. We all gathered in one of those glass meeting rooms at the BBC. I made caveman drawings on a flip chart to story-board the sequence we had in mind.

Andy, not unreasonably, wanted to know that we could actually pull this off before shelling out for a crew to capture footage of a man falling to his death, then being run over and killed all over again. He asked if we had been practising.

'Yes.'

It was only a white lie. Tim had thousands of drops under his belt, and I could drive in a straight line at 50mph, no problemo.

'We ran through it last week. We didn't actually land Tim in the car, but we matched speeds with him alongside it. We know it will work.'

Tim stared at the carpet, determined not to catch my eye.

Top Gear sourced a convertible Mercedes CLK55. It had great acceleration and all the windows folded flat, making it ideal for the job of dropping a man into the back seat from 4,000 feet. Back in those days there was no speculation about me being The Stig, so it seemed logical to do the stunt as Ben Collins. I would be hiding in plain sight.

The location was RAF Bentwaters in Suffolk, home to the RAF's Bomber Command during the Second World War, then used by the American Air Force for keeping an eye on the Russians. The concrete runways were a little ancient but smooth enough to drive on.

I negotiated a day for rehearsals, followed by a day for filming. That way we could figure out if this thing was remotely possible before humiliating ourselves on national television.

Within half an hour of arriving at Bentwaters, my eyeballs were drying in their sockets from the continuous crosswind, and Tim's expression was even darker than usual.

His parachute was a 'Swoop' canopy which could soar like a paraglider. As he approached the ground he would dive to build up speed, turn and slingshot forwards. It would be a bit like falling out of a swing – except he'd be travelling at 130mph just a few feet from the deck.

'What about this wind?' I asked. 'Can you jump in this?'

'If the plane can take off, I can jump. Landing could be tricky, but we won't know until we try.'

Fordy the cameraman, Tim's partner in the sky, reminded me of Captain Scarlet, right down to the dimpled chin. He chewed gum and smiled at us as if he was escorting a pair of loonies on a day out from the Cuckoo's Nest.

We pinged a section of airfield where the main runway was met by another we used for parking the emergency vehicles. It gave me a wider run-up and the converging strips marked a clear X that provided a visible reference at high altitude.

In theory, the grass on either side of it would offer a marginally softer bounce if things went wrong, but realistically, splatting the grass at 130mph wouldn't change the texture of the human jam Tim would be spreading.

We loaded him up with his harness and padded his arms and knees. I softened the landing zone with thick blankets and foam and wound the passenger seat fully forward to give him space. For my own protection, I donned the obligatory Ray Bans.

Tim and Fordy joshed around as they climbed into the Cessna. I cranked up the air con as they took off and backed the car into position. After a few minutes I spotted the ruffled profile of a yellow parachute. It was the first time I'd seen one of these chutes deploying, and for a horrible moment it looked like it might not open. *Time to switch on.* The

countdown began. Tim tacked back and forth until he hit 800 feet. He'd rotate at that point and head for the ground like a Kamikaze pilot on his last hurrah, then swoop alongside the car for a couple of hundred feet before touching down.

At least, that was the plan.

Without warning, Tim spiralled into a turn in front of me. I planted the throttle as he roared overhead at an incredible rate of knots. His speed dropped off within seconds and he landed as I drove past him.

'We'll have to do better than that, Benny boy,' he laughed.

I decided I'd have to start in front of him; there was no other way I could match his speed.

Tim stowed his chute. 'Let's try the next one for real; we might as well get a feel for it.'

I craned my neck around the headrest as Tim dived into his turn and flew towards me in a blur of speed. As our paths collided I fought the urge to veer out of his way.

'Gotta keep it straight, Ben,' he said when he'd kissed the concrete.

'I know,' I said sheepishly. 'It just feels like I'm trying to kill you.'

'Sod it, that's my problem. Just stick the wagon under me whatever.'

We managed three more jumps and sorted the positioning of the Merc relative to Tim's swoop. The big problem was the crosswind. Its strength and direction were changing constantly, which played havoc with his landing distance and speed.

The closest we got was when a gust blew him sideways and his feet nearly caught the inside of the windscreen.

I called Wiseman before the close of play to call off the shoot.

'Don't worry. If you can't do it, you can't do it. The crew's already left. We might as well film whatever you guys get up to tomorrow.'

Another mate of ours arrived to take some photos and found the whole scenario highly entertaining. After a few beers we consoled ourselves that at least Tim's death would be celebrated on global TV. His primary concern, as we rolled out our sleeping bags under the stars, was that he'd forgotten to bring his sponsor's branded T-shirt.

Come the day, the director arrived with the crew. We filmed the Merc doing some sporty cornering to cut in with the stunt itself. Then the mini cameras were rigged to the car and Tim's head.

We had open-mic radios to keep in constant contact, so Tim didn't need to press a button to talk during his descent. He'd give me a cue when to hit the gas according to his airspeed.

The director was bricking his britches. We were talking crosswinds, high-speed swoops and trying not to flip Tim with the windscreen. For some reason he wasn't happy about adding a snuff movie to his showreel.

Tim and Fordy went up for the first run of the day. I visualised and rehearsed the scenarios in my head. If I could get under him early enough and match his top speed, he could drop into the car, then I'd have to decelerate hard because his chute would still be dragging through the air. All this had to happen during a frantic three to five-second window at best.

Tim dropped from the sky, I thundered forward and our paths converged towards the end of his swoop. Tim lobbed across the bow and plopped down on the tarmac.

Jim Wiseman thought it looked 'awesome', which was encouraging news. James May, a man obsessed with anything that flies, arrived to present the stunt. He was always a very warm, genuine fellow who put a spring in everyone's step when he was on set. His eyes glistened with excitement as he met the pilot and our drop zone co-ordinator and checked out Tim's rig. James understood the complexities of what we were trying to achieve. He bounced from one leg to the other as the boys sparked up the Cessna; I couldn't be sure whether that was because of the cold, or from sheer, unbridled anticipation.

On the second jump Tim lined up directly behind the car from the outset. He was lower earlier and managed to bounce his feet off the boot.

The next swoop was slightly higher but a gust of wind caught him and blew him forwards. I had to swerve to avoid him stacking it into the windscreen and as he tugged artfully at the canopy toggles to steer himself through the air. It felt like threading the eye of a needle on a bucking bronco.

With only enough time and fuel left for two more jumps, the pressure was on. Tim came in very fast and bloody low. So low that he skimmed the roof of the ambulance parked in the staging area. His approach was so wild that even the main camera missed the action – and I can count the occasions that happened on one finger. Unsurprisingly, he didn't cue me on that run.

On the final attempt I hit the gas and Tim came in hot. He plonked down as large as life into the rear seat. Just as we rehearsed, I shouted at him to 'Cut away, cut away,' until he came back with 'Clear, I'm clear.' That meant he'd detached his canopy and could no longer be wrenched out of the car by it. It was a perfect run.

The Merc was an auto, so I flicked it right then left and buried the throttle to do a smoking doughnut. Tim bounced around in the back and James whooped with delight. None of us could quite believe it had worked. It was a huge achievement on Tim's part and his habitual frown was replaced by an understated but satisfied smile.

The stunt also entrenched a growing sense of confidence I was gleaning from the Army. The discipline and rigours of military life had broken down my mental barriers by all but killing me and developed an inner reserve of strength that I never knew existed. It was life-changing. After that, there was no fatigue, hunger or mental low that could not be beaten.

Working with people who shared that 'can do' attitude made the impossible possible and it was liberating to view every obstacle as an opportunity.

Tim came along to be filmed with me and Jeremy in the studio, where the business of hiding in plain sight felt mighty uncomfortable. I couldn't wait to get out of there as Jezza congratulated us in front of the live audience. I ran off to get changed into my white suit, straight past Sir Ranulph Fiennes, who I was coaching fifteen minutes later.

I couldn't wait to meet the polar explorer who had sawn off the ends of his own frostbitten fingers rather than wait for surgery; the man who cheated on SAS Selection by hitching a lift in a taxi between checkpoints, and was subsequently booted out of the Regiment for blowing up a film set.

Now this man, who at first appeared more like a retired Geography teacher, was sitting next to me with a demonic expression on his face.

I belted Ranulph into the driver's seat and dashed around to the passenger side when I heard him revving the engine and digging around for a gear. He set off like he was starting a Grand Prix before I had even fastened my belts.

His acute gaze was fixed 1,000 yards down the road. His hands crushed the Liana's steering wheel and he tore through the gearbox.

Ran was only dimly aware of me shouting in the background.

'Ranulph, back off a bit …'

'RAN?'

No response.

'*RRAAANNNN …*'

I was a passenger in every conceivable sense.

I don't know what he would have done next without my intervention, but I didn't want to find out. It was time to get a grip. I rapped hard on the side of his helmet with my knuckles and yelled, 'RANULPH, LOOK … AT … ME …'

Suddenly I was back in the room.

I was determined to keep his attention. I summoned as much authority as I could manage and ordered the legend around the circuit.

His weathered features told me we could have been anywhere – up the side of Everest or running across the Gobi desert. No quarter was asked for or given with the controls of that little car. He wrang its neck and kicked its guts.

Ran's spirit was contagious, and I spent countless additional laps with him in an effort to get him the result he so deserved.

It was sheer bloody-mindedness that drove him. Thirty years of wrestling polar bears meant he couldn't quite acquire the finesse to caress the car towards the ultimate lap time.

I climbed out for his solo runs and watched in awe. Smoke billowed off all four wheels as he screeched through the final corners like no guest we had ever seen. He was every bit the adventurer I had read about, a well-spoken bullfighter, with balls of steel.

As my second series with *TG* came to a close, I was beginning to feel I had more of a role to play, and on surer foundations. Things brightened up elsewhere as well. Georgie moved in and transformed my pigsty into a glowing home.

'What do you *do* with all these boxes?'

'It's where I keep my … stuff.'

'*Storage.*'

With that, my entire collection of … things … was gone. It turned out my place even had wooden floorboards. Having Georgie back made my heart whole again. After all of life's twists and turns, we had found each other again. I couldn't quite believe my luck.

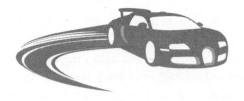

18

STARS IN REASONABLY PRICED CARS

During eight years of *Top Gear* I was privileged to hitch a ride with some of the most renowned personalities from the worlds of movies, TV, music and sports, from tough guys like Christian Slater, Mark Wahlberg and Ewan McGregor to the gorgeous Sienna Miller and Denise Van Outen. Their goal: to become the fastest 'star in a reasonably priced car'.

The front-wheel-drive Suzuki Liana catapulted them all from A-list splendour to Z-list economy travel. Most had never driven a car fast, let alone balls-out around a racing track. Fame is no ally for overcoming fear of the unknown, and there was only so much we could achieve in one and a half hours, but it was my job to tap undiscovered reserves of high-octane talent ...

The first two corners were trials of patience, waiting for front grip in the long gradual turns. Hammerhead tested the discipline to wait for the whites of the cameramen's eyes before braking and not cheat by cutting the corner. The Follow Through was all about faith, keeping your foot to the floor. You had to be a bit crazy in the final two bends. For a good time, all four wheels needed to be drifting at nearly a ton whilst cutting a section of broken tarmac, nearly spinning over the green bit and then running across the finish so fast that the car hit a grass knoll and flew through the air.

When their instincts told them to back off, I urged them to floor it. When the car ran wide on to the grass and they pulled at the steering to regain the tarmac, I told them to straighten up. I saw more clenched teeth and cold sweat in the driving seat than a Harley Street dentist.

Jordan, aka glamour model Katie Price, turned up in a tinted limo. I was expecting an afternoon of crying over broken fingernails. My day hadn't started well. It was belting hot and I'd forgotten to whip my Alpinestars suit out of the tumble drier that morning. The office spare, a manky old cheddar, was three sizes too small, so everything was creaking as I limped over and greeted her. Jordan was dressed top-to-toe in pink, and was good enough not to notice the camel toe arrangement between my legs, so I didn't breathe a word about the white bits under her arms where the spray tan had missed its target.

My first task was Herculean: to strap on her shoulder belts. They ran out of length over the top of her embonpoints, and looked dangerously uncomfortable going round the side. The safest solution was to use the standard seat belt slung underneath, since airbags were already included.

Jordan didn't ask too many questions. I took that as a good sign. After a few practice laps I let her drive solo.

I kept a firm eye on the stars as they wrestled their way around the circuit and could pretty much predict their time before they crossed the line. As Jordan turned through the flat-out right-hander, a concrete hut blocked my line of sight. She should have reappeared less than a second later, but she didn't. Instead there was a shriek of rubber.

She'd spun at the fastest section and was backing towards the building. I felt my stomach lurch. She remembered to mash the brake pedal in an emergency and stopped just in time. Wiseman was biting his fingernails.

'It's all right,' Casper called from his camera position. 'She's heading back to you now.'

'OK,' Jim answered. 'Tell me you got that?'

'Yeah,' Casper replied. As if it was ever in doubt.

Jordan's smile hadn't slipped an inch; she was completely unfazed. We asked if she was OK.

'Yeah. I spun out at that corner. Why was that then?'

'I think you turned the steering too fast,' I said. 'Just remember to be as smooth as possible, like you're lifting a cup of tea.'

I didn't want her spinning there again, it was too dangerous, so I jumped back in the Liana to make sure she took the right line.

She immediately produced her fastest time of the day, a gritty effort following a 100mph near miss.

We also hosted former Spice Girl Geri Halliwell. She was a nervous wreck when she arrived, with an entourage that included her own film crew and a private racing coach.

I knew it wasn't easy. Most of them arrived at Dunsfold knowing only that their PR people had booked them on to some car programme to have a chat and do a bit of driving. One minute they were sipping cappuccinos and basking in the glow of their bestselling book or hit movie, the next they were on a cold, windswept airfield getting intimate with a spaceman in a white suit.

Geri put enormous pressure on herself from the outset to go number one on the board. As always, I wanted to convert her enthusiasm into performance.

The dangers of track driving only dawned on Geri once we started lapping. She hung on my every word, her big eyes looking up at me from inside a helmet that engulfed her. Geri's heart was in the right place, but she was so intense that she over-anticipated everything and kept getting into a muddle. In the course of our conversation I discovered that she had been in a number of car accidents in a short space of time.

The damp track was punishing the smallest mistakes and I had to make sure she stayed on the black stuff. We were on a fast lap; Geri was hitting ninety towards the gap between the tyre barriers at the Follow Through. With a hundred feet to go, I said, 'Just steer left a bit. I don't want you to clip the tyres.'

Eighty feet out she replied, 'If I hit the tyres, will I hit my face?'

Sixty ...

'You might but—'

Forty ...

'I can't hit my face.'

Twenty ...

'Fine. Just steer left. *NOW!*'

I pushed the wheel an extra inch and we wobbled through. A slave to the schedule, there was only so much extra guidance I could give Geri. During the final safety briefing, her hands were shaking. She was so over-psyched that she set quite an average lap time, but she did manage an

unusual pirouette past the crowd on the start line. I knew she was desperate for some sign that she'd done OK.

'You did *really* well,' I said. 'Especially in the quick corners; you were very … brave.' There's a limit to what a chap can do from behind a heavily tinted visor.

My words seemed to fall like daggers. She fought back the tears, thanked us and disappeared off into her motor home.

'You heartless bastard,' Wiseman whispered.

I often forgot that being my passenger could get quite extreme. Eddie Izzard, the transvestite comedian, arrived during a monsoon. He was a stellar bloke; definitely one of the boys.

I took him round the lap and aquaplaned on a puddle. Eddie shouted so loud I thought he was having a heart attack. 'Oh my God, *oh my GOD* … Oooooooohhhh, fuuuuuuuuuuck …' It was an uncanny impression of my mother.

We rattled through a 90-degree slide for about 200 metres, then I gathered it up and carried on. It was no biggy, but it brought on Eddie's motion sickness. He had to climb out of the car after each run to stop himself throwing up, but he never stopped smiling and never gave up. He might dress up in women's clothes, but he was hard as nails.

Some comedians were plain scary. Jimmy Carr arrived by UFO and fluttered down from Outer Space, ready to unleash Armageddon on mankind. Lovely bloke; complete nutter. Don't be fooled by the baby face. Once you looked closer into those counter-sunk chestnut eyes you saw the beast within.

It was Jimmy's second visit to *Top Gear* and he had beaten Simon Cowell to top of the leader board on his first, so we were expecting great things.

He kept jumping on the accelerator too early in the corner, a cardinal sin in my book, and it made the front wheels skid. He wound fifty turns of steering to compensate and eventually I'd had enough. I yanked the Wand of Plenty and spun him off the track.

Jimmy's eyes widened. 'Whoaa, what happened then?'

Hmm. Human after all.

Jimmy drove the hell out of the car and was wildly inconsistent, either super fast or you needed a calendar.

We lost count of the number of times he spun. When we played back his in-car footage he looked totally impassive, even when the thing was flying backwards off the circuit at 100mph. And he never braked when he did that; he totally lacked any sense of self-preservation.

Each time he pulled up to the line for another assault I did my best to get a grip on the situation.

'Are you looking for the braking markers I showed you into that corner on the back straight? You haven't made it round there once yet ...'

'Yes, yes. I think so.' He paused, eyes glinting. 'Hmm. Which ones?'

'Brake at the fifty but don't steer left until you reach the arrow board. If you can do that, you should stop spinning on to the grass. Can you give it a go?'

'I don't see why not.'

I urged the crew to stand well back.

Jimmy made several more wild passes. Unfortunately for him, the rules for that particular episode were that we only counted the time recorded on the sixth lap, rather than the best lap-time overall. Jimmy's sixth included a 300-metre detour across the grass, so his time was over two minutes. His best time would have put him fastest.

As he walked back to his UFO, the mud-caked Liana gave a sigh of relief. A plume of smoke rose from its blown gasket. Pigeons fell dead from the sky and flowers wilted as he ambled by. Jimmy was great sport.

The problem with comedians was you never knew when to take them seriously. Within minutes of meeting me, straight-faced Jack Dee said he wanted to go home.

He was noticeably reserved when we shook hands, so I didn't shoot off with screeching tyres. I showed him where the track went at a gentle pace. After a few hundred metres I turned into the first corner. We were doing no more than 40mph.

'Stop the car, stop. I've gotta get out of here.'

Good old Jack, I thought. He's taking the piss. But he wasn't. He was deadly serious.

I had a feeling that if I let him get out it would be impossible to get him back in it. I didn't fancy explaining to the producer why we had no footage of Jack's lap for his interview with Jeremy. And I was foolish enough to think I could help him.

I slowed down to about 15mph, just too fast for him to open the door and jump out without breaking his legs.

'It's OK, Jack, I'm slowing down. What's wrong?'

'I can't do this.' He was turning green right in front of me. 'I'm getting flashbacks from an accident I had when I was eighteen.'

It was time for Stigmund Freud to look into Jack's psyche and rediscover his lost driver. I asked him what had happened, whether he'd hit another vehicle. It turned out he was a passenger when his friend lost control and flipped his car over.

I peppered him with questions; I needed to understand his phobia, and I needed to keep him talking. By the time we completed the first lap I had it sussed. His friend had lost the back end through a tightening corner, over-corrected and the ensuing tank-slapper, where the car rocks violently from one side of the suspension to the other, was enough to barrel-roll them into the hedge. Not nice.

I explained how he could control that situation by steering gently into the slide or simply by steering straight, rather than fighting the wheel and making things worse.

After a few more laps Jack had settled down and turned a slightly more gentle shade of yellow. It seemed safe to stop and swap seats without him running for the hills.

He built up speed and confidence with each lap. Even at the Follow Through, where he nearly fainted when I drove it at 50mph, he ended up belting through at 75.

By the time he finished I was more than a little proud of him. He overcame his fear. Jack looked as disgruntled as usual, when he climbed out and Wiseman asked him, 'Did you enjoy that?'

'No, not at all.'

I think he was happy to be heading for the relative comfort of Jeremy's leather sofa.

David Walliams was another kettle of fish. As a *Little Britain* fan I thought, wrongly, that I knew all about him. First off, he is a big lad. Just getting a helmet to fit and curling him into the Liana wasn't easy.

We didn't really seem to hit it off. Maybe he was nervous, or I wasn't getting the message across very well. Or perhaps he was suffering the after-effects of a bad vindaloo. But I didn't give up on him.

Walliams put the hammer down, but whereas Jimmy Carr would disappear off the circuit without a prayer of making the corner, this lad would nearly make it, then just lose it at the last moment. It was

agonising to watch; he was so close to getting it right, but his excursions were denting his confidence.

I tried to help him fight fire with fire by recommending that he brake even later for the corners where he was spinning; I thought it would force him to brake harder and therefore make the corner.

The camera crew were set up ten metres to one side to capture him going across the line. I stood between them and the final corner.

Walliams piled into the second to last bend, braked late and skidded sideways and on to the verge, kicking up a plume of dust as he regained the track. Beautiful. I dared to think that my plan had worked.

Then he completely missed the turning-in point for the final corner. He was going way too fast and heading straight across the grass toward us.

He just needed to lift off the accelerator. I jogged backwards as he closed in and tried explaining this with hand signals.

The brain can only process so much new information. Once it reaches overload in a crisis situation, logic leaves the building. In this scenario, Walliams wanted to brake and avoid killing us, but his body was too scared to move its own foot. In fact, all the time he was thinking about braking, his foot was pushing harder on the accelerator, a common cause of accidents on the road.

Within seconds the Liana had chewed up the grass run-off and we were out of time.

With a wire fence behind us and a wide-eyed Walliams inbound, I turned to Wiseman and shouted '*RUN*'. Jim grabbed the soundman, I yanked the camera operator and we darted for cover.

The Liana lurched over the grass rise, all four wheels left the ground, and it landed roughly where I'd been standing. The tyre marks were just an inch wide of the tripod.

Wiseman burst out laughing, apparently entertained by my wildly inventive sign language.

The car came to a rest 40 metres past us. I caught my breath and opened his door. 'It's OK – everyone's OK. Are *you* all right, David?'

His belts were already off and he climbed out of the car looking deeply shocked. It was his final lap anyway so we aimed David in the direction of the tea urn and called it a day.

★　★　★

The cars took a royal pounding over the years. They were invariably launched into the air over the verge at the final corner, landed on the wheel rims and then bounced through the gravel gully. If you weren't using the gully you weren't trying hard enough. We had to keep a watchful eye on the hubs and the suspension.

When Lionel Richie was in the driving seat we heard a strange clanking noise at the first corner. I could just make out his car veering on to the grass. As he hit the brakes, the front wheel fell off, stayed upright and then overtook him. The Liana slumped on to its brake disc, lost all front grip and scraped along the tarmac in a shower of sparks.

There was mild panic at our HQ. The Pop God who had fronted over 100 million records appeared to be bent on giving us the *Top Gear* version of 'Dancing on the Ceiling'.

Jim and I hurtled into the ambulance with the rescue crew, with visions of Lionel's 'people' suing us into oblivion if his French tickler moustache was even fractionally out of shape.

The great man was standing in the middle of the field he had so recently ploughed, his leather jacket still immaculate, staring, mystified, at a car he could buy with his loose change. To our relief, he started to laugh. 'The damn wheel fell off!' We swapped him into the spare Liana and he squeezed out a great time – given that he only used third gear. He had serious issues adjusting to the 'stick shift'.

Lionel may only have driven automatics but he had a major advantage over one guest. Johnny Vegas had yet to pass his driving test. After a few laps I noticed that he was making a silky smooth transition from the brakes to the power, so I had a look in the footwell.

I told him that he was left-foot braking, a technique used by rally and Formula 1 drivers; rather an advanced style for a beginner.

'I'm doin' whaat? Sorry, maaate …' He had no idea what he was doing.

I handed the husky-voiced northerner back to his BSM driving instructor and thought, good luck mate. His test was booked the following month.

After five seasons we had a list of seriously fast times set by the boys from the Big Screen. It fell on one slip of a girl to put them all in their place.

Ellen MacArthur listened intently to every instruction, nodded calmly and said, 'Right', or 'OK'. She wasn't a talker; she just did it. Her expression at breakneck speed was as serene as it must have been when she was watering plants.

It was hard to imagine this tiny, rose-cheeked beauty as a record-breaking loon, circumnavigating the globe single-handed on a boat the size of Lionel Richie's limo.

I asked if she had ever been afraid. She recalled a night in the Southern Ocean when her little trimaran was skimming down waves the size of Alpine valleys at 30 knots, and she had to just rely on the sureness of her touch to prevent it from capsizing. A flat stretch of tarmac couldn't pose much danger after an experience of that magnitude.

Ellen's innate bravery was compounded by the fact that she weighed so little, which assisted the Liana's speed in a straight line. She shot to the top of the board, just seven tenths of a second slower than the Black Stig's benchmark of 1.46.0. Which may have prompted Grant Wardrop's next question, posed to me from behind his mirrored aviators. 'Anyway, what time have *you* done in the Liana?'

He was new to the *TG* production team, but he had a point. I'd never set one.

We'd already hosted two Formula 1 drivers. Damon Hill came along for a laugh, and Aussie star Mark Webber set a sensational time in the rain. Mark recognised me immediately from our Formula 3 days, apparently from the way I walked, so I made him swear not to tell anyone.

Our next guest was World Champion Nigel Mansell.

As he made his way down the tarmac to join us, he grew increasingly agitated. By the time he reached the car, the producer seemed to have his hands full. I walked away to relieve some of the pressure.

Nigel wasn't happy. 'I don't know about this. No one told me I'd be driving this thing for a lap time ... Ooh no, no, no ...' He prowled around the Liana, kicking its tyres.

No one dared say it, but why else was he carrying his personal racing helmet?

Producer: 'Right. Well ... um ... you don't have to drive it, obviously ... but we were really hoping you could ... do a few laps before the interview ...'

Uncomfortable silence.

I decided it was time to break the ice.

'Hi, Nigel, it's really great to meet you. This car is shit ...'

Nigel: 'You're telling me.'

'… but it's quite fun to drive …'

No comment.

Me: 'Have you been busy?'

Nigel: 'Yeah, I've been racing in the new Grand Prix Masters series. I won the last race at Kyalami, actually.' He leant closer. 'In one of the fast corners I was 14kph faster than Jan Lammers.'

Me: 'Awesome.'

Some of the tension dissipated, but we weren't out of the woods. Our Nige made a final inspection of the shitbox, then mumbled something that sounded vaguely conciliatory and put on his familiar Union Jack racing helmet. We were on.

I was a big fan of Mansell in F1 mode. Even Senna and Schumacher had no answer to his attacking style when he was on one, like when he overtook Gerhard Berger around the outside of the sweeping last corner at the 1990 Mexico Grand Prix.

Mansell's physical strength was apparent in shoulders that extended from his ear lobes. During the active suspension era of F1 he was the only driver physically capable of coping with the G-forces. It was rumoured that he clenched his teeth so hard during one qualifying session that it shattered a molar. In the Liana, with no grip to manhandle, I reckoned that approach might slow him down.

Nigel didn't want to be driven, so I hopped in the passenger seat and directed him around a lap of the track to show him the lines. He sparked up on the second lap; I was impressed by how quickly he'd adapted to the car. He was committed every inch of the way.

I left Nigel and joined a giddy Jim Wiseman.

'How was he?'

'He's bloody good, obviously. This could be interesting; he's taking it seriously.'

Nigel dumped the clutch and wheelspun away. The car screeched and groaned from one turn to the next. He completed the lap by neatly slicing the final corner, the rear kicking slightly wide and dropping a wheel into the gravel. It looked precise, tidy and angry. It was also a new record. A high 1.45 on his opening lap.

Jim ran over. Nigel's eyes were round and unblinking, his nostrils flared. It was a look I knew very well. The window slid down and the voice of Jim's boyhood hero spoke to him from behind the helmet he had followed for fifteen years on TV. 'What's me time on that one?'

Jim looked apologetic. 'We can't tell you the times until the interview.'

'Bollocks to that, mate,' Nige said. 'Tell me my bloody time.'

'Um … I can tell you if your times are getting faster or slower, but not the actual time. Sorry …'

The window wound up again.

Nigel drove the Liana, twitching with complaint, to the edge of its physical boundaries and then beyond. But the car looked slow in the straights. Jim let me swap it for the spare.

I gingerly suggested that Nigel braked a bit later at the penultimate turn. Telling a World Champion to brake later was … uncomfortable. He duly did and hooked the car in with bullish gusto, sending up the familiar dust clouds on the apex and exit of the corner. It was his fastest lap of all – 1.44.6.

Nigel launched several equally determined attempts, then wound down the window. 'That's it,' he said. 'I've got no more.'

What an operator. He put everyone around him on tiptoe, delivered a mega performance and wore his heart on his sleeve. He was the most competitive person I'd ever met. You could hear it in his voice, even when he was just talking about his golf handicap.

'Il Leone', as the Ferrari fans called him, had taken a major bite out of the track record to mark the retirement of the faithful Suzuki Liana. She was knackered. The front wheel had been jettisoned three times, with Lionel Richie, footballer Ian Wright and actor Trevor Eve. We blew innumerable clutches (twice in one day with David Soul), cracked the gearbox casing, snapped the gear selector, broke the suspension and dented the panels.

I hoped for a more durable replacement to kick off Series 8. Instead I was handed the keys to a 119bhp Chevrolet Lacetti. It had the worst gearbox money could buy and the paintwork matched the Liana's drab grey/blue.

Jeremy invited seven mad celebs to come along on the same day and set some times. He decided it would be a great idea to host a picnic during lapping, on the verge at the last corner. There was no point arguing; I had my work cut out.

James Hewitt, the love rat, arrived first and canoodled a time, then Alan Davies gurned a lap. Trevor Eve, with his crushing handshake, managed to destroy a clutch before lunchtime, but he was fastest. Rick

Wakeman climbed aboard and casually remarked that he had suffered several heart attacks in the past.

'Are you sure you should be doing this?'

'What do you think, Stig?'

'I think you're mad, but it's your call.'

Off we went.

Jeremy and Hammo were getting stuck into jam tarts and tea whilst I did my best to gather up Jimmy Carr. Rock Star Justin Hawkins joined the mêlée and flat-footed it everywhere with a perma-grin. After that he joined Clarkson in song, with Wakeman tapping out a tune on an electric keyboard. I spent the whole afternoon behind the mask, wondering why no one else found the situation utterly surreal.

Les Ferdinand arrived last. He was a pro footballer, so he'd probably seen a few sights in his time. He spotted the picnic and stopped 50 metres short of it, looking lost. Then he twigged that he was in the right place but it was too late to turn around. His face was a picture. Les narrowly lost out to Trevor Eve and legged it as soon as Jeremy had read out his time.

Coaching the celebs was a hoot. I cried with laughter being driven by Stavros, aka Harry Enfield, and will never forget hearing Joanna Lumley swear. I behaved myself ... most of the time.

The following week I was looking forward to some one-on-one with Gordon Ramsay when, without warning, the Suzuki Liana was wheeled out and I was invited to set a time.

The Stig was hardly going to refuse the challenge. As for me, although both car and track were familiar, there was a distinct sense of pressure. Years of telling other people to drive faster and brake later would come back to haunt me if, for any reason, I failed to beat Nigel Mansell's rather fast time.

Wilman had a mischievous look in his eye that morning. He was loving my moment in the dock; it reminded me of the first day I drove for him. Jim and Grant were wringing their hands with delight and I knew that factors like weight differential, hot weather and tyre wear wouldn't wash. It was put up or shut up.

The Liana was dreadful to drive because it was so roly-poly and gutless. The incessant understeer made it hard to show any flair or balls. Pressing the brakes was like standing on a dead fish. After driving a supercar it was as exciting as filing a tax return.

I climbed aboard the old girl and dragged her to the start line.

'Right then, Stiggy,' Jim said, 'No pressure. *But* ... it would be great telly if you beat Mansell.'

'Thanks, Jim.'

I had been a passenger in the Liana for so long that I'd almost forgotten how to drive it. My first lap was average; I knew it, and Jim's expression confirmed it. He looked genuinely worried for me. Not a good sign.

I pushed harder and remembered how much you had to throw a front-wheel-driven roller pig into the corners. At the end of the straight into Bacharach I barely kissed the brakes. The tail lurched sideways and I put down 100 per cent throttle long before the corner.

I cut a hefty chunk off the inside of the bend, dropped two wheels on to the grass on the way out and carried a shedload of speed towards the final turn. I dabbed the brake in third and hurled it in, slid wide, launched into the air over the verge and crashed on to the wheel rims as I landed.

Jim wouldn't confirm the time, but I knew I had to find more.

'Can we switch cars? I think this one is a dog.'

'OK, sure. Ugh, no actually, we've only got one today.'

I stared at him for a moment, trying not to show my frustration. Grant was talking into the radio. Wilman had some words of encouragement for me, so Grant pointed the speaker in my direction. 'Tell him to think of Damon Hill's quali lap from the '97 Budapest GP,' said Wilman. 'One mighty lap at the eleventh hour is all it takes.' Very encouraging.

'No worries. Let me just cool the engine and give it another go.'

I could really taste the adrenalin now; it had taken its sweet time coming. I waited on the line and pictured the lap in my mind, without squashing the tyres under braking, letting it flow. I opened my eyes and released from the start line with no wheelspin. I braked late for the first corner and released them early. I turned and took the tighter, 'fast in, fast out' racing line. The front barely carried the extra speed.

I straight-lined the Follow Through with minimal steering to scrub as little speed as possible. I nearly lost it into Bacharach but it came good, howled through there, turned into the final corner and flew across the line with both wheels in the gully. I had no more.

Jim was nodding as I drove by and his lips read, 'Yeah, baby.' Stiggy still had it. A few hours later I sat on the sofa to have Jeremy deliver my lap time. He usually tortured his guests by reading it one number at a time. The Stig didn't stand for that kind of nonsense and would never

have waited for applause. As Jeremy started telling the audience my time, I just got up and walked out.

For once I'd caught Jeremy off guard, but he rather liked that. I'd beaten Mansell's time by two tenths of a second.

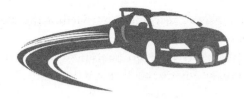

19

DRIVING BLIND

Gordon Ramsay was awesome, even more intense and faster talking than on TV, so I had to shift up a gear to keep with him. He was just a big kid really, and one of the few who swore *less* when he was driving. Only five times a lap.

He bit his lip and stuck in an aggressive but flowing circuit that put him at the top of the board. The balls-out approach doesn't usually work on the reasonably priced car, but he was a natural. He was so excited that he let me blat his Ferrari around the track with his sous-chef riding alongside. He subsequently claimed that I 'fucked his clutch', but you know what, Gordon? I fucking didn't.

Track conditions for the guests varied from hot to not-so-hot, from wet to mildly moist, and that was just the state of the tarmac. When Jamie Oliver came down, Brian the Studio Director took me to one side. 'He really wants to do well. He's a lovely boy; make sure he does a good time, won't you?'

Meeting the Naked One was like catching up with an old mate from school – no airs or graces, just an easy-going dude. He was genuinely pleased to meet us all. Then he saw the track.

'Bollocks, what do you call this, then?'

The whole airfield was covered by three inches of snow. That morning I'd done a power lap in the new Jaguar XKR that was ten seconds slower than normal. At one point it was so thick that when I drove across it at speed, the car was picked up and flung ten metres in the other direction.

Gordon Ramsay had cooked up quite a masterpiece; nothing short of a clear dry run would beat his 1.46.38. But it didn't stop Jamie trying, and as the snow melted he managed to put in a mega time, just a second slower than his arch-rival. As wet laps go it was the best and smoothest I ever saw.

You'd expect elite sportsmen to be good around the track, and that was largely the case, but the Lacetti wasn't the chariot of choice for big units like Lawrence Dallaglio and Usain Bolt.

Rugby legend Dallaglio weighed in at just under 112kg, and Usain was about 95, nearly a tenth of the car's kerb weight and almost two Lewis Hamiltons.

Dallaglio looked ridiculous in the Lacetti. His head was jammed on to the ceiling, his tree-trunk legs filled the entire footwell and his giant hands wrapped around the steering wheel like he was holding a peppermint.

He still managed a lap that was within a second of the fastest time, a storming effort given the weight handicap. I had a go at tackling Lawrence afterwards; it went badly. He lifted me off the ground by my helmet and nearly snapped my neck.

Sprinter Usain Bolt arrived at Dunsfold having set a new world record for the 200 metres in France the night before. After the press conferences he'd gone to bed at 3am, woken up a couple of hours later and got straight on a plane.

Usain is six foot five. You got a stiff neck just looking up at him. But his lilting Jamaican accent made you want to put your feet up, mix a Bacardi and fall asleep. He seemed to be waltzing through life.

He picked up the mechanics of racing in no time and was soon flying solo. He made making an effort seem effortless. He pulled in after setting a blistering time, wound down the window and gave me a sleepy smile. 'Man, this is some scary stuff right here. It's stressful out there.'

'You don't look massively stressed,' I said. 'You're doing really well.'

We pulled him out of the car for a water break and I noticed his shoe-lace was undone. Later on they played a clip of him winning a gold medal in the 100 metres and his laces were undone then as well. Talk about laid back.

I made sure he tied it securely and we sent him out. You only have to get your laces wrapped around the throttle pedal once to realise it's not a good idea.

Usain pulled every ounce of speed out of the car and finished off with his signature pose, pointing skywards with his hands like he was firing an arrow. Had it not been for his weight I'm sure he would have edged Gordon Ramsay out of first place. That honour was claimed by Simon Cowell on his second visit. He surprised himself by topping the times and gave Clarkson a bashing in the interview as they took turns in ribbing one another.

When it came to pure passion, no one could touch the space cowboy known as Jamiroquai. 'Jay' was also a walking supercar encyclopaedia. He'd set the fastest time in the Suzuki on his previous visit, under the guidance of the Black Stig. I'd always felt a bit smug about tearing a second off Jay's time with four of 'my' celebs.

Wherever Jay went after that, people ribbed him about his time being beaten, and now he wanted to put things right. The pressure was on, but he was still carrying a cheeky grin. He arrived wearing some nifty Alpinestars racing boots. I could tell from his handshake that he was pumped.

'Up for it today?' I grinned beneath my helmet.

'Are you kidding? This is WAR, man!'

I knew Jay was wild from a commercial I did with him for an EA Sports game called *Need for Speed*. I was dressed as a State Trooper and thrashing an Eighties Chevy police cruiser, a big mama, around a track. Jay slipped into the role of mad, 'catch me if you can', tearaway speed junkie with remarkable ease. He pulled alongside my car at 120mph in a pimped-out Nissan GTR, shot me the stiff finger, shouted 'Fuck you, Pig,' and roared off cackling with laughter.

As we sat in the Chevy Lacetti, I built Jay up from scratch like he'd never seen the track or driven the car before. I wanted to give him his very best shot. His lines were good, he kept it loose and he pedalled faster lap by lap.

'How's he going?' Wilman asked.

'He's on it. He's just four tenths of a second short of Simon Cowell. He can probably beat it if we stick with him.'

'OK. Keep me posted; I want fireworks out there.'

Jay was super-consistent. I tried everything to pull the extra time out of him and it must have pissed him off big time to be so close, but not quite close enough.

'Keep pushing; you've got to find more in the penultimate corner.'

'I am, man. I'm braking as fucking late as I can in this HEEEAP OF SHIIIIIT. Am I there yet, have I beaten the time, can you just tell me?'

I shook my head. 'All I can say is you haven't done your best time yet. But you will.'

'*C'MON!* You're fucking kidding. *Grrrrrrrr ...*' He banged his head on the steering wheel a few times and blew out a lungful of air. He was working himself up to a performance.

'If you really want this, the money is all in that corner over there. Brake so late that you think you're having an accident, let go, the back end starts sliding, then bury the throttle.'

The producer raised an eyebrow. 'Hmm, I wonder what will happen now ...'

Sure enough, Jay went flying into the weeds. I decided it was time to bring out the spare. It would give the boy a chance to draw breath and gather himself mentally.

Jay went out for two more laps. We remained stony-faced. Grant told him that he could do some more laps if he wanted but that he'd reached a plateau. It was time for the ordeal of the leather sofa. He tapped his foot like a jackhammer throughout the interview, then went still as Jeremy started to read out the time.

As usual, he extracted every last ounce of tension from the announcement.

'One minute ...

'Forty ...

'Five ...

'Point ...

'Eight!'

Jay had pipped Cowell by a tenth of a second. He leapt off the leather sofa and danced an emphatic jig. His passion was utterly infectious.

He expressed his gratitude in the best way he knew how – by scaring the crap out of me and his two mates in a C63 Merc. He shaved the wall at Hammerhead, drifting the car wide through the corner, and I couldn't wait to get my own back. We swapped seats and I returned the favour. He chanted 'Bastard, bastard, bastard ...' throughout the process. I took it as a compliment.

* * *

During eight years of racing around the *Top Gear* circuit, my glittering array of celebrity drivers had to put up with muffled rantings from behind the helmet of their white-clad passenger. There was the odd exception, however, who needed to hear my every word.

I was in plain clothes when I met Wilman in the OB truck, but he still hailed me as per normal.

'Stig … We want to do a lap with a blind guy. Do you reckon he can do it?'

I took a deep breath. 'Um … I don't see why not, if he can hear what I'm saying. Can I sit next to him?'

'Of course. But we don't just want him to crawl around out there. It needs to be a proper lap. I mean we want him to do a time, like close to Richard Whiteley or something.' My most challenging pupil yet was the kind of gentle soul who might run a local toy store. He had a regular, sighted driving partner with whom he'd developed his own arcane communications system. At first, they didn't even want me in the car with them. Listening to them discussing the track and how they'd indicate the required speeds and directions made me feel like an amateur. It was so precisely coded that I couldn't wait to see them in action.

I insisted on at least demonstrating which way the track went, so that the sighted man could take in the layout of the circuit and the blind driver could listen in. I promised to shut up the rest of the time and just observe.

So far, so good …

After a couple of laps I banged in a fast one, fast enough for them to agree I should stay in and keep talking. We swapped seats. The blind man slid behind the wheel with me alongside and his partner in the back.

At that moment Dunsfold looked a lot more twisty than usual and the old Suzuki Liana felt faster too. There were tyre walls, trees and concrete outbuildings that had never concerned me before. I took a reality check. If things went seriously wrong, there was only so much I could do from the passenger seat by grabbing the wheel and yanking the handbrake to spin us to a stop, but even that was not as easy as it sounded. Driving fast made some people nervous, and I imagined blind people would be no exception. I'd instructed 90-year-old ladies who, when I made the slightest correction to the steering, resisted with the strength of Schwarzenegger ripping the pin out of another grenade.

To start us off I indicated speed and distance along a quarter-mile straight. I told them I'd indicate direction changes, raise my voice to suggest an increase in the rate of turn, follow any adjustment with 'Come straight.' 'STOP!' meant just that: slam the brakes and put the clutch in. That was really important.

We pulled away in first gear and veered off to the left. Neither my directional instructions nor the mystical smoke signals coming from his partner in the back seat could keep us off the lawn. I rolled with it for a while, but after twenty seconds of mowing I'd had enough and called for a re-set.

Off we went again. This time when we veered left, shouting 'RIGHT' loudly had a limited effect. We pinballed along the verge for a bit, then triumphantly approached the first corner. The painted lines that defined the track seemed superfluous, but I tried to keep him within them. We flowed off course, back on to the grass. The driver sensed the rough and began panting as I urged him to ease off the gas. He braked instead and we spun.

Trying to explain how to navigate the turns of a fluid race track to a blind man was mind-boggling. I never felt confident of even reaching a corner, let alone driving through one. Adding speed only compounded the problem of direction, because a duff steer for more than a second put us straight into the undergrowth.

A single corner required at least twenty instructions on the steering alone. Sudden corrections of the wheel rocked the suspension and made the front wheels skid; the driver panicked and hit the brakes. We never went faster than 20mph. After a few hours I sensed the driver was over-whelmed, so I threw in the towel.

'What was he like?' Wilman asked.

'I'm not sure,' I said. 'I feel awful saying this, but I've got the impression he wasn't much of a driver *before* he lost his sight …'

The production team, always one step ahead of the game, had found not just one mad blind racing pilot for this mission, but two.

The next contestant was a wonderful man called Billy Baxter.

I spotted him standing in the car park. He was looking into the distance, like he was waiting for a train announcement. His head met his body at the shoulders with the robustness of a front-row forward. He was a stout fellow.

Billy had served the British Army as a member of the Royal Horse Artillery. He lost his sight to a rare disease during the Bosnian conflict, as a result of clearing up the mass graves.

His eyes aimed off as I approached him. He couldn't see me but he was clearly at peace with his surroundings.

'Hi, Billy, I'm The Stig.'

'Hello, Stig.' He held out a firm hand. 'Pleased to meet you.'

His weathered cheeks creased into a broad grin. Crow's feet around his eyes suggested he laughed a lot. He had the husky voice of a smoker and an untraceable accent: part West Country, part London cockney.

Billy had a driving partner too, but he dispatched him as soon as I offered to take him around the track myself. He listened intently as I talked him through each corner, explaining the speeds I would be doing, to listen to the changing wind rush as we accelerated. I put in a lap absolutely flat out and taught him to sense the G-forces as I turned.

Billy took the driver's seat and I read him the riot act. 'Do exactly what I say when I say it.'

'No problem.'

We set off and Billy pointed the car straight ahead. We hit third gear and achieved more in our first minute together than I had during the whole of the previous day. As we headed towards the kink before the first corner, things went slightly pear-shaped; Billy got a tad overexcited and I had to wrestle the wheel back from him before we collided with the concrete hut.

Billy followed my directions precisely and without delay. He had superb feel for brake pressure and graduated his acceleration.

The Liana was rock solid, but the going was still painfully slow. The first lap took us nearly ten minutes. Richard Whiteley's time was two minutes and six seconds.

We began travelling much faster, which meant that when Billy went the wrong way it was more spectacular. We pulled wide at the second corner, with me shouting to lift off the gas, tank-slapped, spun and stopped. Billy fought the steering all the way, his innocent expression unchanged as he stared into the void. He was the salt of the earth.

'Bollocks,' he hissed, then rocked his shoulders like the Muttley character from *Wacky Races*.

The biggest frustration for both of us was when Billy took a corner really well on one lap and then completely screwed it up on the next.

Without sight he had no way of 'learning' the track in the way I was used to. It had to be embedded through a developing sense of timing, in conjunction with the familiar tones of my voice, in a map inside his mind.

By the end of the session we'd made huge progress, but I was still steering much of the lap for him and we were nowhere near a fast time. I really liked Billy and I believed in him. I asked him what his ambition was.

'Well, Stig, I want to beat Richard Whiteley's time, and of course I'd give anything to go even faster. If I got anywhere near Terry Wogan [2.4], that would be amazing.'

I clicked a stopwatch and talked him through a perfect lap on a dictaphone. I closed my eyes and rattled through the sequence of thoughts and manoeuvres that Billy had practised that day: bumps, heavy steers, gears, counting time in the straights. I crossed the imaginary finish line in two minutes and 10 seconds.

'It's a start,' I told him.

I reported our progress to the boss, and heard myself promise that Billy would be able to do a time on his own, in spite of the fact that he couldn't yet hold the steering wheel by himself. In Wilman's world, that put my word on the line.

The next time I saw Billy was to film his performance. I could only keep him in the car for a maximum of an hour and a half, because anything more brought him to the brink of mental exhaustion.

Billy was such a genial character, but his desire to achieve a good time was written in every bullet of sweat that dripped off his nose when he drove. I had to up the ante.

'Billy, I might be quite fierce with you this session. My language might go from PG to 18.'

He smiled and said, 'Don't you worry, Stig, you can throw a few fucks and shits into me! I've been listening to your tape every day. I'm ready.'

Our progress second time round was phenomenal. Billy naturally wanted to ease off the accelerator in the straights, but I dished out so much verbal abuse that it convinced him to keep his foot down until we passed 80mph. Years of military training kicked in and Billy kept the throttle buried. A 'click right' meant a small jab of the wheel and back to straight, which was handy for making small adjustments.

I set him with the correct amount of steering for the corners, but as we went faster the front wheels began to skid. That meant he had to turn more to compensate, but it only worked if he drove at the same speed every lap.

Billy gave everything as the speed piled on the pressure. We made plenty of essential smoke breaks, but I was running out of time with him. He could drive the whole lap by himself, going through all the gears, braking and steering through every corner with the exception of one, the fastest corner of the track, the Follow Through.

I placed a single finger at the base of the steering wheel and told him, 'IT'S LOCKED.' It was too dangerous for Billy to drive that section unaided. The tyre barrier left just enough room for two cars' breadths, and at 100mph it could go wrong too quickly for him to recover it. The system worked so well, and his driving was so smooth, that I had to take a look at him to remind myself he really couldn't see.

We took our final break and I explained how close we were. Forget Richard Whiteley, we were only one second away from Wogan. Billy sparked up another roll-up. His hands were shaking. I felt a rush of admiration and affection for him. He had sacrificed so much for his country, and still had the balls to be televised in pursuit of a personal milestone.

Back in the car I did a final talk-through, highlighting areas he could improve. I got him to paint a mental picture of the perfect lap and run a commentary. Then a silent thumbs up to the camera and one simple word to Billy: '*Go!*'

Billy lit up the tyres and after a few 'small lefts' and 'small rights' we made it to the first corner. Our approach was a bit wide, but I risked sticking with it and called for a late brake and shouted 'TURN NOW.' I didn't have to tell him twice. The car scythed through the corner, the front wheels pleading for mercy. *Click left, left, straighten.*

'Keep it flat, Billy. Don't lift, kink left, more left and BRAKE.'

We just missed the tyre wall at Chicago as the ABS braking clawed at the tarmac. Billy applied heaps of right lock and we exited the corner a little too far to the right.

I bellowed at him to keep his foot hard down along the fast back straight. The hair on the back of my neck began to tingle as it often did on a good run in qualifying. It was still a long way to the finish.

Billy skidded through Hammerhead chicane without cheating by cutting the corner, and powered through the gears to the super-fast Follow Through.

'Really good, Billy – dead straight, straight, straight now, don't blow it, don't lift, don't lift AND TURN …'

Billy flat-footed it through the right-hander, a corner that a third of sighted drivers never took flat.

We approached the perilous 100mph left.

'A little left, go straight, little left, hold that, OK, it's LOCKED …'

My thumb hovered over the base of the steering wheel as we screamed through the corner. Billy never lifted. Both of us knew this lap was the one.

We made a sensible approach under braking for the penultimate corner but Billy turned too much. We cut all the way across the grass and by some miracle the car didn't spin.

One last jab of the brakes at Gambon corner, 'TURN,' and nothing could go wrong any more.

Billy crossed the line and I told him to stop.

I cradled the stopwatch for a moment in my hand.

'That was a good one, it felt like a good one. How fast was it, Stig?'

Billy had become the focus of my thoughts, and for the past week his goal, his dream, had become almost as much mine as his. He had set out to drive a racing lap as well as a sighted man. But he had achieved far, far more.

'Well, the first thing you need to know is that I never touched the steering wheel on that lap, even at the Follow Through.'

I let that hang for a moment as his chin buckled and another bullet of sweat dropped from his eyebrow. The gravity of his achievement washed through him.

'And you didn't just beat Wogan. You're under the two-minute barrier. Your time was one minute and 58 seconds.'

It was all too much for Billy, but even war heroes are allowed to shed a tear now and again. I hugged him and thanked him for being such a top man.

In the background I could see the long shadow of the world's tallest TV presenter approaching and decided to make a quick exit before my emotions got the better of me. I handed Billy over to Clarkson.

Jezza armed himself with a fifteen-second briefing from me on the terminology required to help Billy navigate the circuit, introduced himself to Billy and climbed into the car. As I walked off, Billy zig-zagged down the straight before piling off on to the grass. 'Good luck, Jezza.'

I gripped my fist in celebration of Billy's success. His time was faster than five sighted celebrities. It meant more to me than any lap I could have driven.

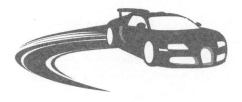

20

TAKING THE ROUGH
WITH THE SMOOTH

The reason *Top Gear* felt so exciting and personal to me was because the camera crews gave their all to capturing every moment.

It required something special not to tear yourself away from the monocle as some lunatic headed towards your kneecaps at ramming speed. Most mortals would be running for cover or asking the director to leave the rig unmanned. *TG* crews stayed put, because they could pull the image into crisper focus – and the results were there for all to see. We built up a high level of trust and I never felt complacent about the risks they took to get the perfect shot.

On Series 6 of *TG* the presenters splashed out on three dreadful coupés for less than £1500 a throw. I went to the alpine handling track at Millbrook to test their suspension and handling flaws. The Hill Route was soaking wet, and encompassed every kind of treacherous bend. The fastest machine around a closed loop would be deemed the winner.

The three musketeers duly arrived with three old heaps. Jeremy had a Mitsubishi Starion, James a Jaguar XJS and Richard a BMW 635. I made a cursory inspection of them all. Judging by the amount of rust and gaffer tape not quite holding them together, I reckoned I had a one in six chance of spearing off. I passed this on to the crew: 'If it sounds or looks wrong, start running.'

James's XJS was an utter shed. It was all I could do to hold it in a gear and count the minutes as she struggled to make it up the hill. Gravity kindly guided it down the other side.

Clarkson's clapped-out ball of metal was the fastest and boasted a vague semblance of handling. Hammond's BMW was a mean old dog that still liked to bite. It was the most powerful of the three, but 300kg heavier and designed back in the days before ABS braking systems. Time had not been kind to it in other ways; she was inclined to turn right even when you spun the steering left.

Millbrook boasted a famous jump where you went airborne and landed at a sharp left-hander. We had a camera located directly ahead, tucked behind the barriers. The man operating it normally worked at Dunsfold, so a location shoot was new territory. He was also pushing seventeen stone.

With the presenters in eager anticipation I wiped the condensation from inside my visor, took the cue to go over the radio and sped up the hill. The BM had the sweet cocktail scent of old air fresheners and wallowed like a Cross-Channel ferry. The engine's rattle suggested the ignition timing was counting it down to oblivion. I arrived at the presenters' viewpoint, hit the brakes and nearly joined them when the BM wobbled into its suspension and locked a rear wheel. Clarkson yelled, 'Run for your lives!'

I turned down the hill and nailed the throttle. As I powered up the jump the BM lurched into the air and started to turn right before I'd even landed. The suspension made a loud groan as its groggy parts stretched out of their sockets. Before the car cleared the crest, our stocky cameraman had his Nikes on and was pegging it into the trees faster than Linford Christie, knees pumping at chest height. I couldn't eject, I still had to land this disaster.

The BM slewed to 45 degrees in the air and pulled further right as she cannoned into the tarmac. Copious opposite lock countered the slide but the sheer weight of the machine pulled it down the slope at increasing speed towards the recently vacated Armco barrier. I broke the rules of car control and hit the brake pedal to reduce speed mid-slide. The front wheels locked abruptly and the engine spurted oil across the tyres. I wasn't confident of braking any time soon.

I'd lost count of the steering revolutions, but with plenty of left-hand lock still on, the BM made a brutish swerve and climbed the left-hander.

I was in so deep that I resigned myself to swiping the barrier. I waited ... and it just missed. The tank-slapper came to an end some 50 metres further on.

Clarkson's Starion won the contest comfortably.

The next three-way shoot was on the Isle of Man and involved three brand-new speedsters: Aston Martin's 8 Vantage, BMW's M6 and Porsche's Carrera S. You have to take the rough with the smooth.

The stark landscape reminded me of the Welsh mountains, with brooding cliff faces highlighted by silver-lined clouds. The locals seemed oblivious to the scenic beauty; instead of pottering around on foot, they enjoyed the faster pace permitted by the island's relaxed attitude to speed limits. There weren't any.

Top Gear arrived in force at this driver's paradise, and naturally The Stig came too. I arrived on the baggage conveyor belt at the airport.

I whetted my appetite for the Vantage by blasting it along the section of mountain road out of Douglas Harbour. Sitting in the Aston was like taking a pew in a nightclub, with red stitching on shining black leather and a gleaming metal trim. The sun was shimmering across the inky sea, and for a few minutes the barren single carriageway belonged only to me. I filled the sloping landscape of boulders and long grass with the rasping valve song of the V8, smacking it around its rev limiter in every gear and topping out at 145mph.

There was promise of power aplenty in the exhaust note, and I punished the engine for under-delivering on it by nailing the pedal to the metal and scrabbling through the open corners on the edge of adhesion. The Vantage rolled more than the DB9, squatting into the rear tyres and shooting me plenty of warning signals. Fun, but a hairdresser's car.

I arrived at the top of the island all too quickly and hooked up with the crew. We knocked out a series of in-car camera shots, including a lively one of the heads-up display in the BMW reading 141mph across a cattle grid.

The M6 had all kinds of stability controls and traction systems. Once you turned that lot off, punched in the power elevation button and expressed the paddle shift, the V10 motor set about tearing flakes out of the black stuff to the wanton howl of 501 horsepower. It was too try-hard-techy for me. When you bent it out of shape the fly-by-wire throttle

reported you to the nanny ABS system, which cut out the brakes when you tried to slow down.

We based ourselves out of Jeremy's house to shoot the other pieces. He lived at a wonderful spot on the shore where you could pluck a crab or a fish right out of the sea, clearly demonstrated by the numerous photos of his children doing just that. All the more frustrating when the lobster pot that Jeremy's wife Francie lent me came back empty after two days. 'A first,' she told me, clearly unimpressed.

To determine which was the fastest sports coupé, Production locked off a section of the prestigious TT bike racing course from Ramsey to the rail crossing, so that we could record a flat-out time in each one. Timing beacons would monitor my speed and time precisely.

I studied some in-car footage and noted that the roads were bordered by drops of 50 feet into rocky heather. Even with a helmet, if I went off in a standard road car without racing belts, that would hurt.

Back at Jeremy's I sipped beers with the boys and chatted through the filming schedule with the director. I was also waiting to hear more news about a NASCAR opportunity in the US. It looked like my ship was coming in. After months of discussion, my team racing overalls were on order.

I went outside into the weather to get some reception and discovered that the financial backing for the new team had fallen apart.

I went back inside and Hammond asked what was up, so I told him. He badgered Wilman all night about finding a way to help me out, which was a kind gesture, but I festered inside until the following morning, when I lined up for blast-off.

Minutes before I was sent up the hill in the BMW the heavens opened and the fog swooped in. With two slow recce runs under my belt I could have done with a bit of vision, but to hell with it. Fuelled with anger and frustration, I disconnected brain and kicked the M6 in the guts. The dazzling fog lights were useless in the white-out. I just barrelled up at the corners and reacted on arrival with a stab of the brake and in. The M6 relied on stiff suspension for support, which cost it dearly in traction and grip in the wet. I forced the throttle open and dared it to fly off the road.

The silver Porsche 911 went through next. Its powerful brakes and chassis developed over generations of racing at inclement venues like Le Mans saw it revel in the wet conditions, mullering the time set by the M6 by six seconds at an average speed of 84mph. Doesn't sound much, but when I tipped into the fast left at 'Black Hut' and ran wide towards the

verge it felt plenty quick. I could have had an excellent crash there. Part of me wanted to.

I rounded off with the Aston and maxed it to an identical time to the BMW. Wilman, the wily fox, eyed each timed run carefully and refused to let me do any more. I got changed and joined the presenters. They were borderline hypothermic by that point, each of them quivering like a dog crapping a peach stone. They carried on filming all day and night with the longest discussion of cars I had ever witnessed. The crew were on their chin straps by the end.

I was getting into *TG*. The cameras felt less intrusive and more like a protective bubble. I think the show was getting me too; my direct approach worked for the producers. Most of the time.

You can walk through any security cordon and enter any building in the world if you're carrying a bucket of water. It makes you look purposeful, like you're there to put out a fire or water flowers. The White Suit did all this and more. It made me virtually bullet-proof, even when tangling with the Law.

The guys wanted to build a Caterham kit car in less time than it took The Stig to drive a prefab Caterham from Kent to Knockhill racing circuit in Scotland. If I arrived before they finished, I won. The distance between the two was 465 miles.

The Caterham was one of the best track cars on the market, especially the R500. You could drive endless flat-out laps without killing the brakes or blowing the engine, or spend a day driving sideways without the rear differential exploding. Doughnuts and powerslides were tea with two sugars for this bad boy. Driving it on the road was more challenging – unless you hated your wife; you wouldn't hear a thing she said over the engine and wind noise.

I banged along the motorway north out of London behind a Range Rover full of TV crew. Ben Joiner was filming me from inside the tailgate. His *Mad Max* cycling mask helped him cope with the fumes. Passengers in passing cars occasionally clocked the storm trooper in the middle lane and waved.

The Caterham's plastic door had refused to close properly since we left Kent. As I blatted up behind the Range Rover for another shot, the whole thing flew off, spun 30 feet into the air and landed on the hard shoulder.

'Nigel, my door just blew off. Now the roof's got the shakes.'

'Sorry, Stiggy, you're just going to have to hold on. We're a bit under the whip …'

Nigel Simpkiss was the original director and one of the creators of *Top Gear*'s look and feel. He had a rare talent for framing cars against landscape, which made his films wonderfully fresh. I loved Nigel's shoots because they never lacked pace, and beneath his focus lay a deep fascination with everyone and everything around him. But it paid not to forget that a flicker of his hazel eyes could send a King Cobra scuttling home to Mummy when his temper was fraying.

A minute later I detected a blue light in my wing mirror.

'Nigel, we've got company …'

'Pull over. We'll film this.'

With me sandwiched between the Range Rover and the Law, we pulled in to the hard shoulder. The crew were out with the camera in a flash, ready to home in on the action.

Two coppers walked up alongside the Caterham.

I stayed put.

'Is that your door that just fell off?'

'Yes, it is. Sorry about that.'

'Is this your car?'

'No.'

Pause.

'Have you got your licence on you?'

'No.'

Another pause.

'What's your name?'

I thought about it for a moment, then leant across to really spell it out for them.

'THE STIG.'

That broke the ice. They very kindly returned my door. The pressure of Ben's camera lens bearing down on them precipitated their rapid withdrawal, and Nigel thanked them for their understanding.

* * *

We once filmed one of Jeremy's DVDs in the desert a mile from Edwards Air Force Base, the ultra-sensitive location of the US military's experimental aircraft facility. This was where they developed and operated the Stealth Fighter, the new F-22 Raptor and other Deep Black weapons systems no one has yet seen.

The crusty surface of Rogers Lake was cracked into plates of dried mud as far as the eye could see. It was like the surface of another planet. The setting was too stunning to resist, despite the fact that we were within a restricted area.

'Guys, we really shouldn't be here,' pleaded our American fixer. 'The military don't have a sense of humour about this kinda thing …' He was a gentle man, mid-forties, with a career in soap operas and a closet full of Hawaiian shirts. His protests fell on deaf ears.

I slipped into character and marched out on to the very lakebed where, according to respected astronaut Gordon Cooper of NASA's Mercury Program, an alien UFO had been filmed landing by a military research team under his command in 1957. The footage he reviewed from their cinetheodolite cameras depicted a silent saucer-shaped craft which, when approached, 'took off at a great rate of speed'.

I slid my radio into my pocket and walked 300 metres, a satisfying crunch of mud flakes underfoot, then turned and headed back through the heat haze towards the camera. It was our homage to legendary test pilot Chuck Yeager, who first broke the sound barrier at Edwards aboard the X-1. There were no little green men running around, but I couldn't quite shake off the eerie feeling that we were being watched.

As I reached our crew, a cluster of big 4x4s with blacked-out windows swung to a halt alongside us. The guys jumping out weren't local rent-acops with lazy hip holsters and beer guts. These dudes were wearing assault vests and black berets, shouldering M4 carbines – with rounds in the chamber, judging by the way one of them was checking the breech.

To a casual observer the soldiers spilled randomly from their vehicles. In fact their patrol sergeant, a black bruiser with sharp sideburns and wrap-around shades, covered us vehicle by vehicle. Two emphatic fingers sent two men running towards our lead Ford Galaxy; another two cut off the rear.

I walked as casually as possible off the lakebed and joined the group where our American fixer was trying to pick up the pieces. There was plenty of 'yes sir, no sir, three bags full'. It was hard to hear much inside

the helmet, but judging by the body language it seemed best that everyone did exactly what they were told. I took a seat on the tailgate of our Suburban and marvelled at the process whereby this quick reaction force assessed the situation. There was no *Top Gear* on US TV at this point, so it took a little longer to explain that the guy in the spacesuit and helmet wasn't a Korean fighter pilot trying to steal one of their latest aircraft.

Iain May leaned over and whispered, 'Looks like you might be spending the night with these guys. Wanna borrow some soap?'

'No, thanks; I know where you keep it.'

The sergeant nodded, circled a gloved finger in the air and his men saddled up. We were escorted five miles away from the base, then released and given back our identity cards.

Iain grinned. 'Shall we nip back?'

The fixer buried his face in his hands. If we went back he wouldn't come with us, and we 'wouldn't be so lucky next time'.

I spent most time around the presenters in the course of filming their escapades from various tracking vehicles. You probably never heard the one about the glamour model, the dwarf, the Spaniard and the three stooges. These six characters were the stars of the Classic Rally of Mallorca 2009.

I spent a day doing a recce of the route with the other tracking drivers to gauge time and traffic flow, and to recognise key route markers. The presenters had been paired with co-drivers that in some way parodied their persona.

For some reason Hammond was hooked up with the dwarf, and May (the beast!) got the glamour model. Clarkson was given the Spaniard who couldn't speak English, which made two of them who were incapable of listening. The co-drivers were responsible for navigating the presenters around the perils of the Mallorcan rally stages.

The supercharged Range Rover was the ultimate tracking weapon. It provided a moving platform for the camera crews to film whatever the presenters got up to in their cars. It was big, ridiculously fast and had a tailgate, allowing a cameraman to shoot from the back without falling out.

At six the following morning, the crew were busy rigging at the start line in Palma, surrounded by palm trees swaying in the morning breeze

under a clear blue sky. Complementing the Titanic yachts in the harbour were numerous Porsches and muscle cars, any of which boasted more power in their headlights than the bhp of our three entries put together.

I was charged with filming James May with Barbie doll Madison Welch aboard their 1970 Citroën Ami 8. It would take more than clever tracking to make that little biscuit tin look dynamic. James played on his Captain Slow character and hammed up his eccentric, mad professor image, but his real personality was never far from the act.

Before the cameras started rolling, he was trying to look in every direction other than the bulging Page 3 breasts bobbing next to him. When Madison asked for some help to tighten the shoulder harnesses that clicked into her waist belts, the set came to a standstill. Our sound operator was first to drop his bacon roll and dive in through the passenger window to assist her. Whilst he craned his head around in our direction to have his picture taken, James shifted uncomfortably in his seat and snuck a sideways peep at what he dubbed 'the work of the divine potter'.

Having secured Madison's breasts, it was time to start the rally. Everyone climbed aboard, with Casper filming from the boot, his assistant and the sound recordist in the back seat, and Phil, the young up-and-coming director, alongside me.

We rolled out of Palma in convoy, with the other Rangies leading Jeremy in his little Austin Healey Sprite and Hammond in the lumbering Lanchester. Casper, Ben and Iain blazed away with their cameras, cleaning up Grand Vistas of the glistening beach, the rugged yellow stone mountains and close-ups of the star cars, with Phil monitoring the dialogue via the soundman.

'Fast Porsche coming through on your right, Casper,' I shouted.

'Thanks, Buddy. Casper hoovered a shot of James being zapped.

'EYES, RRRIGHT …' An anonymous voice over the crew channel. The spotting game was off to an early start, with a hot blonde in heels and a snug bikini strolling the ocean drive.

'What's he saying in there?' Phil asked.

'He's asking her to calculate speed and distance formulas, and she's telling him to shut up and drive faster,' replied the soundman.

'Beard …' the radio crackled as we passed a pedestrian in a trench coat with a set of outrageously bushy mutton chops.

'*Bearded woman with DOG*,' Iain called.

That spot was declared a winner.

'Jeremy's making a phone call to James,' the soundman reported.

I turned to Phil. 'I'm indicating right but James isn't.'

James was prattling away whilst Madison gazed out of her window. Neither seemed too concerned about the direction they were travelling. All they really needed to do was follow the Rangie. I slowed in front of him and pointed to the slip road. James flew straight past and missed the junction, blinded by the headlights in his passenger seat.

I put the supercharger to work and caught him up again.

'We're going the *wrong way*,' James squeaked. 'We should have turned off the motorway by now.'

'Er, we know. Just follow the tracking vehicle from now on, Jimbo. We have to make a U-turn.'

The rally course followed the coast for a while before peeling up into the tree-lined mountain roads. 'Rally' exaggerated our mission. The aim was simply to mark the most precise time and speed over a set distance, although that rule didn't apply to anything with a Porsche badge. Those guys were taking huge risks on the closed mountain passes and waiting at the end of the stage to set the correct average.

James and Madison were the picture of a dysfunctional couple. With the corners tightening into hairpin bends, James put in some spirited helmsmanship, rolling the car into its suspension so much that the wing mirrors scraped the tarmac. Maddie fiddled with her lipstick and looked singularly uninterested. We stopped at a checkpoint and I asked what she thought of James's driving.

''E's awful. I thought I was gonna be sick. In them corners I looked out the window and all I could see was road.'

'You should be fine. Just keep your arms inside the car if it really leans over.'

'No shit, Sherlock.'

God knows what a young girl like Maddie made of a clique of eccentric blokes filming cars, but her previous experience certainly came in handy. Phil fidgeted and gnawed his nails as he summoned up the courage to explain a delightfully gratuitous shot of her working her magic with some soap and water.

'Basically, you'll be leaning over the car in a tight, er, white T-shirt. And as you're wiping the car, you know, um, well, some of the water will, er, you know, get on your shirt ...'

'Oh, wet T-shirt,' Maddie chirped. 'Yeah, I done that one. No problem.'

We bolted a small camera to the front of the Rangie, so I could chase the farting French supermini through the corners and get some forward tracking shots. Casper had been glued to his viewfinder monocle for nearly three hours, which was murder for motion sickness and would bubble chunks in the hardiest of men.

I had to match James's speed precisely to keep the nose of the Rangie a few feet from the Citroën as we belted through some dense woodland.

With James leading the way, we inevitably got lost in the town centre and arrived too late to enter some of the stages. The rally rounded off with a few circuits. I joined Grant, who was busy tanning his biceps, to watch the presenters pound around in a chase scene from an Inspector Clouseau movie. Clarkson's helmet poked out of his convertible like a cartoon character as he was harassed by a Ford Mustang.

James finished off his day with Madison over a delectable picnic of strawberries, foie gras and chilled Chardonnay. Madison swooned in the love scene; after five takes the sun and the plonk had taken their toll.

Brian the dwarf announced that he was unusually accomplished at handling liquor for a man of his stature, but was very concerned for Madison's wellbeing. We helped her trot indoors to drink some water in the shade. I was looking forward to dinner.

The patron of the rustic hacienda reserved a special table for the twenty-five film crew and guests in the far corner of his restaurant. Brian tucked straight into the vino rosso and Madison did her best to focus on her soup. On the arrival of the second dish, Brian appeared excessively disgruntled by the temperature of his spaghetti. When he rejected it a third time and his noggin started circumnavigating the rafters, I suspected that his gazpacho was due a second coming.

I hustled Brian into the fresh air with Grant, and we propped him up against the garden table. We really needed to get him back to the hotel, but not before a final showdown of man pride.

I had already laid waste the crew champ in an arm-wrestling match: now it was Grant's turn to feel the burn. As we clapped our paws together and took the strain, I began to regret my recent enthusiasm for the wine and garlic mussels.

Iain helpfully chanted in my ear, 'Go on, Grant, *have 'iiim …*'

Russell, the cockney soundman, offered me some cool instruction. 'All you gotta do, Ben, is go over the top. Seen it a million times; it's all in the wrist.'

Grant stayed as firm as the pillars of Zeus. It was a dead heat.

'Well,' Russell said, 'seems the only way to settle this one, fellas, is a good old-fashioned fistfight. Chop chop.'

We completed the night in a taxi with a paralytic dwarf, a broken stiletto and a sore arm instead.

21

IF IT'S GOT WHEELS

The crew were as adaptable as they were wicked. By land, sea and air, from the polar icecaps to exploding volcanoes in Iceland, they conquered the sights and sounds of the world for the purpose of light entertainment on a Sunday night.

My favourite method of filming was by helicopter; it offered so much perspective at speed and could follow the action almost wherever it led.

I flew out to Valencia to film Sauber's new Formula 1 car. Felipe Massa was driving and it was the first time I'd caught up with him since Formula 3. He was still down to earth and smiling at a world of opportunity that was opening up for him.

I was driving a BMW that had been hurriedly modified with a ton of scaffolding to act as a tracking vehicle. The camera was rigged too close to the exhaust, which blew condensation over the camera lens. Also Iain's camera operating console was malfunctioning, so we kept getting fixed shots of either sky or tarmac.

By the time an F1 engine was switched on it cost the team around £50,000, so every lap counted. I had to drive the BMW flat out just to prevent Massa's engine overheating. And the track was damp.

Iain rode in the back cursing the equipment, and I had Phil directing from the passenger seat. It was his first time on track with me. To communicate with Massa he had to relay everything via the team, so they could pass it on through Massa's earpieces. Phil was having a shocker getting his shots and our allotted laps were counting down.

'Can you get alongside the F1 coming out of this next corner?'

'Yep, but he's not making it easy,' I replied. 'He keeps pulling up on the way out …'

The BMW sank low on its wheel arches as it struggled through the turns under the burden of the metal cage and camera. It was an embarrassing contrast with the thoroughbred F1 bird trundling alongside on idle.

Determined to drive out of the corner ahead of Massa, I had the traction control off and squeezed hard on the gas. The tyres spun and I ended up sideways on the slippery painted exit kerbs, just as he popped up alongside for a close-up. The rear snapped back into line and the Sauber promptly romped away.

'Phil, this camera is shit,' Iain chimed, oblivious to everything else.

Phil turned slowly towards me as I chased after Massa and said, 'Are you OK?'

'Yeah, no problem.'

'You sure? Do you need to pull over for a minute? Because from where I'm sitting, we nearly just hit a Formula 1 car.' The colour had drained from his face.

'No, we're fine, I had options.' I fought to keep a straight face.

'Phil, this camera's shit. I can't pan or focus; all I'm getting is sky,' Iain said.

We took a five-minute break which turned into two hours of watching the local technicians try in vain to resolve the camera system. I explained to Massa the track positioning we were trying to achieve, and we managed another sketchy run with more footage of sky, tarmac and glimpses of Sauber.

Phil hopped into a helicopter to shoot from the air. As it crabbed sideways down the pit straight, all eyes were on the Formula 1 car as it exited the last corner and sped into view.

Phil sensed something was wrong, glanced up from his viewer and felt the air sucked out of his lungs by what he saw.

'BRIIIIIIIIDGE …'

The pilot swivelled his head to the right and clocked the walkway over the middle of the pit straight, now metres away from the airframe and only feet below the spinning blades. His wrist snapped at the cyclic stick

and he cranked the collective to gain altitude, hopping the bridge just in time.

'Thank you, Señor.'

Most helicopter shots were achieved using a stabilised head operated by an onboard specialist or by a guy hanging his ass out of the door with the recorder on his shoulder. It required a combination of skill and balls to sit in the fresh air with both hands on the camera, with a false view of the horizon, and still manage to keep the target in focus.

Iain May lived for these occasions. He was *da man* when it came to reading oncoming traffic so that I could overtake with impunity and scythe through the countryside.

One of the finest scenic drives in the world was the Flüelapass from Davos to Susch in Switzerland, a 17-mile stretch of stunning alpine road. Wave upon wave of heavenly corners punctuated long straights and a scattering of cambered hairpins. The medley of juicy bends flowed through a seam of green and snow-capped peaks, so high that if you were about to meet your maker it was only a short trip.

I was driving a 200mph Mercedes CLK63 Black automatic, one of the most nimble weapons in the AMG armoury. It was jacked with brute power, boasted a telepathic feel through the tyre to the road, and flew through the mountains like a Messerschmitt. Its carbon-fibre cockpit contained a moulded racing seat that fused you to the ride. The tight suspension and direct brakes made it ideal for arriving late into the turns, pointing in and blasting off on to the next straight. The massive torque of the Affalterbach motor was over-zealous for its tyres; you hung on with both hands.

Iain took to the skies with a two-way radio that he kept live so he could operate the camera joystick and talk me through the traffic without moving his hands. With my eye in the sky, blind corners were no more and I kept a constant picture of the terrain.

Zip, zip, zip to a thundering rpm in fifth gear, running parallel to the rail tracks approaching a bundle of traffic, into a wooded hill with no line of sight.

'All clear, clear ahead, splash 'em.'

No need to brake, straight past the lot and down the hill.

'90 left coming up, then two cars, don't pass.'

Braked down to third, slightly threw the steering, big powerslide, straightened and held behind the two cars. I could see the parallel road coming out the other side of the next hairpin was clear, booted it past the obstruction and entered the corner.

'Nice one, Ben. All clear.'

I caught a group of bikers strewn along the road like a Hell's Angels chapter of the pinstriped variety. Some rode in pairs, side by side; the rest were linear and offered little room to overtake. I eased past them one at a time to ensure none of the organ donors fell off their mounts, then caught the two leaders. Alerted to the presence of an infiltrator, they sped up, beards and ponytails whipping in the airstream.

The road rejoined the railway for a straight run and the Merc splashed past with ease. This riled Ponytail, who wound back the throttle on his Milwaukee vibrator and tagged along. It was *CHiPS*, Swiss cheese style, versus me in a 460 horsepower race-tuned Merc with a helicopter in my pocket …

Iain updated me on a section where the road curled left downhill and crossed the train tracks. The flat level cutting through the road would act like a jump, the sharp drop that followed like a landing ramp.

As I arrived at the tracks I braked, dropped two cogs to third, released the pins and took off. All four rubbers left the deck on a slight angle across their axis, with some lift on the front left owing to the diagonal cut of the tarmac.

My head kissed the sunroof as I vaulted out of the seat and banged back into the deck, no dramas. And Ponytail …?

I looked up to the head mirror at the wall of tarmac, pine trees and sky behind. It really was a *big* drop. Suddenly the fat hog flew into view about two metres off the ground. Ponytail was clinging on for dear life. His saddle bags extended from their side mounts like wings, the left one reaching up over the back of his seat. The dynamic effect of his weight over the handlebars kept the nose pointing earthwards, the saddlebags tilted his rear wheel high and to the side, so that I could the spokes spinning.

Ponytail landed his machine with bags and moustache in some disarray. He popped the white flag and cautiously applied the brakes, no doubt scanning for a lay-by in which to hose off the river of gravy running down the inside of his leathers.

At lunch on top of a mountain the following day the boot was on the other foot. Clarkson had been driving the Merc and had somehow annoyed a cyclist on the way up. Jeremy arrived at the top considerably faster than the cyclist, parked up and slurped back another espresso from Heidi's tavern. Meanwhile the cyclist pumped his pedals for another fifteen minutes and visualised ways of murdering the Mercedes driver.

I was chatting with the crew in the lay-by at the top of the hill when I clocked a goliath of a man stepping off his racing bike on the other side of the road. He looked *pissed* and he was scowling in our direction.

He was at least six five and 220 pounds, and he was solid. Once the traffic cleared he strode purposefully across the road. He wore a mankini, like Borat's, only his was high-vis yellow over black leggings. He was a terrifying sight. Jeremy copped it first.

'Who is driving the *fucking Mercedes*?'

This was the first occasion I'd seen Jeremy lost for words. And as he turned to face him, he appeared to have shrunk at least six inches.

'Is it you, huh? You're driving this car like a fucking idiot?'

'No, it's not me. I don't know what you're talking about.'

It was a good opener, but Mankini wasn't to be put off that easily.

'This car is going up and down like stupid. Who is the driver?'

'I don't know, but I think he went that way …' Jezza pointed randomly back down the mountain. Good work, mate; just don't start pointing in my direction.

Mankini was livid at being denied a righteous kill. He lectured us on the sanctity of two-wheeled travel, yelled, 'Fuck all of you,' and loped back to his nut-hugging Lycra buddies.

Our visit to Switzerland was not entirely unwelcome. Brian Klein, *TG*'s studio director, was helming Clarkson's DVD and led our convoy of supercars to another location at the base of the mountain. As Brian climbed out of the Aston Martin DBS, the female proprietor of a local restaurant came running out and refused to let go of his arm.

Brian was wearing an urban cowboy ensemble, with pointy boots, bleached jeans and a stripy top over his well matured physique. After we ordered some food and the rest of the proprietor's family had been assembled, the cause of the commotion became clear.

'She thinks I'm Timothy Dalton.' Brian slipped on some sunglasses, adding to his mystique.

He had his photo taken with the extended family Robinson and signed autographs whilst the rest of us chewed down the kind of pasta pesto the Romans would have used as building mortar.

We flew to Malaga in Spain and stayed at the opulent Ascari Resort. The circuit nestled inside a range of rugged mountains dotted with sparse Andalusian foliage. It was designed by the owner and my former team boss, Klaas Zwart, and replicated twenty-six of the most challenging corners from Grand Prix venues like Spa and Zandvoort. With sun all year round, it was the perfect setting to assess the true performance of three of the latest road cars: a BMW M3, an Audi RS4 and a Mercedes-Benz C63 AMG.

As I walked down the pit lane I passed a familiar shape peering from underneath the metal shutters to one of the garages. I stared longingly at the aggressive dive planes covering the wheel arches of Ascari's Le Mans racing prototype. It sent me back to the time I drove it around Le Mans. The desire to race stung like a wasp, and it was all I could do to drag my focus back to the day's objectives.

Clarkson was hunched over his laptop, sucking on a Marlboro as he rocked back in deep contemplation of the script he'd been working on with *TG*'s other wordsmith, Richard Porter. Jeremy was the architectural powerhouse behind all his work, so I left him to it. I needed to make a decision that would affect the rest of my day: Cappuccino or Americano.

The Ascari lair with its marble floors, manicured gardens, 'Cortijo' clubhouse, swimming pool and sleeping hammocks compared very favourably to the spit and sawdust of Dunsfold. The crew enjoyed it so much that we lobbied Wilman to shoot the whole series out there. Predictably enough, he refused to 'become a shareholder in EasyJet'.

Having satiated myself at the breakfast buffet I moved back towards the presenters, who were embroiled in a mock debate about their cars in a build-up to filming their comments.

Clarkson turned to me. 'Have you driven it?'

'What's that?'

'The Merc.'

'Not yet.'

'You'll love it. It's got loads more power than the others; it's insane.' Big draw on his fag and back to the laptop.

The statistically correct script labelled the Merc as a winner by virtue of its 450-odd horsepower, against the Audi on 420 and the BMW a nickel short. The Audi was four-wheel drive, which might throw in a curve ball, but the BM seemed destined for third place in the performance stakes.

Whilst the presenters got to grips with their lines, the director got me on to mine. We filmed all three cars going flat out around the circuit. The crew had already dispatched instinctively and were filming Grand Vista shots of the countryside before the rest of us had even arrived.

It was no surprise to see that Iain had found a cherry picker. Ben panned artistically across the hillside, through the branches of an oak tree. Casper was shooting from on high to absorb the bleached panorama.

First up was Clarkson's Merc. I climbed in and moved the seat forward for about five minutes until I reached the pedals. It was a big heavy unit, with a 6.2-litre engine that could power a supertanker. I shifted into gear and positioned alongside Phil, who was busy with his radio, his sunbaked forehead turning the colour of beetroot. He gave me the thumbs up and 'Action.'

I skipped my left foot off the brake and simultaneously pinned the accelerator to the floor. A cloud of smoke billowed in my rear-view mirror as Daimler's finest horses roared towards the first corner of the day. I braked earlier than I felt I needed to, but the Merc sopped up the margin; its lumbering weight folded into the soft suspension. Yuk.

The front of the car washed out mid-corner as the chassis lolled about, front first, followed by the rear. With so much roll and so much power, I knew that a touch of the throttle would produce a filthy slide, so I opened the floodgate. There was a screech of rubber bordering on the sociopathic and two bubbling black stains across the pristine grey road surface.

Being inch perfect was difficult as the volume of power overcame the rear differential and shoved the remaining surge through one wheel, spinning it faster than the other. Overpowered, with soggy brakes and wobbly suspension. What an old nail.

Next up was the sales rep's wet dream. Hammond's M3 sat firm on its suspension, with a smooth ride from shock absorbers that clamped the rubber to the tarmac. The tender brakes reacted quickly to my input. The acutely sensitive power delivery was stunning and controllable. It drifted sideways through the corners like it was on casters. Every detail, from the

cross-stitched leather steering wheel to the flawless gear-change and reduced upper body weight, was bang on. It was such a gem I wanted to kiss the designer.

I hopped into James's Audi RS4. As an Audi fan I expected to be impressed. The four-wheel drive gripped and bogged down on the fast pull away, then kangaroo hopped along the pit lane. Even with a 40/60 front to rear torque split, I never liked four-wheel-drive sports cars. They only functioned properly if the bias was substantially in favour of the rear wheels, otherwise the two axles competed for supremacy at the cost of cornering stability.

Once I was up to ramming speed, the engine torque punched the Audi nicely through every gear. Minor inputs of the wheel were met by jarring returns from the suspension and cornering became mundanely predictable. The RS4 juddered with understeer through every turn.

I donned the white suit for a time attack to determine which of these V8 bullets was the fastest. I already knew the answer. I tried to warn Jeremy that he had picked a dog.

'Rubbish, you've no idea what you're talking about,' he replied.

When it came to posting a time in front of camera, the Merc rolled over on its wheel arches and flashed its undercarriage at every opportunity. Its time was 2.43.5.

Next I pushed the Audi to the brink, flat-footed it through the kink on to the back straight and reached a top speed of 145 into a fast, tightening right-hander.

Braking and turning from high speed tested the driver's confidence as much as the essence of the machine. I went in flat, cogged down and braked lightly to prevent the ABS activating, then gradually increased the brake pressure. The ABS triggered as I reached for the apex at about 110, resulting in a deadening of the pedal. Then the electronics gave up, no longer caring to moderate the percentage changes of fluid pressure to slow each individual wheel. That sent all the braking to the least loaded wheel, the inside rear, locking it instantly as if someone had hooliganed the handbrake. It sent the car completely sideways.

The Polaroid moment that followed saw The Stig in a flat spin, exiting stage left off the circuit towards a gravel trap and tyre barrier. And it was only 10.30 in the morning …

The gremlin in the system's electronics had more to offer. I piled on the opposite lock, slammed the steering into the rack stop and applied

100 per cent brakes, scanning desperately for a solution to save the car either by swivelling it around or trying to accelerate away from the wall. At that critical moment the ignition switched itself off, taking with it the power steering and assisted brake. I had to push them both twice as hard to achieve the same effect, manhandling the controls like a gorilla at feeding time.

Scraping the tarmac ran my speed down another 40mph to a manageable 70 by the time I slid across the border of the gravel trap, missed the deep stuff next to the wall and brought the car to a stop on the grass. The engine and electronics were totally dead. *Naughty car*, but you had to laugh. These things happened.

I removed and replaced the key. She switched on and drove back to the start line as if nothing had happened – and still managed a time just 0.4 of a second slower than the Merc.

The M3 tore a ferocious pace thanks to its poise and balance in every corner, and aggressive braking. The time was a full five seconds faster than the other two.

I went out with Klaas and the presenters for tapas in the medieval town of Rhonda, overlooking the spectacular 'El Taho' gorge. It was a rough existence.

Jeremy was so irked by the day's events that he accused me of deliberately missing an apex to foul the lap time of his meat wagon. I told him that if I put an apple on the apex he could drive at it all day and never hit it. Jezza swallowed the bait whole.

We lined up the cameras on a sharp corner and I placed the apple at the latter part of the apex kerb. I stood right on the corner to goad the big man further.

Jeremy went at it hammer and tongs, drifting sideways into the corner on different lines and somehow managing to miss every time. He was excruciatingly close, but no strudel. I bit my lip hard, trying desperately not to laugh. After the fifth attempt he gave up and it was my turn in the BMW. If I hit the apple, Jeremy was prepared to eat it.

I flicked the M3 into the turn, lit up the rear tyres and squelched it on the first take. At Jeremy's request we filmed it from another angle. I nailed it and the big man took a big bite of humble pie. He picked up a grubby piece of crushed apple from the kerb and guzzled it down.

* * *

Nothing daunted, Jeremy handed me the keys to a Lamborghini Gallardo 560-4 Spyder, issued himself a Ford Focus and demanded a race down the Rhonda mountain pass to the port of Marbella. The winner of course was a foregone conclusion; he must have figured The Stig needed a night out. So we decamped to the harbourside to film some atmosphere.

Marbella was everything that *TG*'s home turf was not. It was loaded with minted Russian oligarchs and country-sized yachts crewed by orange people wearing Gucci goggles. The only cleavage we saw at Dunsfold was the 'mighty sarlacc' of Steve Howard's rump as he put his back into salvaging another scrapheap challenge. The army of party poppers gracing the bars and clubs of Puerto Banus were all slinky-hipped underwear models staring at their own reflections in the Cartier and Bulgari windows.

I made a lightning change of clothes inside the phone booth of a petrol station, boarded the lime green Gallardo as The Stig and put the roof down. Locals and beachcombers alike whipped out their cameras and I felt like a movie star. I snapped the throttle and kicked up the notes of the V10 motor to clear a path through the crowd filling the main drag. People darted left and right, oversized heels stumbled, mouths full of gold bullion rattled.

My directions, 'eighth bar on the left', seemed vague at night as I strained to see even the neon lights through my visor. The helmet had to stay shut. Some of the friendlier oranges were slapping my shoulder and taking flash photos through the open cabin. Amidst the sea of people I recognised Dan De Castro the Spanish yeti, biceps burning as he legged it with his camera.

With the cameras rolling I cracked the throttle a final time, switched off and marched towards the nearest bar.

'Not that one, the other one,' Iain shouted from camera 2.

A few minutes later I made myself at home in the Ten Bar with a cocktail. It wouldn't be long before The Stig's sex appeal attracted plenty of attention, and sure enough as Jeremy made his entrance I was suitably dripping with fans getting their pictures taken.

Jeremy clocked me at the candle-lit table and doubled up laughing.

'We're in Puerto Banus, in a bar heaving with fanny, and you've managed to pull four blokes ...' He raised both palms to the heavens and then waved at the scousers I'd met in the course of their stag do.

'No, honestly, before you came in there were girls here, I swear.'

Thanks to the magic of TV, The Stig's honour was soon restored. A group of scantily clad chicks were waiting upstairs with the other cameras, and we filmed the kind of shots footballers' wives see of their husbands every week: champagne, bling and boobs.

With the filming over, I made the transition from Superman back to Clark Kent in the urinals and joined the lads in the open-deck bar. The boys switched their heavy cameras for lager and melted into the leather sofas. Brian Klein was grinning from ear to ear.

'Did you see him with those blokes? I mean, honestly, Ben, you're like the Pied Piper for *Sun* readers.'

'Well, I saw something tonight I would never have dreamt possible,' Jezza gasped. 'A Spaniard running, *actually* running. Welcome to the English way of life, De Castro.'

'Fuck you, Jeremy, at least our government isn't run by a bunch of Scots gits.'

Jeremy laughed so hard he choked on his beer.

To make good our departure without giving my game away, Jeremy drove off stealthily in the lime green Lambo. I ran through the back alleys, caught him up and swapped seats for the journey up the mountain.

Weirdly, it was the first time I'd ever driven with Uncle J on the open road. The ribbon of polished tarmac that led up to Rhonda from the coast is one of the most breathtaking in Europe. It was a clear night, and the soft moonlight showed just enough of the rock face lining the road to see ahead without drowning out the stars. I didn't worry about the drop into oblivion to my left because the Lambo was sensational at following precisely the path I ordered. The V10 bellowed at the moon and we just flowed up the winding road on a magic carpet.

Jeremy called his wife and held his phone into the air. 'Can you hear that? Ben's driving us up the mountain. It's just epic.'

Epic or not, as soon as we got into town he started busting my balls about the route, insisting we take his one.

'So which way now, Sherlock?' I asked.

'I don't know, you've come in the wrong way, man, turn left. No. Right.'

'Well, which one is it, Jeremy? Left or right?'

'Are all racing drivers devoid of brains *and* sense of direction, or is it just you?'

I never argued with Jeremy, he was too bloody good at it.

'Shut up … you … fucking talky man …'

He roared with laughter at his own expense for the second time that day, and the name has stuck with him ever since. Crucially, it bought me twenty seconds in which to figure out the way to our hotel.

I found the Bull Ring and then home.

The close of another day in paradise.

22

BITTEN BY THE BUG

Some days I maxed as many as fifteen different cars with no lead-in. With the time constraints of filming, I learnt to skip the foreplay and adapt quickly to all comers. The Ron Jeremy of cars.

In a racing car the belts welded your body to the chassis, and you felt the reaction to every bump or force physically. A road car was more subtle. You hung loose like a surfer harnessing the power of a wave.

Whether I raced a car for years or drove it for a few minutes, I developed a connection with its soul. The secrets poured out once you knew how to listen. Some spoke softly, others shouted from the pulpit with a loudhailer.

There was only one Tyrannosaurus Rex. The Bugatti Veyron was just as extinct the moment it rolled out of the factory, a relic of our time. Future generations, driving small gas- and electric-powered cellophane composite cubes, will look at the Veyron in museums and say, 'Wow, those guys in the Oil Age were cray-zee, but clever.'

For once, statistics really painted the picture with the Veyron.

Its heart was a mighty 16-cylinder engine. A normal car had four cylinders, so that was like having four engines under the bonnet. Four turbochargers spun maximum power instantly from the 8-litre motor, with ten radiators cooling all the systems.

It developed a gargantuan 1,001bhp and 1250 NM of torque at the stroke of the pedal, *from any speed*, to bend space-time and blur the road at 253mph. The engine didn't propel the wheels as much as shove millions of cubic litres of the earth's atmosphere out of the way at one third of the speed of sound.

The tyres were only rated to run at top speed for fifteen minutes, but at 250 you emptied the fuel tank in twelve minutes anyway. My favourite stat: the motor consumed an estimated 45,000 litres of air per hour.

Complicated physics and supercars normally equalled frequent and catastrophic mechanical failure. Volkswagen group, owner of Audi and Lamborghini, bought Bugatti and provided the Veyron with the metronomic reliability of a Swiss watch in a way that only German engineers could.

There will never be another production car so dedicated to the purity of speed, so perfectly delivered, and the economics of selling a car for £850,000 that costs more like £3m to produce are unlikely to return soon, unless the Pharaohs make a comeback.

In 2005 I knew none of this bar the price tag, which failed to impress me. Racing cars were far more valuable and were built to be thrashed, not worshipped. I had to get to the basement of the NatWest Tower, locate the car and drive it, fast, from London to Milan.

The three presenters had raced across Europe from Alba in Northern Italy to determine the fastest way of transporting a fresh truffle to England. Contrary to popular belief, the *Top Gear* races were for real. Hammond and May flew in a small Cessna and hitched a ride on the Eurostar; Clarkson drove the Bugatti over the Alps, crossing Italy, Switzerland and France.

A tracking crew had chased Jeremy across thousands of kilometres of countryside to record his journey. My job was to recreate the trip in reverse with another crew to capture the necessary pick-up shots.

The clock approached midnight as I headed through the giant glass doors that opened into the Tower foyer. The place was deserted apart from a uniformed guard on the front desk. It felt like Bruce Willis wandering around the Nakatomi building in *Die Hard*. I scaled a smart escalator and took a long ride in the main elevator to reach the Vertigo bar on the 42nd floor.

The lift doors opened into the dim blue lighting of the reception area. Camera kit was strewn across the carpet, surrounded by a throng of soundmen, cameramen, producers and directors.

Iain May, beer in hand, spotted me and began singing, 'It's only just begun – for you …' His shift was over.

The first objective was to get the Bugatti keys off Clarkson and go film 'some footage of London'. I wandered around the oval room and found the presenters steadying themselves with a few bevvies with Andy Wilman and Nigel Simpkiss.

Hammond and May looked relieved to be standing more than two inches apart, after thirty-six hours crammed into the tiny Cessna. They hadn't reached the stage of the Russian cosmonauts on the MIR space station, who passed written notes to one another so they didn't have to speak, but they were close. May hunched over a cocktail table with his hair draped over the ashtray, and Hammo leant against the bar, sinking Belgium's finest without letting it touch the sides.

Clarkson had won, so he was in jubilant form, propping his fag up in the air like an antenna and reminiscing about the last couple of days. He handed me the key and grinned. It weighed heavy in my hand, solid metal bound in red patent leather, the Bugatti oval enamelled in the centre.

'You'll fucking love that.'

'Really?'

'Oh …' He shook his head. 'Epic.'

The inbound crew were soaking up the booze. It looked like the makings of a damn good party, but we had orders from Nigel to get moving.

Down in the basement, producer Alex Renton and a giddy Jim Wiseman were circling the Bugatti like frenzied hornets. Wiseman was wearing a shocking set of Elvis sunglasses.

'Nice shades, Jim.'

'With a future this bright, you know it makes sense. Speaking of which, *mmm*, I see you're holding the keys to a *Vey*-Ron. We'll see you out of here, mind the kerbs.'

I climbed inside the cabin and landed in the U-boat captain's chair. I shut the door and felt the cockpit pressurise. Gauges and dials littered the maroon leather dash, poised to confirm when every one of the 1001 horses had been deployed. The main console was made of tortoiseshell-patterned steel. A pistol-grip gear selector at its centre looked primed to fire torpedoes. The wheel was so sturdy it must have been solid cast metal. All the controls were hard-wired to the functions of steering, gearbox and engine.

I pushed the start button, and a heavy-duty starter motor screeched the engine reactor into life.

The Veyron had been boxed in, nose into the wall of the underground car park. Rear vision was poor, probably because nothing stayed close enough to worry about. But it meant that my first minutes behind the wheel were spent sweating bullets, reversing it up a narrow parking ramp at less than one mile an hour.

Casper and I finally headed into the amber night. A single wallop of the throttle dealt with the Blackwall Tunnel, then we headed east into the City. The crew stopped somewhere near 'Wall' at 2am to set up an elevated tripod, to get a glimpse of the Bugatti hammering around a big roundabout system. Then the police turned up.

Casper's brow furrowed as he climbed out of the passenger seat. A few minutes later he was back. 'Spoken to the Law. They've got a message for you: "Give it some shit".'

My pleasure.

With adult supervision, I floored the Bug around this roundabout for the next twenty minutes. In a straight line the four-wheel drive could accelerate the rig from 0 to 60mph and back to 0 again in less than five seconds.

I reached under the steering wheel and depressed an innocuous silver button to disengage the traction control and dumped the throttle at the traffic lights. The four wheels clawed at the greasy road then shot off. I aimed around the corner and clung on to the wheel just to stay in my chair. It grappled its way across the wet manhole covers with a few minor slippages along what was otherwise a 90mph tramline.

My exuberance got the better of me that night as the warm glow emanating from Casper's camera encouraged my right foot to slip on the empty carriageways. The kidney pinching thrust that went with every impulse of the accelerator was in a class of its own, and compellingly addictive. Even the strobing flashes through the Limehouse Link tunnel failed to bring me back to the real world. F1, eat your heart out.

We picked up our German escort from VW some hours later and began the two-day journey to Italy. Getting from A to B took longer than the actual race, because we kept stopping to position film crew and because every traffic cop in Western Eurpope wanted to see how fast it would go.

The Bug had a paddle shift to pick from seven gears or you could leave it in automatic and take pot luck. It paid to remember which one you

were in. If you floored it in 'D' there was a slight delay as the gearbox considered the most powerful cog. By the time you realised what was going on, the acceleration thumped you into the back of the seat and you entered warp speed. Nothing on the autoroute moved like this. It was like flying a UFO after someone had pressed the pause button on the rest of the traffic.

For any good road trip, you needed a wingman. Frenchie was a loveable wide-boy from the production team who, as he constantly reminded me, had once owned an MX-5: 'Rear-wheel drive, did doughnuts, my pride and joy, *tragically* caught fire and burned to a cinder one day …' He wiped his eye.

Frenchie took his duties seriously, kept the Bug brimmed with snacks and occasionally noted signposts between bursts of neck-breaking laughter every time I so much as tickled the throttle.

There was a burst of static from the radio. 'Turn right at this junction, please, we're going left to film you …' We'd almost forgotten Nigel was there. 'No, sorry, come with us now. Take the left.'

The left lane was heaving with traffic at a red light whilst my lane was green. I hooked the indicator to a chorus of French horns.

'I feel your pain. A thousand pairs of Gallic eyes burning into the side of your faces.'

'Thanks, Nige.'

Actually, the eyes didn't give a monkey's about the side of our faces. They were simply captivated by the Veyron. We drew a crowd wherever we went. As we thundered through the bucolic countryside people waved from the fields, and children ran towards it as we cruised slowly through the villages. Back on the open road, tree-lined boulevards whirled by as I snapped at the gear paddle like a junkie on a crack pipe.

We stopped to film at a remote wood and a crowd gathered within minutes, young and old, some taking photos, some just marvelling that such things could be. The Bug made everyone smile; it conjured anew the innocent delight we can all feel when admiring a beautifully crafted automobile.

'OK, Mr Collins, time to move on.'

Nigel set up a camera in a copse for a panoramic shot of the Bugatti crossing a small suspension bridge over a sparkling river. I zapped across in the blink of an eye.

'Fuck me,' Frenchie groaned from the footwell, 'did you feel the G as we came round the bend?'

I was grinning like an idiot. 'Mega, isn't it?'

Nigel was back on the radio almost immediately. 'Let me know as soon as you've turned, please.'

We had a specific time permit to film through the Mont Blanc tunnel, crossing the border from France to Italy, so we couldn't hang around.

After a brisk contretemps with a construction truck we made it back on to the main drag and overtook everything except the fuel stations. I coasted down every mountain in neutral to save fuel, using modest blats to sail past other cars like they were signposts. Even so, we guzzled fuel. Nigel was beginning to tire of my incessant requests for a top-up.

We made it to the tunnel in the nick of time. Ben Joiner hopped in with me to film as the orange lighting danced around the interior. With CCTV monitoring every millimetre, I didn't break the speed limit, but I flicked the throttle as soon as we were out and watched Ben's smile spread from ear to ear.

We set up at a motorway service station to do an all-wheel-drive launch to 100mph, which the Bug achieved in five seconds. The VW engineers had to phone Bugatti's head office in Germany for permission to engage the launch control system. We changed the setting from stun to kill by turning a magic key behind the seat. The whale tail wing rose behind me and the Bug's active suspension lowered the nose into the ground like a raging bull, ready to charge.

'Nigel, why don't you hop in for this one?' I said.

He climbed in reluctantly, scooched his long body into the passenger footwell so he couldn't be seen, and set the cameras running. I applied the brake with my left foot, which acted like a clutch, floored the gas with my right and then lifted the anchor.

The car charged forward like the *Millennium Falcon* going into hyperspace, and the wide expanse of tarmac suddenly narrowed on to the motorway. Sure enough, the Bug transported Nigel into another world. He said nothing. He just rocked back with fits of carefree laughter.

For most of the shoot I ran the Bug in handling mode, which was good for 233mph, only switching to speed mode, with the wing down, when I needed a bit of extra juice. As you passed around 140 the downforce sucked the car into the road and the suspension reassuringly locked itself in. The amount of powered rubber in contact with the ground meant the

Bug was always poised to take a direction. You held on and drove it, 100 per cent of the time.

Beyond 180, ahem, the aero balance started to favour the rear and made it less willing to dart around.

As we crossed the border into Switzerland we started seeing more German plates and seriously powerful Porsches. Good sport.

I noticed an orange ant in my mirror, closing at a rate of about 80mph. Appropriately enough, some hard Haus music started pounding out of the radio. You only live once.

'Watch this, Frenchie.'

I notched down to fourth and let the 911 Turbo run past at flat chat, then nailed the throttle. We matched his speed within a second, then splash, bye-bye Porker. For good measure I opened the tap all the way, leaving the boy marooned in the fast lane.

The Bug firmed up, tyres hissing and roaring. At 230mph, a sparsely populated autobahn metamorphosed into a Grand Prix circuit. Dotted white lines became a seamless blur. Cat's-eyes pummelled the undercarriage like speed bumps. The slightest kink in the carriageway became a corner.

Your eyes only moved from the road's horizon for milliseconds, anticipating the cumbersome trajectories of the other 'static' road users well in advance as the Bug gobbled tarmac at a rate of 340 feet per second, the length of a football pitch in a blink of an eye.

A line of flashing lights whipped into view, blocking the fast lane. Traffic accumulated. I pulled the ripcord and hit the brakes, knocking the Bug out of speed mode. The rear wing went vertical to form an airbrake, the suspension adjusted smoothly to the interruption and the ABS crackled underfoot.

They told me it could stop dead from 250 in ten seconds. What bull. It took less than that.

If the Bugatti was the fastest car in the world, the second fastest was the Audi RS6 containing the VW engineers who were trying to keep an eye on us. Whenever I sped off, the Audi would loom into view a few moments later. As our journey progressed, a mutual respect developed between the *TG* crew and the Teutonic boffins who were supporting us.

I lost count of how many times we up and passed the camera and the number of roads we did them on. Through kaleidoscopic tunnels, stunning archways of trees, tiny Italian villages, across open fields, up

twisting mountain roads, past wind farms, vineyards and fast-flowing rivers, the visual feast of continental Europe unfolded before our windscreen.

The trip seemed to end as suddenly as it had begun. In Milan I reluctantly handed back the keys for the final time. My life would never be the same again. The Bug was being snatched away from us by a journo for review. He'd been hounding Nigel all week.

To say I was jealous would be like claiming that Cindy Crawford was mildly attractive. I could only console myself with the hope that my rival for the Bug's affections might be a plump, balding man with glasses. In that, at least, I wasn't disappointed.

23

TRACK RECORD

I was reunited with the Bug when the time came to spank it around the Dunsfold circuit. Bugatti didn't have one available, so *Top Gear* convinced a private owner to hand over his keys. Amazingly, he only had one stipulation ...

Our new fast-talking Series Producer, Pat Doyle, had been around the TV block; he was as canny as a one-armed snake catcher. His thankless task was to try and control our spiralling budget and keep a leash on the pack of hounds chasing editorial nirvana. He had a curly brown mullet and a mouth that beamed whenever something unconscionable or surreal was unfolding. With *TG* that meant most of the time, and now was no exception.

'How many laps do you think you need, Stig?'

'That's as long as a piece of string. At least six or seven; as many as it takes to get the tyres working.'

'OK, six laps. The owner's over there ...' His brow furrowed. 'He's giving me chapter and verse of his life story; he's only just bought the car, yada yada, and the deal is we have to pay for these tyres if you screw 'em. So, less laps is good. Can you do less laps?'

'I can try. It depends on track conditions and how accurate you want the time to be. Can I use launch control?'

'Um ... Yeah ... Will that screw the tyres?'

After grappling with rubber it was time to talk fuel. We needed some. I didn't fancy driving this guy's brand-new baby on the open road in case someone drove into the back of it, so we dispatched him to the petrol station. He returned with a gouge running down the length of the right side, having had a minor disagreement with the concrete plinth beside the pump. I still had to watch those tyres, though.

I wanted the Bug to do well on the track, but in spite of its unrivalled power-to-weight ratio it still weighed a ton more than a Ferrari 430 and it proved hard going to stop, point and squirt it out of the tight corners at Dunsfold. On the straights, it was phenomenal, but out of the corners the all-wheel drive hunted fruitlessly for traction before being blown out by the massive engine torque.

The Bug was the King of the Road, the most awesome car ever made. But my granny could have popped her dentures in the cup holder and driven a more electric lap with her mobility chair.

I arrived early another morning for a different powertest altogether, grabbed a coffee and hooked up with Wiseman.

'We've got the Big Daddy today, Stiggy. We've got the Koenigsegg.'

'Sounds great. What is it?'

For driving on the edge, nothing was more fearsome or difficult to pronounce than the Koenigsegg CCX. This 806 horsepower Swedish landmine was the brainchild of the company's founder Christian von Koenigsegg, who dreamt of making a car that would break world records. In 2005 the CCX scalped Guinness records for both the fastest and most powerful production car in the world. In 2006 they brought the car to *TG* for a crack at posting the fastest time on our leaderboard.

As Jim filled me in, Jeremy appeared from the other end of the office in a haze of smoke. 'Be careful in that car. Look, I know you're a good driver but, trust me, this is like nothing you have ever driven before. It's a beast. The cornering is ... *something else*. Just wait; you'll see what I mean.'

That was odd. Jeremy never did that.

Jim and I made our way down to the start to see how things were shaping up. The camera crews were busily making their way around the track in their little black vans. I could make out a large square object hogging a big section of the parking area. A flurry of men in dark overalls hovered around it NASA style, probing things. They opened an enormous engine cover, and for a moment it looked as though the car might transform into an aircraft-carrier.

It sat on fat 20-inch tyres that neatly fell in line with the square side profile, but the car seemed noticeably shy of downforce. There was no sign of any wings that would generate high-speed grip, and the bodywork was too flat. As I quizzed Christian von K, the car's ethos became clear. It was designed to avoid drag at all costs, in order to go as fast as physically possible in a straight line and break the world record.

Christian could easily have passed for Ernst Stavro Blofeld's cheery cousin. He was passionate about his baby, showering me with facts and figures to illustrate its prowess. He was living out a boyhood dream to build a dominant supercar. His team anticipated another striking performance around Dunsfold, but as the Bug had discovered, the track could be a cruel mistress.

I peered into the engine bay to have a look at what would shortly be pushing me along the strip at 170mph. Once you hit the track you were either totally committed or you shouldn't be there at all.

The 4.7-litre V8 engine was locked into the rear bulkhead, in a similar layout to a Le Mans car, with the springs and dampers clearly visible over the double wishbone suspension. The all-carbon air scoop snaked across the top of the engine like the taut neck of a body-builder.

I lifted the door up, not out, towards the sky, and was surprised to find my helmet wedged into the upholstered ceiling when I sat inside. I squidged around to find a less claustrophobic position and strapped myself into the belts.

I gunned the engine and felt the brawn of the cylinders rumbling behind the seat.

I gave Jim the thumbs up. He grinned. 'Be careful out there!'

'Never.'

'Stand by to roll, everyone, track is going live in 3, 2, 1 …'

I dropped the clutch at just over 4,000 revs and shot off with the rear bouncing. Aboard the Koenigsegg you actually felt the spinning wheels patting the tarmac. The engine barked a raw note as the revs peaked and fell each time the wheels broke traction. In just over three seconds the car reached 60mph, and a few seconds after that it was running at 120 into the first corner. I squeezed the brake pedal and felt the weight swing across the rear axle. With minimal downforce to keep it in check, the rear twitched and my world started rocking.

Changing gears required the dexterity of a brain surgeon to avoid crossing the gate and grabbing the wrong gear. A fumbled down-change

would lock the rear wheels in an instant and could spit the car off the track. On the up-change, it might over-rev and blow the engine to bits.

As I exited the first corner I short-shifted a gear to reduce the wheel-spin and make life easier. There was so much grunt that she still let loose and I strained into the belts as the back swung away.

The steering wheel felt as small as a beer mat when I whipped it over and struggled to find the return point, the moment in the slide when the grip came back and required me to straighten the front wheels. Leave it too late and the slide would go into transition and spit me off. The CCX had a slow steering rack, which meant I had to work the wheel twice as much as normal. I was aware of the flurry of my white gloves and suffered the added indignity of accidentally setting off the horn buttons on the wheel handles.

I stroked her up to about 145 on the back straight towards the heavy braking area for Hammerhead. I pressed the pedal and it moved towards the floor, but the car didn't slow down. Tyre wall, landing lights, field, trees ahead.

I had to lift my foot and apply it again twice to build fluid pressure and slow the car in time for the corner. I straight-lined the chicane and took a close-up of the catch net they used to put up for snagging greedy jets that gobbled up too much runway.

I motored on towards the Follow Through, checked the brakes and turned in. The car felt very light at the rear as I powered through and towards the tyre wall corner. I gave a big lift and then floored it on to the main straight towards the final corners. As we straightened up it felt like the main body was still leaning from the previous corner. The bodywork was acting like an aerofoil as the speed built up over 160. It was so light on downforce that nothing prevented it from squirming around.

I needed to speak to Jim.

'It sounds amazing; what's it like?'

'It's … amazing all right. It's got a braking problem; the pedal is going long at the Hammerhead chicane. Feels like I might lose them completely. Also, there's something wrong with the power steering; it suddenly goes heavy when I'm sliding.'

Jim translated this into Koenigsegg and came back with his response.

'They say that their driver, well, their engineer, warmed the car up this morning and it was fine. It's up to you. If it's not safe, obviously don't drive it.'

I stared at the dashboard for an answer. It would be a major blow to Koenigsegg if I refused to drive. Then again, I didn't fancy brake failure and being flat-packed at the Hammerhead tyre wall.

'It's cool. Let's crack on, but if it gets worse we might have to stop.'

I closed the door and lined up, with Jim ready on the stopwatch. It was all or nothing now. My heart picked up a notch and the adrenalin ramped up.

Three, two, one …

I kept a watching brief on the brake pedal, tapping it up with my left foot on the approach to every corner to check it was still there. It was, but only just.

The car was never easy. It had so much power that I had to change gear with the frequency of a hummingbird on acid. Every time it crested the rise into the first corner I nearly disappeared down the escape road. We had to re-position the camera twice as far back.

Under heavy braking it wanted to slide; as soon as I turned, it wanted to slide, accelerate, slide. The sheer weight of the car meant that once it went off line, dragging it back was impossible.

Most supercars went through the flat-out kink towards Chicago, well, flat out. The Koenigsegg rolled in with the suggestion that it might swap ends at any moment. Braking on the other side was spirited, in the way that slow dancing with a rattlesnake can be.

In the slower corners the front wouldn't turn, then as I tried to balance the car on the throttle the rear viciously broke traction. I sent a hand to catch it, usually the one that was already busy changing gear, which was like threading a piece of bendy cotton through the eye of a burning needle.

As I reached Hammerhead for the second time I was determined to show the scary bitch who was boss. I brought the brake pedal up with my left foot but held off the brakes till the last moment. If they didn't do the business, I'd be chewing bark.

Eyes wide, I flicked my left foot out of the way and stamped on the pedal. In a dead straight line the rear stayed put and the front wheels flickered under my feet as they bled the speed.

Made it. On the exit the throttle balanced the car into a satisfying four-wheel drift whilst I changed gear and whistled Dixie. I played the

steering wheel like a flute but it was too much for the motor. As the power assistance failed, the steering switched from feather light to arm wrestling with a silverback gorilla, with equally dire consequences if I lost.

Jim had enough shots for his film, but I knew I could shave a few tenths off my best time of 1.20.4. I was going fast enough at the Follow Through to produce some downforce, and with a bit more effort it might just take some extra mph.

It didn't seem right to stop yet. I visualised the perfect lap and dropped the clutch one more time.

I kept the tail neat and tidy, held my breath through the kink and squared the car up for Chicago. I was dialled in. I took another big risk at Hammerhead. The pedal went soft but the brakes worked. She scorched her way out, twitching and snatching and forcing me to brawl with the heavy steering as the power assistance faded.

As I sped towards the Follow Through I knew I was on a mega lap. If I could carry a tad more speed through the fast section, I would surely post a 1.19. I turned in with a few extra mph, willing the car to hold it and stay neutral.

Before I reached the painted chevrons at the apex the rear slipped big time. I steered into it but only just enough to halt a spin. The longer it travelled sideways the more speed the tyres would bleed off and the better my chances of recovering. I kept my sights fixed on the tarmac I wanted to stay on.

As I went to pull the steering straight, an invisible hand pulled the wheel in the opposite direction. The assisted steering had completely gone. With the wheels pointing left just at the point of grip return, that's exactly where it sent me.

I adjusted to the new scenery. Green, concrete building, tyre wall. I had always wondered what that wall was there for. Now I knew and my interest in it was growing exponentially. At 130mph on wet grass the Swedish tonne had a snowball's chance in hell of missing it.

I squeezed the brakes and waved the wheel about, but the rate of closing with this immovable object was unchanged. I hit the wall square on. Luckily it kind of exploded, tyres went skywards and the metal frame was flattened. The £500K supercar jumped slightly into the air and eventually staggered to a halt.

Shit. I'd get the sack for this.

I climbed out to inspect the damage. It was relatively light, given the circumstances. The most striking feature was a whacking great tyre that had wedged itself into the front air scoop, as though the Koenigsegg was biting a giant doughnut.

Christian von K arrived on the scene and wanted to know what had happened. I apologised profusely. My most earnest expression was totally lost on him behind the visor. As the car was mopped up I prepared for the walk of shame into the production office to face Andy Wilman. He was talking to Clarkson, and as I opened the door he whipped around to face me.

This was the first time I had even dented a car with *TG*. I had no idea how much of a big deal it was to them. A racing team would understand, but a TV show that borrowed cars from manufacturers based on good-will was completely different.

'I am so, so sorry, Andy.'

'Oh, don't worry about it.' Jeremy treated me to the mother of all smiles. 'I told you it's bloody awful, didn't I? I'm surprised you held on to it that long.'

You had to love this bloke. A lesser man could have hung me out to dry.

'Did you get a good time out of it?' Andy asked.

'Reasonable. If they stuck a rear wing on it and sorted the brakes it would go about three seconds faster round here.'

'*Three seconds*? Bollocks.'

'Seriously. It's massively short of downforce; you can feel the body rolling and walking on the straights. If they nail it down with a proper wing and sort the other problems, three seconds.'

Andy shrugged and exchanged glances with Clarkson. These two had known each other since school. Thick as thieves. Andy went straight to Christian von K and booked another run. Several weeks later. They were determined to beat the fastest time set by the Pagani Zonda.

I'd be sad to see the Zonda defeated. It was possibly the most beautiful supercar in the world, from the stunning carbon-weave body to the leather-bound steering wheel.

Mr Pagani took a personal interest in every detail of every car he designed. The Zonda was relentlessly polished and primed prior to filming.

'Oi, mate, what car's that, then?' a besuited spectator had shouted to the man with the duster from behind the track barrier.

The Italian politely upturned his hands. '*Mi dispiace, che io non parlano Inglese …*'

'What, no speaky English?' The suit looked left and right for an audience that failed to materialise. The laugh was on him anyway. He was insulting Mr Pagani himself, a gentleman wealthy enough to leave a platinum horse's head on his pillow.

I made my way to the Koenigsegg, now fitted with its rear wing and some brake fluid. I thought the mechanic would look daggers at the white-suited hooligan pacing towards his baby, but he welcomed me with a smile and a vigorous handshake.

The wing stabilised the car so much under braking that I could carry lots more speed into all the corners. The power steering worked and the brakes were faultless. The car was no less dramatic to drive and had me sweating profusely. As I chipped away at the times I was always relieved to cross the finish line.

Jim Wiseman gave me the thumbs up, we had all been waiting for, and confirmed that the car had 'gone fastest'. I'm not sure there's such a thing as a perfect lap in the CCX, but it was the closest I could get that day on 1.17.9.

I parked up whilst Jim gave Christian von K the good news. He practically levitated with joy. His head rocked back and gazed at the sky, thrusting both fists upwards. His crew shook all our hands repeatedly. I was even given a signed copy of the *Koenigsegg Storybook* and a Koenigsegg bobble hat.

TG had pulled out all the stops to make the run happen, and Christian felt it personally. I changed into civvies and found Jim Wiseman outside the greenroom looking very stressed indeed.

'*Fuck* …' He covered his mouth with a cocked finger.

'What's wrong?'

'You just did 1.17.9, right?'

I nodded. 'One tenth faster than the Zonda.'

'That's the thing. It's one tenth *slower* than the Zonda. I just called it in. And now I've got to go and tell him.' I followed Jim's pointed finger to where Christian von K was swapping high fives with the paramedics in the car park.

'What the hell do I do now?'

'Come on, I'll go with you. But you'd better do the hard part.'

The blood drained from Christian's cherubic face. 'I must phone my wife.'

An unprecedented third and final session was arranged. Judging by the ominous clouds, we had ten minutes to make this happen before rain removed any chance of a fast time.

I asked the mechanics to lower the suspension's ride height. There were no cameras. It was just me, the car and Jim with his stopwatch.

I flicked on the radio. Chris Evans immediately obliged with a personal favourite: 'Buck Rogers' by Feeder. Wiseman got on his air guitar and after fine-tuning the tyre pressures it was time to go.

The adrenalin was flowing and I was zoned. The CCX tended to focus the mind, a bit like dancing the tango with a hammerhead shark.

I'd been running laps with this machine in my head for so long that I needed no time to settle in. I did two and knew that the second was unbeatable. 1.17.6 was two tenths faster than the Zonda – pole position at last.

The Koenigsegg shunt was the only one I ever had on *TG*. But there were times when I came mighty close.

The Ferrari factory brought two stunning new £130,000 F430s to the track, a Coupé and a convertible Spider. When Ferrari brought an automobile to the track, it was always just so. It started on the button and the V8 maelstrom filled the air.

The 430's body styling was a touch more complicated than the 360 and produced more downforce, hugging the road like a hovercraft. Wilman was so excited that he took over the stopwatch to get closer to proceedings.

I took the Coupé for a blast and got into the groove. Its mid-rear-engine configuration made it perfectly balanced, a kick-ass weapon of mass destruction. You could pitch her in, tramp on the gas and defecate sound and rubber through every curve.

Switching off the traction systems was easy. You simply turned a dial to 'CST', which also sped up the paddle gear-shift and made the throttle more responsive.

It was the windiest day I had ever known at Dunsfold. There was a twister at the Follow Through and my times were a full two seconds short

of the older 360, as Wilman was first to point out. The pressure was on me to deliver.

The front of the car abjectly refused to turn into the medium speed stuff. I was certain the older 360 model had never handled like this. As the laps ticked by, Wilman's expression grew more grim.

'This car should be faster. What's the problem?'

I didn't know. The 430 was supposed to be a second faster than the 360, and I was going flat out.

'If you think you *can't* drive it any faster, just say the word.'

'I can always find more – let's give it another shot.'

Wilman clutched his stopwatch and straddled an imaginary chair. Suggesting that I couldn't drive any faster was intended to get a rise out of me. And it worked.

I couldn't force any more time out of the slower corners and I was braking so late that I was barely staying on the circuit. My only option was to give it rock all in the fast stuff and hope it stuck.

I was already taking a much wider line on entry to counter the effect of the wind, aiming straight at the tyre wall on the right-hand side until the last possible moment, then cutting back hard to carry speed through the left-hander. I decided not to lift off the throttle at all.

This would propel the car faster and generate more aero grip, whilst also keeping the rear differential fully locked and more stable. I imagined how it would feel, the extra resistance to turning, how it would just clear the tyres and I would finish with an extraordinary time. It sent a fresh wash of adrenalin through my system.

I pounded around the lap in anticipation of the big moment. It suddenly arrived; the tyres were coming up fast. I mashed my foot into the carpet, aimed in and the force of the wind pushed the car into a 120mph four-wheel drift.

The Ferrari was heading inexorably for the wall on the right, the same side as my seat. My mouth tightened and I made myself as small as possible, as if this would somehow prevent the sacrilege of smearing Ferrari red down the length of a grubby tyre wall. I pulled in my elbows, clenched my knees together and held my breath.

I caught the wall with the front right panel and rubbed it as far back as the rear wheel arch. In racing we call it a 'sticker rub' and it's no big deal. Abusing a beautiful supercar, *a Ferrari*, was something else. But the lap wasn't over yet.

Parachuting into a car.

Car ice hockey. Great for five minutes until the snow turned to porridge.

Tim Carter with his aerial buddy and photographer Andy Ford.

Filming on a frozen lake in Norway.

Army toys. The Evo fared well until the Army opened fire.

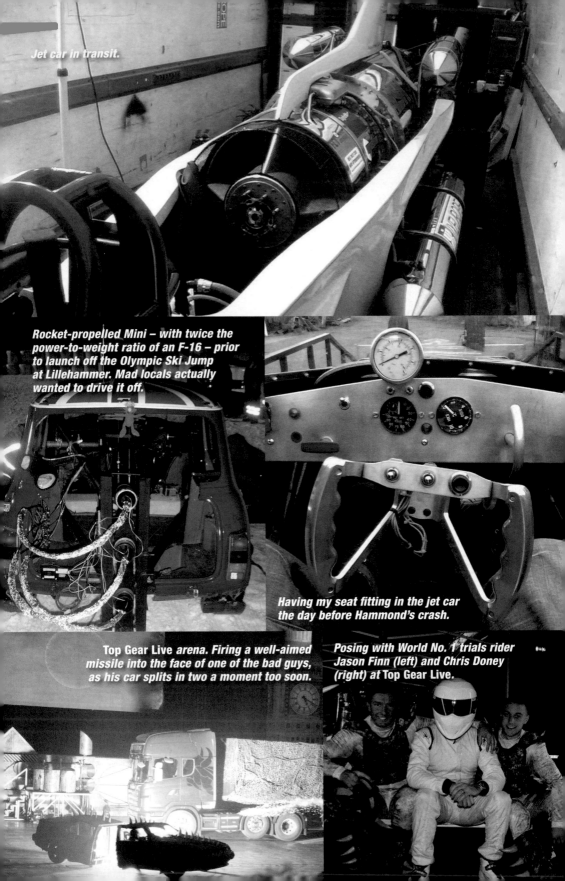

Jet car in transit.

Rocket-propelled Mini – with twice the power-to-weight ratio of an F-16 – prior to launch off the Olympic Ski Jump at Lillehammer. Mad locals actually wanted to drive it off.

Having my seat fitting in the jet car the day before Hammond's crash.

Top Gear Live arena. Firing a well-aimed missile into the face of one of the bad guys, as his car splits in two a moment too soon.

Posing with World No. 1 trials rider Jason Finn (left) and Chris Doney (right) at Top Gear Live.

Walking across the dry Rogers Lake, moments before the Men in Black arrived and took us away.

Lt Nick Arkle and his Harrier jump jet.

The Stig 'hates' scouts.

Stig in Boots.

T. Rex. I still have no idea what this shoot was about.

Arriving at Puerto Banus in a Lambo Gallardo.

Stig hits the town and decides the future is orange.

GREY GOOSE VODKA

Bugatti smokes all four tyres. 0–60mph in 2.5 seconds.

Vauxhall VXR8 Bathurst Edition.

Drifting a Pagani Zonda.

Ford GT burns rubber.

Koenigsegg CCX takes out the tyre wall during a time attack. Christian von Koenigsegg receives my explanation in the background.

Jaguar XKR.

Filming at the Ascari Resort.
Jeremy is about to fail the 'apple test'.

Volvo S60 commercial.

I jammed the car through the final two corners to clock a 1.22.9; a full second faster, but still short of the 360CS.

I prostrated myself before the Ferrari engineers and apologised profusely. Their young test driver was the first to greet me as I went to inspect the damage.

'Stiiiga, donta worry, Stiiiga. You are a driver, you are pooshing. At Fiorano, we have many cars. We damage many cars; it's OK.'

Top man.

Ferrari was no shop window, it was a stable of racers. Urban legend had it that if you returned a bag of wreckage bearing the prancing horse emblem to the factory gates at Maranello, red-suited worker bees would always gather to repair it. The spirit of competition was in their blood.

'The car is fantastic, but it just won't turn in like the 360. I don't understand it.'

He scratched his chin in deep contemplation.

'Before you hada Pirelli tyres, Stiiiga. That's iit! Today you hava Bridgestone.'

Eureka. Pirelli tyres were two seconds a lap faster than Bridgestones back then.

I gave Wilman the good news. 'We should do a feature on tyres, don't you think? Look at the difference it makes …'

'Not if you actually expect anyone to watch the programme,' he said.

24

MATCH OF THE DAY

Going from a 200mph Ferrari one week to a diesel Golf the next was a major change of pace. Pushing small everyday motors to their limit felt cruel at first. Their front wheels begged for mercy and their underpowered engines strained through every gear with an asthmatic wheeze. But I got used to it. I took inspiration from another breed of racing driver. Men with no remorse or mechanical sympathy.

Touring car racing, I decided, was different from any other category. It permitted drivers to do to each other all the nasty things that were forbidden elsewhere. Touring cars were graced with minimal aerodynamic bodywork because they were loosely based on the small production road cars they resembled. As a result, they were employed more like a weapon than a surgical instrument.

If someone barged you out of the way to take the win, there was no headmaster to whinge to. You noted the name and number on the door and repaid the favour at the earliest opportunity. The drivers were … assertive.

'Remember your idea about *TG* doing something with football?' Wiseman said.

'Absolutely. Which footballers are you talking to?'

'Well, it's not exactly what you suggested, but it does involve football … kind of. It should be really mega.'

Car football consisted of a giant ball, two teams of five cars liveried in red and blue and a bag of nuts behind the wheel, which included Matt Neal, Tim Harvey, Dan Eaves, Rob Huff, Tom Chilton, Russ Swift and me. Russ and I were the odd ones out, as pro drivers but not touring car racers. He looked docile enough, but was a legendary stunt driver who pulled twenty handbrake turns before breakfast and spun J turns through impossibly tight spaces for elevenses. I was keen to see his voodoo in action and take him on.

The venue needed to be big enough to host a bunch of speeding cars trying to outscore one another. We figured that if Bruntingthorpe airfield was long enough to land the Vulcan nuclear bomber, it would suffice.

James May captained one team and made his selections. The Stig couldn't play in this game, he hates football, so I joined Hammond's team as myself. Hammo and I were a little nervous about me being visible on *TG* again; we'd only just recorded another film together with a skateboarder against a rally car. It was tricky pretending not to know each other, so we avoided eye contact.

We made our way over to an unremarkable fleet of brand-new Toyota Aygos, the type of box your dotty aunt might call a 'sweet runabout'. Little bug-eyed headlights looked nervously at the prospect of pillage at the hands of ten twisted joyriders.

We knew we hadn't been called in to drive within the DSA guidelines, but no one really expected to write off ten brand-new cars …

James 'Boicey' Bryce, a protégé of Ridley Scott, was directing the shoot and explained the format: 'What we want to do today is start off with some precise driving shots, hitting the ball to see if you can actually knock it into the goal, with no contact. We'll stop the game after about ten minutes to check cameras. Then we might allow a little contact and gradually build up the tempo.'

Sideways grins suggested otherwise.

My Aygo was a demonstrator fresh out of the dealership and still smelt of sweet silicon. The plastic steering wheel and reasonably priced instruments gleamed. She had been carefully delivered with paper sheets in the footwells and plastic seat covers.

I chucked those out straightaway, wedged a couple of pennies into the handbrake button and taped them down with gaffer – *et voilà*, a flyaway handle.

At first no one knew what to do; it was the school disco with everyone hanging around the sidelines to see what would happen next. I weaved my car around the pitch and pinched the waist-high inflatable ball from Wiseman, who was marshalling on foot.

You could dribble by knocking the ball forward and accelerating behind it. It was so light that the air speed would raise the ball off the ground and you could carefully place it on the nose or windscreen to drive it along. The trick was anticipating when the ball would roll off centre, steering into it and using the wind to line it up again. Straightforward, until someone suddenly parked in front of you.

The more confident drivers became with the ball, the less willing they were to share it with anyone else. Stealing and 'tackling' became increasingly aggressive and Russ was taking no prisoners. He shot across my bonnet so fast I thought I'd accidentally driven across a motorway. I had to brake and swerve hard to avoid him. He was utterly ruthless. I admired the fact that he was defending his territory. Two could play that game.

The only problem with car footie was that the damn ball kept blowing away in the wind. The cameramen, Wiseman and Boicey, spent much of their time booting it back into play and trying not to get run over. When Wiseman found himself holding the ball surrounded by a gaggle of impatient Aygos, Boicey radio'd a stop.

'We've got some great stuff here, guys. We're just going to keep filming now. Keep an eye on your in-car cameras. If the light goes out, get it recharged and watch out for the marshals. You can make a little contact now.'

Ahem.

I wasn't comfortable with scratching the immaculate Aygo and laboured under the pretence that I could score the most goals without putting a mark on it. After all, the competition was just a bunch of touring car biffs, two TV presenters and one old man.

We formed two semicircles around the ball for the kick-off. I punted it over the other side and slipped through a gap, caught up with the ball and dribbled it beautifully towards the goal at 30mph. Suddenly Hammond shot across me, hit the ball away and stopped dead. I jammed the brakes to avoid him and saw red.

'I'm on *your* team, you lunatic.'

'Hahaaa, *sorreee* ...'

Off he went.

A couple of cars crowded the ball, nudging it and then reversing but going nowhere. Nobody would cede ground. I joined from the left and bounced it into the air. As it landed, my car was rocked to the right as Russ Swift drove into my front left wheel arch and punted the ball away. My space had been invaded. It was First Blood, and the rest of the sharks tasted it in the water.

After that first dent, the tempo wound right up. Minor scrapes at first, then full-on wheel banging. No one cared to look behind before reversing flat out to re-position, and it was OK to tap another car into a spin to steal the ball. It was mass road rage.

I found myself in a remote part of the airfield with my opponent Matt Neal, the tallest racing driver in the world. Blue smoke billowed from his front wheel arches as I dumped the clutch on mine and we surged towards the ball. In a game of chicken, someone had to have the brains to back off first.

The ball exploded with a mighty pop and we collided nose on nose. My bonnet crumpled and snapped up, headlights smashed and the grill embedded into the steel radiator. I was rocking in the seat with laughter and saw Matt hanging off his wheel, grinning at me through his windscreen.

'Drivers, we only have three balls left; please try to preserve them.'

The carnage continued unabated. James May kept reversing into people by mistake. They would have monstrous accidents in his wake attempting to avoid him.

I chased Hammond as wingman when another player drove into his path, forcing him to stop. I jammed the brakes and skidded sideways to miss him just as Chilton, the spiky blond from *Baywatch*, tail-ended me. He flew over my rear wheel and landed alongside, all neatly captured on my rear-facing camera.

Shortly afterwards I was speeding across the middle of the pitch when another car reversed into my path, probably May, and speared into the driver's side just behind the door. Bang went the rear window, and the rear wheel didn't fare much better.

I was glad to see my Aygo stretchered off. Judging by the temperature gauge she'd been running without radiator fluid for the past ten minutes. I hopped into a spare that had been vacated by an absolute animal who had been riding the clutch. The left pedal was on the floor and the stench of burning clutch plates hung in the cabin.

A few goals were scored, usually by hoofing the ball over the top of the opposition, chasing around and banging it into the net.

At the end of the game, the tarmac was littered with broken glass, door handles, wing mirrors, bumpers and fluids. I kicked my crumpled door open to climb out. Matt Neal's vehicle was comically pigeon-toed. The rest of the fleet were KIA or walking wounded. We'd completely ruined ten new cars and there were a few stiff necks.

I'd also formed an intimate knowledge of the Aygo. It was superbly agile and resilient. The gearbox was quick and easy and the ABS had patiently accepted all the abuse I hurled at it. Sweet runabout.

I also began to see cars in a new light when manufacturers started tinkering with the format. BMW brought an ordinary looking 330i to *TG*, which they claimed could learn the track and drive it by itself.

Over the years the Bavarian coneheads had pioneered slick automatic gearboxes, fly-by-wire throttle backed with traction control, servo-assisted brakes controlled by anti-locking software, and active power steering that hardened and softened as you steered. These became *standard* systems fitted to all BMWs and unbelievably could operate all the functions of the car without the need for a driver. All it needed was a tweak to the software …

Men in blue coats plugged computers with fat glowing cables into the car's brain and asked me to drive three laps of Dunsfold, one slow, one fairly quick and one fast. The onboard GPS tracking system logged the lines I was using around the circuit along with the lateral G-forces, speeds and steering angles. After the initial laps, the BMW engineers told me I no longer needed to steer, change gear, accelerate or brake. The car would do it by itself.

From personal experience, I preferred doing the driving to leaving it to a robot with ideas above its station. For the most part safety features did what they were supposed to: make driving safer. But all machines are fallible. I climbed aboard the BM half expecting it to wrap its auto-tightening seat belts around my throat, bind my arms and legs, then accelerate into a tree. I asked the German engineers if they wanted me to start with a slow lap to test the system first.

'No, we make normal speed for the first run. Then we try a little faster.'

I could wrest control from the car at any time by pressing any of the pedals or grabbing the steering. The car started the lap by flooring it and nipping through the gears. I had to hold my hands together to override the temptation to touch the wheel. It dealt with the first few corners with remarkably late braking, so much so that I could feel the ABS working to control a locking tyre.

LED lights on either side of the dashboard indicated when the car was deviating from its optimal line. As we sped into the Follow Through the lights went green, yellow, orange and quickly red before the computer let go of the steering and I had to take hold. The software was only programmed to turn the wheel a certain amount, so when the excess speed made the car understeer, it was unable to add enough steering to compensate.

I drove back to the BMW boys. They dialled out some speed at the Follow Through and added a little at a few places where we felt the car could cope. It ran perfectly; not as fast as I could drive the lap, but close enough.

It was pretty spooky watching the wheel spinning around by itself, but I really warmed to the technology. It was a snapshot of the future.

Radar technology from aviation was also being used in cars, acting as a collision warning system and triggering the brakes when it sensed another car was too close. At low speeds it was programmed to detect pedestrians and make an emergency stop. Ford based their Radar system on the one used by the F-22 Raptor, a stealth fighter so canny that it automatically tracked and identified people on the ground.

An integrated system that married the auto driving capability of the BMW with satellite navigation and radar tracking would mean we could all just plug in the destination and fall asleep at the wheel. Road deaths would be a thing of the past, as would the boredom of driving on motorways littered with surveillance cameras.

The only problem is that the government would probably make it illegal to switch the system off, so you would go to jail for enjoying yourself on a country road. But it would be worth it. Imagine swerving in and out of traffic and watching all the other cars automatically twitching to a standstill, waking their passengers and jarring them back into the real world, forcing them to log on to Facebook all over again.

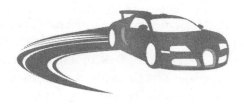

25

SMOKE AND MIRRORS

'Time to lock and load, boys. Good luck out there tonight …'
I was just out for a late-night cruise in my car, minding my own
business. The streets were derelict and poorly lit, oppressive. I turned
through a warren of alleys that led to a dead end and drew a bead on a
pair of badasses on motorbikes who were looking for trouble. They
clocked me and started bunny-hopping towards me, laughing and sneer-
ing to one another.

Both wore filthy helmets bristling with long silver spikes, lime green
tights and olive body armour. As you would. Within seconds they'd
surrounded my car and started banging at the windows, invading my
space, thinking they could intimidate me. Big … mistake …

I dropped the clutch and spun through 180 degrees. The skinny
one fell off his bike; the bigger lad made a run for it. I drove head on
at the stricken biker, missing his leg by inches as he kicked the rear
of the bike clear and accelerated away in the opposite direction to join
his mate. I should have left it there and then, but I didn't. I yanked the
handbrake to turn and face them. It was a Mexican stand-off, fight or
flight.

I sensed movement behind me; a car crept out of a side alley I hadn't
seen. It took up position at my five o'clock, blocking my escape. I looked
ahead as a beaten old sedan covered in algae flew into view alongside the
bikers. It was a trap.

A blinding flash of light pierced the darkness to my right. The explosion engulfed a fuel tanker.

To my surprise, a 30-foot monster with skin like a toad, bulging red eyes and a flame-thrower for a tongue rose from the conflagration. It gave a venomous howl and waved its claws in my direction. Time to skip town.

I dumped the clutch and made a chicken run at the renegade trio. The bikes flinched first and split around me towards the other end of the alley. I tugged the handbrake gently to make a quarter turn and slide right in behind them.

We sped down the street. The sedan shot out from the right and nearly T-boned me. I counter-slid around the obstacle and continued the chase.

The muscular biker flew through the air and crashed on to my bonnet. I tasted two-stroke as his sump smashed the windscreen. He spun his wheel and rode over the roof, then the sedan smacked into me from behind.

I booted it away and went after the skinny rider who was struggling to turn in the confines of the alley. I slapped his rear wheel with enough force to knock him through a wall. One down, four to go. The flame-breathing, bog-eyed swamp creature wasn't pleased.

The power band kicked into third gear and I surged ahead. The sedan flew out in front of me, partially blocking the street and offering a perfect target. I accelerated towards it, took aim at his passenger window and pressed the firing toggle on my steering wheel.

A missile spewed from the bazooka above my right ear, rattling my eardrums as it scythed through the sedan. The rear section dropped away and the front spun off to my left, so I hammered through the middle. With a clear line of attack towards the big biker and Car Two, I kept on the gas and sped through the debris.

Car Two hesitated and I slammed into his rear quarter hard enough to destabilise him. The driver wrestled with the steering, then tank-slapped hard into the wall. The biker had nowhere to run. We were just a metre apart, so I dropped the clutch and lunged forward. He scrabbled around me, kicking at the ground to get away. We revolved around one another in a deadly tango until he had enough momentum to set off into the back street.

We plunged into darkness and grime, both struggling for traction, but I was gaining on him. Just inches from his rear wheel, a gentle kiss on his

chain would unseat him. The rider's leg dropped and nearly went under my wheel.

He shot a nervous glance over his shoulder before turning left towards the fuel tanker. I pulled alongside and squeezed him straight into it. The bike thundered into solid metal, flinging the rider over the handlebars. He landed like a rag doll.

That just left the 30-foot fire-breathing monster. Its cloaked arms lashed out, filling the air with burning petrol.

'Perrrfect!' Colin purred inside my earpieces. 'Now for the money shot, Stiggy.'

I pulled my final handbrake turn to face the creature and fire my last missile, striking 'Swampy' in its evil heart. The strike was so close that the burning embers rained down through the open caged frame of my Rage Buggy.

I swatted them off my white overalls and spun around to face the 4,000-strong audience.

Richard and James strode back on to the stage as Jeremy brought another *Top Gear Live* show to an end.

'The Stig is *victorious,* ladies and gentlemen. You've all seen a lot of crazy car stunts tonight, so please remember on your way home … *drive fast*. Good night!'

I tilted my visor open a fraction to make eye contact with the defeated biker, Jason Finn, lying in a heap on the side of the tanker. His chest bobbed as he fought to get his breath back without visibly moving. He looked across and pouted at me.

The Stig's battle to save the universe from speed cameras and like-minded forces of evil played out according to the script above, mostly. The live theatre was part of a tour that began in Earl's Court and was taking in Europe, Australia, New Zealand, Hong Kong and South Africa.

The good burghers of Johannesburg cleared off muttering, 'Yessus, man, some lekker cars there, hey,' and Jason, the world's number one freestyle trials rider from Essex, hobbled towards me backstage with Chris, his young apprentice. Jason took off his sweat-soaked helmet to reveal his pop star good looks. His Lycra tights were bursting at the seams, evidenced by the number of golf balls smuggled in his front pocket.

'Awright, Benny Boy? You was right close before the tanker.'

'I thought I could see you twitching. Must be old age.'

'I smashed me ribs on them bars that time.' He tugged at his vest. 'Just as well I'm wearing me Fisher Price pads, innit?'

Colin appeared from behind the curtain, his waist-mounted man-bag leading the charge. As the genius who choreographed our timings, he was the one independent critic we aimed to please.

'Superb, boys. Ben, even your little missiles went off this time, the sedan fell apart on cue and Jason showed the punters his arse. Are you all right, Jason? You look out of breath.'

'Yeaaah. Think I caught me nads, but I'll be awright.'

'Thanks, Colin, you did an awesome job,' I said.

He knew our routines backwards. We meticulously choreographed every move to chime with the music and pyrotechnics. With so many near misses in a tight space, timing was everything.

Doing it live meant we had to be prepared to improvise within a split second, and with up to five shows a day it created some tension backstage. I slept as much as I could between performances to maintain my focus. We spent most of our time at the arena, but did manage to slip into Jo'burg once or twice.

Outside the dome I passed out under the African sun with a tumorous hangover from a dinner party the night before. Just two bottles of Windhoek beer had reduced my brain to a pulsating bag of snot after a third day of breathing exhaust fumes inside the closed arena.

Hammond had swallowed his own vomit on stage during the show and Jeremy was moving around like someone was operating his limbs remotely with strings. James's whereabouts were still unknown.

The dry heat roasted my limp carcass and I shaded my eye sockets with some light reading, *The End of Oil*. The impending fuel crisis had been of great concern to me, until I read the bit about the dawn of hydrogen fuel cells and the very fast, very powerful electric vehicles of the future. Then I slept like a baby.

'Has anyone seen Ben? *BEN, you're ON for f …!*'

I peeled my sweaty bones off my cardboard floor mat and tried to remember where I was. I pulled focus on cargo containers full of gearboxes, a gazebo covering an Apache gunship with wheels and a Ninja dressed top to toe in white silk. Ninja was doing a standing splits and whirling a double-ended sword through the air with phenomenal

co-ordination. My watch alarm went off and it all came back to me: drive time, third show of the day.

I ran past Ninja, a freakishly talented young girl called Chloe. Her slender arms and legs fired through a sequence of graceful kicks and swipes, with a final thrust of two fingers towards her eyes and a single point at me. I returned her salute and slipped on a black balaclava.

Backstage was blacked out but it didn't silence the thrum of my V8. I inspected the climbing handles on the rear deck of the jet-black Vauxhall Monaro 'Ute', then double-checked each individual tyre by hand for signs of blistering or bare canvas. I pumped the flyaway handbrake, disarmed the TCS and armed the smoke box. The familiar green LED dials all read true, and I pulled forward with my heart running a million beats a minute. I always dreaded this sequence, in a good way.

We lined up silently on the stage, hidden from the audience in a sea of darkness. A crashing drum roll introduced Chloe under a strobing white light, then the spotlight hit me. I unleashed 450bhp, nipped some left-foot brake to exaggerate the wheelspin and slewed off my mark. Chloe stepped aside at the last moment, allowing the fender to brush her sword as I yanked the wand and rotated the bonnet around her legs.

The Monaro began its circle fully sideways as I powered the rear wheels and took my hands off the steering. The wheel spun itself through 720 degrees in the blink of an eye until it found the appropriate degree of opposite lock, a peculiar technique I had picked up in the course of the tour. I caught the wheel one-handed and began the perilous triple lap around Chloe as her right leg darted skywards and she balanced precariously on the left. With the bumper inches from her shins, I could see nothing below her waist between intermittent bursts of blinding spotlight. The largely male audience saw rather more of Chloe's nubile figure as she spread her sinewy legs in a standing splits. The aisles were regularly swept clean of fallen chewing gum.

An irregular note in the music coming through my earphones informed me I was running a second too fast into the routine, so I eased on some left-foot brake to slow the rate of turn and increased the throttle by a gnat's whisker. My Ute had a few special modifications, including a solid welded rear differential that allowed the rear wheels to turn at the same speed and spin consistently every time.

I separated from Chloe and drifted around a lap of the arena whilst she threw Ninja grenades at me with coinciding pyrotechnics going off

around the stage. The finale involved a rolling burn-out: the Monaro crept forward with the rears spinning at 70mph, burning more rubber than a Durex factory. Chloe jumped on to the car, 'killed' it with her sword and walked off. Or so she thought.

The V8 sprang back to life and into a smoking doughnut, with a little help from the machine belching out the pyro. The Ninja searched the cloud in vain for her prey, whilst I circled around to come at her from behind and tap her calf with the bumper. That concluded our business and we bowed out.

There were so many occasions during the sequence when I could easily have run her down that I welcomed the relief after each run.

The producers had their work cut out too. Cars had to be out of the door on time, routines memorised and logistics executed to the second. Machinery could and would always break down, and *Top Gear*'s technology record was notoriously 'ambitious but crap'. They worked all hours to keep wounded vehicles operational, but if the Stig Buggy died for any reason, I was under orders to stop one of my pursuers, punch the driver and commandeer his vehicle.

My favourite variable was the sedan, an ancient Alfa Romeo 75 that split apart when I shot it. If the driver hit the gas a fraction of a second too late when I drove towards him we would have a severe T-bone. I trusted him, but I couldn't say the same about his motor. The Alfa's designers never imagined it would be deployed in a pitched street battle twenty years after leaving the factory.

Frenchie had become the live show's executive producer. He even wore a pressed, collared shirt these days. He'd kept a completely straight face when he described the stunt during the concept stage.

'Basically, the two halves of the Alfa are held together by magnets … Why are you laughing?'

'Magnets?' I snorted. 'You, we, *Top Gear* have a car that's held together by *magnets* and plan to use it in a live show? That's hysterical.'

'Yes. So anyway, the car is held together by *magnets* and we can use one of the rockets on your buggy to blow it up. You've got two buggies, two bikes and the 'Swampy' tanker, which has to die at the end. Have a word with the drivers and see what kind of sequence you can come up with …'

There were a million diverging opinions on how to turn our second-hand car lot into an action sequence. Everyone contributed. We made

drawings of the best suggestions, pushed matchbox cars through the moves, then rehearsed them on foot in the arena, before driving them, slowly at first, then flat out.

Top Gear's version of NASA, aka the Euphoria Race Team, had busied themselves preparing the magnetic Alfa and were ready to put a driver in it to do a systems check. Neil Cunningham, who'd spent much of his early life being chased by the New Zealand police around country roads, slipped on his brain bucket and warily climbed aboard our equivalent of Apollo 13. A muffled Kiwi voice came from inside: 'How d'ya turn this thing on?'

The technicians remained unsympathetic. 'Turn the bloody master switch, you nugget.'

'I've done *that*.'

'Oh.'

The launch was stood down. The Alfa went away for further development and reappeared ten minutes later.

Neil gunned the engine, which ticked over like a basket of choleric cobras. The plan was to drive it in one piece around the stage before moving on to the next stage: detachment. The Alfa accelerated away reluctantly and shed its rear section almost immediately, as the crew gave a round of mock applause.

The technicians worked their nuts off with the limited resources available, and in true MacGyver style they managed to get the magnets to hold the car together and to detach on demand about 50 per cent of the time. The rest of the time I took evasive action.

I drove flat out towards it, waiting until the last moment to fire my rocket and activate the car splitting in two. Firing at close range was essential, because it looked more realistic and it gave me a better chance of hitting Neil in the head with the flaming projectile.

The downside was that if the car didn't fall apart, there was a very real chance of slamming into the side of it. If it split early I nearly hit the front end as it sped up; if it split late it was a case of waiting to shoot through the middle or near missing the back half. Doing a three-way 'elk test' time and again was counterintuitive, as common sense urged you to slow down, but I really enjoyed the challenge.

The presenters always watched the grand finale of the Stig battle, and Jeremy never tired of announcing it: 'And now for the moment you've all been waiting for. Some say that he's terrified of ducks and that his penis

has a chicane in it. And a four-mile straight. And a hairpin. All we know is, he's called The Stig …'

The presenters watched in bemusement from behind the curtain as bikes jumped over buggies, cars fell apart and spurted oil everywhere and we slithered around to keep the sequence going.

The preparation area that supported these efforts resembled 007's 'Q' branch, with pyro engineers, mechanics and stunts going off in every direction. Flame-throwers and detonators were tested in one corner; in another a milk float was being fitted with a rolling lead weight so it could do a wheelie, and the whine of a jet engine suggested that Clarkson's bicycle was operational. Front of stage, Frenchie was getting to grips with a new precision biker who had shaved Hammond's balls a little too close to the follicle during one of the stunts.

Frenchie lay on the floor face up, to give the offending rider a human dummy to practise with. The biker rode towards his head, and his mount lurched clumsily into the air. I winced as it clattered down between Frenchie's legs and the rear wheel horse-nipped the inside of his thigh. He was the boss, so this was no time for laughter. I buried my face in my hands.

Car football was such a popular feature from the TV show that we had to incorporate it into the theatre. After thirty-odd matches all the drivers were so adept at flicking the ball around that the damage inflicted to the cars was relatively minor. But occasionally we would get a tad carried away and accidentally enjoy ourselves.

Frenchie rushed down from his ivory tower after one show and pulled us all together. 'Lads, that was a fucking bloodbath out there tonight. The guys from Suzuki have basically told me that if we break another front suspension arm in one of these games, they'll pull the cars.'

We clasped our hands together and looked skywards like errant schoolboys. Personally, I was still glad that I'd stopped Paul Swift from scoring a goal by reversing into his front radiator at 30mph. Secretly, he was content to have repaid the favour moments later by clouting my front right wheel and breaking my steering arm so that I could only turn left.

Although that bollocking was deserved, most of the damage inflicted on us came courtesy of the presenters. They drove around talking into microphones that transmitted every moment live to the baying audience. I don't have a problem with people that can talk on a mobile phone

and drive at the same time, but car football was no time for added distractions.

There was nothing more alarming than dribbling the ball towards the goal, only to look out of the side window and see Richard Hammond bearing down for the kill. He talked a running commentary as he hit me in the side so hard that I went up on to two wheels and bounced across the floor like a hockey puck. As we came to a rest, all I could see was a mop of hair, a set of sparkling teeth and a pair of laughing tonsils. In those moments neither of us could honestly say we were working. Hammond is a very physical kind of guy and he didn't miss a trick.

I drew a short straw for the job of rolling over in an old BMW M5 converted into an abominable wheel-clamping machine. Heavily reinforced with sheet metal, a sealed fuel tank and a completely flat side so that it could flip off a ramp and skid along on its flank, it looked like a mating of Mad Max's interceptor with a door wedge.

I could see just enough through the scratched polymer and wire mesh windscreen to manoeuvre around the arena and harass the other cars before meeting my 'death'. I disappeared behind the stage, peering out in search of the five foot tall launch ramp. I had to hit it in a dead straight line. The engine misfired from the hammering it had taken, so sometimes it would dribble off the end of the ramp, but at other times I could drive on two wheels for a while and then slam into the deck. Being banged in the side of the head every time it clanged into the concrete was a touch monotonous, but someone had to do it.

Eventually the engine conked out part way up the ramp. I teetered on the edge and plopped off the side next to the stage. I unbuckled my harness and fell out of the inverted seat to stand on the passenger door, which was resting on the ground. I smelt the usual whiffs of pyro and oil but no fuel leaks, so I scanned through the windscreen to make eye contact with the mechanics and give them a thumbs up. As I did so, I noticed a gigantic box of pyrotechnics with coloured wires coming out of it, less than a metre away from the windscreen. It looked nuclear and was due to go off at the end of the sequence to send a percussion wave towards the audience.

I had no radio to contact the producer, so I tried using telepathy: 'Frenchie, please tell me you've disarmed the pyro—'

'BOOOOOOMMMMM …'

The shock wave rang through my metal cage and a cymbal-clashing monkey was let loose in my brain. Ears ringing like church bells, I kicked my way out of the armoured door and leapt down on to the arena as the three presenters ambled past. I ripped my helmet off and took a deep, quivering breath.

Hammond had obviously seen the whole thing. 'Mmm,' he said. 'Was that nice?'

'Outstanding.'

Jeremy was also in his element. He proudly announced our arrival in the former colonies with the line: 'Britain used to be a Kingdom, ruled by a King; then it was an Empire, ruled by an Empress; and now we're just a Country.' He leapt around the floor as referee for the football games and narrowly missed having his feet flattened on numerous occasions. He waxed lyrical about the hotbed of supercars we had on display with undimmed enthusiasm throughout the tour. He even kept going when his voice went, and all he could do was squeak.

I spied Jeremy screaming around the arena on a jet-powered bicycle with a riotous grin on his face, run across stage to introduce another act and head behind the curtain for a short break. The Red Bull was on ice for him, so I handed him one as he lit up. He stubbed out the fag after four deep drags, wiped the sweat from his brow and went back on stage.

We were allowed right off the leash to create a pure driving spectacle. We even tried to make the commercials (which live performance allowed) unforgettable.

With the 'Navman' we unquestionably succeeded in that – but not necessarily in a good way. It was unique to the Sydney shows and it was horrible. It started with a man and wife driving on to the stage arguing about directions. Eight thousand confused Australian punters looked on from the packed grandstands of the Olympic stadium. Then Navman galloped to the rescue.

Or rather sidled down the aisles dressed in a tuxedo, singing, *'You're too good to be true-hoo. Can't take my eyes off of you-hoo. You'd be like h-heaven to touch. I want to hold you so-ho much …'*

I was sitting in a fake Ferrari ready to do a three-car drifting display and unplugged my earpieces to cop a better take on just how out of tune he really was. The presenters were sitting close by, laughing and goading Frenchie via their closed loop radio mikes.

'*French*,' bellowed Clarkson, 'get me a Glock 9mm. I'm going to shoot this man in the back of the fucking head. On stage. Back of head. Booofff, brains over the floor. Yes, I am. Because this is absolutely the worst thing I have ever seen.'

Frenchie cackled: 'You would not believe what I'm hearing on my cans. If the guys on stage could hear Hammond and Jeremy right now …' Then: 'What's that? The singer has ears on? Well, I fucking hope he can't hear us; if he can, the guy must be a stallion to keep going …'

Navman finished off his dodgy solo by straining for a high note and dropping an octave, then handing out free satellite navigation devices to the crowd. The now happy couple finally pissed off in the right direction to a chorus of boos. There was a scuffle in the grandstands and a section of the crowd had to be removed by security. One Australian voice echoed the mood of the audience. 'No more facking adverts, you c***s!'

Ouch. There were still four more to go before the show started …

I got my comeuppance for laughing at Navman when I starred in a luxury yacht commercial in Hong Kong. The build-up took place on screen. A champagne-quaffing mincer with orange skin dressed like James Bond carved up the waters in a mini action movie then switched from boat to car; as he exited the main screen, I appeared in a real live Aston Martin DB9.

Dressed from head to toe in black, I slid the DB9 across the stage on full opposite lock, threw it into a 360-degree spin, stopped, climbed out, drew my replica pistol and pulled the trigger. As giant bullet holes miraculously appeared on the screen, my heroics were greeted with a disconcerting amount of laughter from a predominantly male audience and whistles from a mixed crowd. Either way, I fought to hold a straight face as Colin whispered into my earpiece: 'Ooooh, Big Boy … Big Boy with your *Big Gun* … Bang, Bang, oooohhhh yeeesss …'

After five performances we hit the town like inmates on a day break from Alcatraz. And suffice it to say that until you've heard Hammond on bass, May on keys, Jezza on the drums and Tiff Needell giving everything to his Sex Pistols impression, you haven't lived.

Wherever we went the public viewed the presenters as their mates. The show was averaging 6–8 million viewers in the UK, with a global audience of some 500 million; the goodwill was awesome. The great thing about the live event was that it gave foreign fans an opportunity to see the

show up close. In the UK, the waiting list to attend the studio was twenty years long …

It was rather reassuring that three middle-aged men cocking around with stuff could become so popular. I struggled to see them as sex symbols, but there was a unique chemistry between the presenters that was lightning in a bottle. People greeted them like rock stars. Women covered their mouths in giddy excitement and blokes sidled up to ask what the best car was. They promptly disagreed with the answer, whatever it was, hoping perhaps to engage in the kind of spirited debate they had seen so often on screen. I relished my anonymity and happily stepped aside whenever someone cut past me for a moment of their time.

It wasn't all cakes and ale, though. In one particular bar a throng of blokes in suits and open collars, photocopier salesmen all, gathered around Hammond in a distinctly unfriendly fashion. As I made my way over to him I noticed most of them were holding mobile phones behind their backs. The screens were lit and set on video, ready to capture some celebrity happy slapping.

I'd never seen Hammond snap, but it was obvious from the look in his eye that the countdown had begun. One idiot was trying to embrace him like an old pal. I managed to intervene, slid an arm around Hammo's waist and tried to lead him off. His body was as rigid as a Rottweiler but he did come with me, mumbling curses all the way to the exit.

Clarkson was a force of nature, but the other two were pretty regular guys who happened to be superb at presenting information to camera. Hammond's ability to consume a script and thoughtfully regurgitate it on to the screen was uncanny, whilst James had to, if anything, dampen his encyclopaedic mechanical knowledge to a level that befitted light entertainment. Me? I was having a ball. My responsibilities had expanded into choreography and co-ordination, so no two days were ever the same.

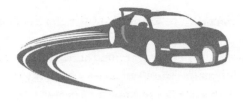

26

JET MAN

The plan was simple: drive a jet car as fast as it would go, which meant 300mph and then some.

'The car is basically a dragster,' Grant explained. 'Giant wheels at the back, little wheels at the front – you know the kind of thing. The difference,' he chuckled, 'is that this baby is powered by a jet engine like the one they used for the Red Arrows.'

'Sounds … interesting …' I said, not believing for a second that this would come to anything.

'It's called a Vampire. It's been purpose built and customised by the owner. It would be the fastest thing we've ever featured. Ideally we'd like a presenter to drive it, with a bit of help from you.'

I asked who was running it, naively expecting the answer to be McLaren or Williams. It wasn't.

Schemes like this came and went with *Top Gear*, and the Vampire wheeze looked as flimsy as a paper fire-fighting suit. A TV presenter in a 300mph dragster? No chance. I wondered for a moment if they might drop the presenter bit and send me up and down the runway for the footage. My stomach tightened.

'Er … Let me know how you get on …' I said.

Two weeks later the phone rang again. This wasn't going away. Hammond might not be available, what did I think about James May driving it?

'No way; he won't do it.' The words came out without me thinking.

'Really, why do you say that?'

James was a sensible bloke who flew aeroplanes and pretended he couldn't drive; he wasn't exactly an adrenalin junky. You needed to be slightly unhinged to want to drive down a runway at 300mph like spam in a can. Sure, it took some skill launching off the line and holding the car straight, but no amount of it could save you if the engine exploded, the wheels fell off, the parachute failed or if you involuntarily shat out your kidneys with fear. You either needed to be immune to the consequences of mechanical failure, or have balls the size of space hoppers.

'300mph is a huge speed. It's not like anything you experience in a normal car. I'm not saying James isn't brave, but his idea of exercise is similar to Clarkson's – a glass of wine and a fag. We crack 225mph at Le Mans, and even that's a long way short of what this thing can do.'

'I know. This thing will do 330mph. The British record is, like, 300. Officially we're not actually going for it – but it would be nice if it happened.'

I imagined being at the airfield with a mirage part way down the gigantic runway. I pictured James's doe eyes peering out of his visor, with 5,000 pounds of thrust breathing down the back of his neck. He'd flick a switch and hit 270mph within six seconds.

'If anything goes wrong, it'll be a mighty big shunt; then it'll come down to fitness. Hammond is tough. I'd be happy doing it with him, but not James.'

Core stability and strength literally held all your bits and pieces together on impact. There would be no small shunts at 300mph; why else did they pack a parachute?

Grant was on the dog again the following week.

'We've got Hammond; he's really up for it. I'm sorting some kit out. We've got some overalls kicking around in the office, think they're Nomex. Hammond says he's got a motorbike helmet that he's comfortable with—'

'He needs a proper F1 helmet, an Arai GP5. Not the toy one he's got for his bike; don't let him use that. How old are the overalls?'

'Not sure. Couple of years …'

I explained that they wouldn't be fire retardant any more. He needed a new triple-layer Nomex suit. If the jet fuel ignited, every second would count.

'Triple … layer …' Grant dutifully took notes. That was the last I heard of it until I was dispatched to a goose-infested farmyard the day before the shoot, to inspect the car and meet Hammond. I'm cool with ducks, but not geese. I hate geese. They're evil.

Colin Fallows had built Vampire and set the British land speed record. He emerged from a metal cargo container wearing a boiler suit and thick round glasses. He was very amenable, more of a Penfold character than a speed freak. We had tea.

Colin had no idea who I was, and I used that to my advantage to quiz him about the project. I needed to know that he wasn't some bipolar lunatic looking to win a Darwin Award.

Legend had it that a dude once drove into the Arizona desert in an old Chevy Impala. Nothing unusual there, except that he'd strapped a solid fuel rocket with comparable thrust to an F-16 fighter plane to the roof. Forensic evidence subsequently revealed that Impala man made it up to 50mph using conventional means before he lit the candle. The Chevy then accelerated past 250.

He realised almost immediately that this was not good, slammed the brakes, melting them instantly and blowing the tyres before the car became airborne. The incinerated remains of car and driver were found three miles away, three feet deep in the side of a cliff, 125 feet from the ground. That was the funny thing about solid fuel rockets. Once you pressed go, you kept going until they ran out of fuel.

Vampire on afterburner would behave much the same, except that you could shut off the thrust controls, killing the propulsion and popping the parachute air brake. Assuming the parachute opened, you slowed down.

Colin swung open the corrugated steel doors to reveal his modest workshop. Vampire was smaller than I imagined but still 30 feet long.

I gazed into the gaping chasm of the metal turbine. It had more steel veins, couplings and rivets than Michael McIntyre's Man Drawer. It looked like a NASA experiment crossed with something out of *Thunderbirds*. I pelted Colin with questions about every aspect of the build and preparation. What kept the car on the ground rather than turning it into a missile? What did he know about jet engines? How was it fitted to the car, where was the fuel, would it blow up and kill everyone? He answered each question in detail, and with extreme patience.

He'd spent twenty years as an engineer in the Royal Air force – twelve of them on the Rolls-Royce powerplant that would be sending Richard and me down the road at 300mph.

The engine installation was angled so that the faster it went, the more it pressed the middle of the chassis into the road. Colin picked the engine up 'cheap' when it was retired from the RAF, describing it as 'thirty years young'. The propulsion system was fuelled by heating oil, of all things.

The tubular frame chassis completely encased the cockpit and was similar to NASCAR racers I had driven. Simple technology – wheels, springs, dampers and metal suspension attached to a metal frame that supported the whopping engine.

No stone was left unturned. What would stop the engine flying out of the frame? Had the suspension ever broken? What problems had he encountered thus far?

Colin admitted that Vampire did have a tendency to attract wildlife, having recently spilt the blood of an eight-pound rabbit. It also emerged that there had been a problem with the rear suspension in the past. A joint had shown signs of damage and might have caused an incident involving Vampire's sister vehicle, Hellbender.

I scribbled away furiously. 'But no one was hurt?'

'Well, yes …'

Mark Woodley had been at the helm of Hellbender when it veered off course during a high-speed run at Santa Pod. It struck the barriers, killing him instantly.

Colin showed me the modifications to the suspension which seemed to have fixed the problem. I was no engineer, but the joints looked thick and solid.

Elvington was a big open airfield without walls, so at least there was less to hit if it did break. The downside there was the curvature of the runway. The driver had to apply a significant steering angle to counter the camber and keep in a straight line, putting additional load into the front right wheel.

I inspected the tyres and recognised the Hoosiers from racing on oval tracks. They looked pretty old, but Colin explained that they skimmed the tread to reduce the build-up of heat. Using older tyres was counter-intuitive but it made sense, despite the basic appearance. The construction of a new tyre heated more under severe loading; it was part of the reason that new rubber produced faster lap times over short distances. In

this scenario, that would increase the likelihood of delamination and tyre failure. And tyre failure would convert the car into a projectile.

I stared long and hard at each tyre.

The only unknown was the runway itself. I asked about track sweeping procedures, inspecting for debris after every run to remove anything that might puncture a tyre or collide with the machinery. It was already on his agenda.

All that remained was to do a seat fitting. I wanted to get comfortable with the belts and think about where the camera mounts would fit inside the cockpit. I also wanted to familiarise myself with the controls.

The sparse cockpit was fresh out of *Flash Gordon*, with a few gauges dotted around a metal console. At the centre lay the solid aluminium 'butterfly' steering bars, like a pair of upturned shovel handles joined together. My left foot held down a dead man's pedal, which would cut the engine the instant you released pressure on it. The right foot controlled the brake pedal, which operated a standard disc from a road car. It held the beast steady at the start line whilst the engine built up revs, in the same way a commercial airliner does before take-off.

Acceleration was controlled by a pair of levers like the ones on the *Millennium Falcon*. The first of these wound up the jet using conventional thrust, gradually accelerating down the runway up to 170mph. The second applied the afterburner. Afterburn worked by pumping unspent fuel into the engine and igniting a flame that substantially increased the rate of burn and thrust. You applied both levers and held station on the footbrake, then you lit the candle by flicking a switch on the steering wheel and vanished into the distance. Your only concern thereafter was stopping.

Releasing the dead man's pedal cut power but not your speed, and at 300 the footbrake would melt if you touched it. To stop, you had to pull back both thrust levers to deploy the parachute.

As far as I was concerned, stopping at the first hint of trouble was the only thing that mattered. I practised whipping my hand from the steering to the levers and knocking them back, until it became second nature. I visualised an unsettling vibration and using a reflex action to shut down in a nanosecond. Colin agreed that this would be the key part of the training at Elvington.

The sun was setting and there was still no sign of Hammond, so I rang Grant. Hammo was still filming and wouldn't be able to join us. Also, my

presence was no longer required at Elvington. I was needed at Dunsfold with Jeremy instead.

The tension sprung off my shoulders the way that it did following a pressurised race weekend. But I was leaving Hammond to fend for himself, and that didn't feel at all comfortable.

I briefed Wilman at length. 'He needs to sit in this thing. And don't be surprised if he takes one look at it, turns around and goes home. This car is serious. It's like nothing any of us has ever seen or done before.'

I ran through all the details of how the car needed to be controlled, the systems, and what Hammond and the crew should expect. How vitally prepared he needed to be to rip back the thrust bar and release that parachute if he even sniffed a problem. The jet car crew had to have priority over filming to stop and check for debris on the runway after every run, and the director had to be really careful with the placement of the static cameras.

Wilman got me to write it all down and send it to him. Hammond was really up for it, so he asked if I thought he could do it. I said he could, as long as he did as few runs as possible.

I turned back to Colin and thanked him. I said I'd speak to the director, but that, on reflection, I thought he shouldn't allow cameras to be mounted inside the cockpit.

'One last thing,' I said. 'I'd like *you* to do the first run tomorrow.'

I emailed my report before heading to Dunsfold the following morning to film the new Jaguar XKR with Jezza. Richard arrived at Elvington and got to grips with his shoot. It was like a scene out of *Sliding Doors*.

Richard met up with Colin and familiarised himself with the procedures. Colin banged in the first run of the day, as he had promised. Richard's early runs were textbook as he gradually built up his speeds using standard thrust. He practised the emergency shutdown drills before putting in a maximum speed afterburner run, during which he howled down the runway at 314mph. Space hoppers.

He was unperturbed by the punch in the back as the car bolted from its mark, unfazed by how much steering force he had to apply to keep it pointed straight, resolute in the face of mind-bending speed. As he popped the parachute at the end of that run, his body slammed into the five-point harness at twelve times its normal weight.

Richard climbed aboard Vampire for his final run, lucky number seven. She guzzled a load of fuel as he slipped on his blue Sparco driving gloves one more time. The crew lit his inferno. An ear-splitting roar grew into a shriek as he reached maximum rpm. He reached across the blurred, throbbing steering controls and lit the afterburner.

Richard's neck absorbed the doubling weight of his head and helmet as he shot down the runway as a yellow streak towards the camera crew. Molecules of air blasted his helmet and shook it violently as he kept an eye on the horizon and a firm grip at the helm, steering hard to the left to drive straight.

At 288mph, Richard noticed the car pulling even more than usual. Just half a second later, the time it takes to blink, he was in the middle of a colossal accident and fighting for his life.

At Dunsfold the Jag was spinning its wheels in fourth and producing enough smoke to fill a pop concert. The good light meant we finished a little after 5pm. That was when news was filtering in via the camera crews that there had been an accident at Elvington.

I remembered standing on the rugby pitch at school next to one of my pals. A typical redhead, his wiry frame punched well above his weight. With a ball in hand he was unstoppable; he would take anyone on. He lay on the ground in front of me as motionless as a corpse. My initial shock turned to horror as his head injury caused him to convulse until the paramedics loaded him into their wagon and took him away. The hours that followed felt like days.

Russell tugged me back into the present. 'Do you think it's serious, Ben?'

'Of course it's fucking serious,' I snapped. 'He was doing 300 miles an hour.'

When we came to investigate the accident with the Health and Safety Executive, I met a spaced-out Hammond near a café in Bristol. He'd lost some weight and looked understandably fragile.

I hadn't seen or spoken to him since his accident. I had wanted to badly. I was told to stay clear of the hospital because my appearance would have stoked the media frenzy that was already hard to control. The presenters and many of the *TG* team had gone to see him and show their support. Mindy, Richard's ebullient wife, was at his bedside throughout, enduring the agony of watching her husband pass in and out of consciousness. Not knowing if he would slip away for good.

In the end I'd gone anyway, to smuggle him some junk food – chocolate, Coke, crisps – that Mindy told me he was desperate for. But I couldn't see him.

Now he was staring peacefully out across the docks. Part of me expected him to be angry or cold towards me, but seeing him alive was all that mattered.

'Hey, mate,' he said a fraction slower than usual. 'I think I got here a *bit* early.'

We stopped for a coffee at the waterside and I couldn't escape the feeling that he'd copped it on my behalf. Then again, it was his daft idea in the first place.

He signed autographs for the staff and told them he felt all right and was 'much better'.

He told me he couldn't remember the accident clearly – except that he'd been fighting something – reaching for something maybe – when the car rolled. He desperately wanted to know if he had done it right on the day, or whether he had just cocked things up and risked never seeing his family again.

We ambled across to the HSE building and met some gentlemen in suits. They escorted us to a small meeting room with a white board and a laptop containing all the data from Vampire's black box.

We proceeded to run through the same old questions about Richard's preparation and the build-up to the shoot. Richard calmly replied that he had felt prepared, he couldn't speak highly enough of the rescue crew that saved his life, that the accident just came out of nowhere. He didn't believe there was anything he could have done to avoid it.

I was itching to get hold of the data. I couldn't see the screen. Some photos appeared on the desk and I pulled them across. All I wanted to know was whether Richard had reacted fast enough in the crisis. If I knew that his actions had been true, it meant that we'd armed him with a fighting chance. I needed to see that he'd pulled his parachute.

I surveyed the first image of the wrecked machine, lying on its side on the shredded field. Hanging out of their pods were the telltale white strands and the limp remains of the parachute.

The second photo was of the cockpit. The position of the thrust levers confirmed that he'd been fighting to reach the thrust levers to deploy his chute. What a fighter. He had done it right.

The telemetry recorded the speed and G-forces, and the HSE guys were doing their best to interpret them by the letter. I was keen to take my own view.

Richard was bombing down the straight when he felt the first unusual tug at the steering. Just 0.4 of a second later, the front right tyre exploded, affirmed by a drop in the car's ride height. What impressed me was that before the tyre blew, his speed trace was *already* dropping. It suggested that Richard had already lifted his foot to cut thrust.

BANG. The tyre exploded.

Subsequent footage revealed that a blister had formed during the penultimate run, perhaps due to the extra forces exerted by the surface camber.

As the rubber flew apart it exposed the metal rim of the front right wheel, which nose-dived, lifting the rear left wheel into the air. That sent him sideways and hard right. Hammo applied intuitive counter-steering with his hands and applied the brake with his foot, registering as a longitudinal G-force. As the machine turned into the airstream it slewed across the runway at an acute angle. Vapour trails formed around the bodywork's leading edges. Less than a second had passed.

Richard began to experience lateral G-forces beyond those of fighter pilots engaged in a dogfight. He ditched the steering and reached for the thrust levers. Exponential forces of air density flooded the cockpit as it jolted, rotated and flipped. Somehow, he grabbed the levers and pulled them down. The chute deployed but collapsed before it could arrest his speed.

The impact with the ground came from behind; the earth hammered through the roll cage and Richard's helmet absorbed the brunt of the blow. Sid Watkins, the renowned F1 neurosurgeon, believed that had it not been for the quality of his headgear, Hammo would have bought the farm.

HSE's report concluded: 'As RH sat in Vampire's cab there was significant clearance between the rollover cage and the top of his crash helmet.' It was a polite way of saying Hamster was on the short side, another factor that reduced the blow to his swede. I wondered if I would have been so 'lucky'.

HSE decided that no one would face a legal charge for the incident and they gave us some spiel about how 'Safety Management Systems' and risk assessments could have saved the planet. I was tempted to ask where

'Health and Safety' stood on natural selection, but decided to keep schtum.

For good measure, the powers that be published their findings and attached my name as someone who 'worked closely with *Top Gear* as a high performance driver and consultant'. It didn't leave much to the imagination about my day job.

27

STREET FIGHTING

I didn't pay much attention to the history of Bucharest until I saw the street circuit wind its way around a building that made the White House like a Barbie Mini Mansion. Romania's Parliament was housed in the second largest building in the world, originally built by its deposed dictator, Ceausescu, as his personal palace. The madman laid waste to 7,000 houses, churches, monasteries and a hospital to create a lavish neoclassical leviathan crammed with hundreds of chandeliers, more gold leaf than you could shake a stick at and nearly one million cubic metres of local wood. He left nothing in the budget for the roads, which were as pockmarked as the surface of the Moon. Golf courses were in short supply too.

'What's the hotel like, son?'

'It's great, Dad. Klaas booked it; it's the best.'

The tapping of keys suggested he was Googling. This could take some time.

'It's a long way from a golf course; I fancy taking my clubs. Is the food any good?'

'So far I've had a burger and fries.'

'*Burger*? FAT BOY. Well, I might fly out …'

'Let me know. I plan on winning this one. The track's a real shithole.'

'It does look wild. Your sort of place, I should think. Give me a call after qualifying.'

* * *

The FIA GT Championship was holding a street race around the capital with a grid of race-tuned versions of every kind of supercar from Aston to Lamborghini, Maserati, Ferrari, Corvette and, not least, my humble Ascari KZ1.

Ascari's newly formed team included old sweats like Spencer mixed with new talent in the form of the highly organised crew chief Neil Leyton. Gurus all, their car was so immaculately prepared you could eat your breakfast off it. Even though we were being penalised with excessive performance ballast, she was fast and nimble.

I was on top of the world. Georgie was expecting a baby and we were getting married. The popular myth in motorsport was that kids and family slowed you down, but they had the opposite effect on me. Points made prizes, and prizes quite simply paid the bills. I was feeling aggressive, ready to tear it up.

With the car on stands I had a slightly better view of the pit lane. I could see how many cars were due to go on track, and how many were changing tyres for another run at the pole time. I was sixteenth out of forty. With only five minutes left in the session I couldn't afford to get caught in traffic during my final shot on new tyres. On a street track, qualifying *was* the race. It was nearly impossible to overtake once the flag dropped.

The pit lane opened and the racers filed out on cold tyres.

Spencer frowned. 'You sure you don't wanna go?'

Not yet.

Waiting for the others to get further around the course increased the risk of running out of time if someone clouted the wall, but provided space for a balls-out attack on the tight streets. Five cars had already been smashed to pieces in this qualifying session alone.

I'd made a costly error in the morning; I slid on to the dusty marbles, clipped the wall and tore off a rear wishbone. It was doubly frustrating because there was never enough practice time on a street course. The grip level changed all the time as the cars laid down rubber, so I lost vital set-up time when we missed the second session. I was going into qualifying blind.

In the final seconds before departure I visualised the perfect lap one last time, braking later to make the most of the new tyres, stretching them to breaking point, squeezing past the tight walls and rolling the dice through the tricky final corners.

The clock never stops. I signalled Spencer to drop me on to the deck, pulled off and lit up the waxy new tyres.

The circuit was covered with oil stains, white lines, road markings and grit. The surface was a patchwork of concrete, stone-clad bitumen and blotches of fresh asphalt. There were tight, fast chicanes, heavy downhill braking areas and bumps that shook your fillings loose. Some downshifts under heavy braking would catch a manhole cover or a bump, causing the rear to drift. You had to ride it out. There was rarely any run-off, just concrete. Traction was equally transient over the surface changes and dust. Big licks of oversteer were running me hard up to the walls and it was a fight to keep on top of it.

The opening lap on new tyres was critical. They were the most significant factor in how a car handled. The bottom gripped the road, the side supported the weight as the car cornered and rolled. When you braked or accelerated, the tyre stretched lengthwise like a balloon.

Accelerating warmed the rears, but pushing too hard too soon overheated them and cost grip when it mattered most. If you didn't work the front tyres it created an imbalance; they had to be pliable and tacky enough to cope with the super late braking and corner entry speeds of qualifying. The trick was to work the sidewall and surface simultaneously. If you overcooked it when they were cold, the wheels locked up. That was bad news when you were still moving at 80mph because it burnt a flat spot that could later blister or puncture.

It was a delicate process, not to be rushed, but with other cars fast approaching on their flying laps, I couldn't afford to hang around.

I flew past the pit board and my adrenalin surged as I saw I had slipped to 22nd, one and a half seconds off the pole with only two minutes remaining. There was no more time for reflection; this was the moment of truth.

I pulled sixth gear and the LED rpm lights lit up like a Christmas tree. I slipped into another world – there was no sound, no car, no me. Nothing but pure movement. The first corner was closing and I didn't have to think. I trusted my body to know what to do.

Braking for Turn One was a last-minute showdown to slow from 170 to 90. A single error, a duff down-change, too much brake pressure whilst the tyre carcass was cold and hard, and you bashed into the wall twenty metres ahead. The first touch of the brake was everything, like a striker connecting with a football. It shifted inertia forward and generated G.

The tyres stretched and took the load. The brain sensed the grip, synapses flickered and signalled more or less brake pressure. You rode the tyre stretch through the seat of your pants and adjusted within nanoseconds, instinctively. When it worked perfectly, you reached the speed at which you could barely make the corner by releasing the brakes in the nick of time to turn in.

The car fired towards the apex with some new-tyre understeer. I reduced throttle, which shifted the balance back to the front, then slammed it home to drift out of the corner. I approached a tight, right-left walled chicane, braked late into the right and added some ambitious extra speed which sent the rear gliding – so much so that there was no need to turn in the middle of the chicane to nose it through. With the steering straight the car made a graceful transition slide through the corner.

I kept on it and sidled up to the concrete barrier on opposite lock, straightening at the last moment to prevent slipping further to the right and to protect the front suspension if it kissed concrete. With millimetres to spare, plumes of dirt and marbles blew through the wheel arches and into the air.

Two tough corners were in the bag and there was no traffic in sight. I was buzzing. For the rest of the lap I played an aggressive game of point and squirt, bounced on to two wheels over high kerbs and slithered across bumpy side roads. I even had time to contemplate the final corner. The undulations in the road there were playing havoc with the brakes, making the pedal soft and treacherous and prone to locking the rear wheels. I could play safe and drop a few tenths to bank a lap that would still be good for the top five, or go for it. A split-second decision and an easy one.

The last corner bent round to the left then doubled back on itself, which meant there was no run-off whatsoever. I improved the pedal pressure by pumping it and took the plunge on the brakes outrageously deep into the corner, right on top of the nastiest bumps. The back wheels locked before I had a chance to shift down. The engine note dropped and the gearbox clattered. I popped the clutch, modulated the brake and heard the revs spin up again. Then the inside front locked.

I was running out of road, but no more than I had expected. I released the pedal pressure a fraction and extended the speed into the left-hander. It stuck. I whipped by the wall, braked some more and plucked second

gear to change direction. I cracked the throttle a few times to hustle the rear as the pit straight opened up ahead and then nailed it, short-shifting to third for traction and bolting past my dent in the wall from the earlier session. I searched for the pit board and waited to hear the result.

The pit to car radio crackled into life: 'That's it, Ben,' Neil stammered. 'You have pole position.'

It was the best feeling, bringing home the bacon for the crew. With no time left on the clock I could relax a little, but you never switched off on a street circuit. I drove through the first corner and was joined by another car leaving the pit lane. I sped uphill towards the next horizon and saw yellow flags waving beside a stricken Lamborghini Gallardo. I took the edge off the throttle. That was when the car behind hit me.

I was slammed back hard into the seat. My metal cocoon was propelled forwards and violently to the right, giving me a bird's-eye view of the stationary car I was approaching driver side first.

130 to 0 in one second. A searing pain exploded in my spine. The impact was sledgehammer brutal. As the Lambo's solid gearbox met the door of my Ascari, the energy passed through me like a wrecking ball. In spite of the harness binding me to the seat, my head and shoulder managed to smash through the Perspex window and split the door open.

The air stopped moving through the cabin and the heat from the engine was stifling. My spine was gripped by an intense burning cramp, a spasm of muscle contracting around a white-hot core. My lungs seemed no longer to exist and air could only be swallowed, not breathed. A great weight clamped my chest shut, but the pain was so overwhelming that the breathing issue paled into insignificance. I wanted to pass out, but the sadistic survival instinct kept me wildly alert. I gathered my strength to gesticulate urgently to the nearest track marshal, but then realised I couldn't move my arms. My right hand just bobbed limply in my lap.

The world was foggy. Sweat poured from my throbbing head as the blood continued to crash around my system. The visor on my helmet was bent shut by the impact and I couldn't open it for the tiny amount of air it might let in. I still couldn't breathe. I'd been winded badly before, but this was different; this felt like I was paralysed.

I slipped into delirium, but fear forced me to focus and seize on the slightest encouraging sign. I managed a squeak of air but no more. Panic would only make things worse, so I kept trying.

An orange-clad marshal opened the passenger door and slowly made his way inside. I couldn't bring his face into focus or understand him, but his presence was reassuring. It meant the car probably wasn't on fire.

My door was wrapped around someone's gearbox and the racing seat extended around my head in a horseshoe, curved forward of my chest and up from my hips. That meant I'd have to be dragged forwards then sideways across the centre console.

Another marshal appeared brandishing a large orange rescue board, big enough to go surfing on. They couldn't seriously be aiming that into this little space. They were. He peeled away my belts and rustled his fingers inside my race suit. I couldn't stop him even if I'd wanted to. I was slowly suffocating. Someone pulled my legs to the right and it tore a hole in my spine. My left shoulder was nudged gently forward, ripping open a cavern in my back. Train tracks were being pulled out of their sleepers, bent, twisted and wrenched away. The pain was medieval and I wanted to vomit.

I never saw how they solved the conundrum of getting me over the gear-stick. As my head was drawn forward I passed out. The heroes in the orange suits somehow got me on to the tarmac, where a new thought invaded my mind: *Stupid selfish fool if I can't walk when my baby is born ...*

'Hello, can you hear me? My name is Anika. You will feel something in your arm, OK?'

'OK.'

The army medical training rotated in my subconscious. *A chest wound typically involves air in the lung cavity. Lightness of breath ... you hear the blood rattle on the lungs ... signs the lining has been breached ... If things start to go wrong it can happen fast, you need to act quickly to perform a lumbar puncture ...*

To my relief, no one ran at me with an eight-inch needle to punch a hole through my ribcage, yet every breath felt like a belt was being ratcheted around my chest. Anything was better than this. The stabbing in my spine refused to be ignored. I focused on staying calm. I couldn't move my legs.

I was taken to Romanian A&E on the orange plank. My back wasn't damaged; I'd snapped four ribs very close to my spine. Once the shock and swelling calmed down, I could move my limbs. The Romanian medics were fantastic, especially the doctor who allayed my worst fears. But there were a couple of unexpected challenges. The first was that to

call for food or any kind of help I had to reach a button on the wall two metres behind my head. The second manifested itself the following morning …

Two very butch mamas bowled up, dressed like cleaning ladies. One was Rosa Klebb and her mate was an Olympic shot-putter. They were gesticulating furiously and muttering what sounded suspiciously like, *'Il presidente, bloshloka, bretishlokkka!'*

Their frenetic gesturing and vice-like grip on my arms suggested I was about to evacuate my rather posh room whether I liked it or not. Bearing in mind that the biggest movement I had managed until this point was to turn my head from one side to the other, standing up would be easier said than done.

I fended Klebb away from my left arm and begged for time from the Olympian. Perhaps I could slide off the right-hand side of the bed. I motioned to the right.

JEEEEEESSSSSS … NO WAY.

Left, then.

Gripping the sheets with my right hand, I clawed forward with a series of snail-like movements and banshee cries to bring myself upright. The mamas clicked their fingers impatiently. My feet couldn't reach the floor and pleading my case for them to lower me down got me nowhere. I had to jump.

I exercised every millimetre of my butt cheeks to slide as close to the floor as humanly possible. Then a muscle I never knew existed – and I suddenly wished it didn't – tautened across my ribs. I plummeted involuntarily off the bed and landed uncertainly on my feet. The spasm lancing through my back sent dominoes of fire tumbling around my body. My legs buckled and I managed something between a whimper and a groan. The mamas looked on unmoved as I took my first faltering steps into what I hoped might turn out to be a friendlier world.

Klebb wasn't leaving anything to chance; she led me out of the room by my elbow. It seemed that my private room, complete with TV, was reserved for the Romanian President. She marched me along the corridor in search of more modest accommodation at triple my speed limit. One look at the wards confirmed that whatever state I was in, I was better off making a run for it and flying back to England.

I rang my old man. He'd been following my progress and we had an unusually long chat.

'As long as you're OK. What a shame, though. How bad's the car?'

'It's FUBAR. Could you pick me up from the airport? I've seen enough of this place.'

'Of course. I'll see you in the morning.' He paused. 'Love you, Son.'

I rang Georgie next to let her know I was coming home. A pregnant lady had enough to worry about, so I lied about my injury.

'Are you sure you're OK? What aren't you telling me?'

'I'm just annoyed about the busted car. See you really soon.'

Braam, Ascari's short-stacked South African Team Manager, swung by the hospital.

'Ben-jamin. Grab your shit and let's get out of 'ere.'

I pulled myself up.

'Jeez, boy, you ain't gonna dance the Macarena for some time, eh?'

We boarded Romania's most dilapidated taxi. Carpet oddments covered rusted-out holes in the floor and its shock absorbers didn't absorb. The driver spotted the racing logos on our shirts, dropped a gear and gave us the Grand Prix treatment over every pothole in the city. His overtaking technique was novel. He rode the rear bumper of the car in front and accelerated repeatedly into oncoming traffic until they waved a white flag. Mike Tyson worked my torso for ten rounds until we made it to the airport and boarded the plane to London.

After the short flight to Luton airport, the effect of the mysterious painkillers in glass vials had worn off. I clicked on my mobile to call my old man and it rang within seconds. I heard the quiet, apologetic voice of an old family friend, and knew immediately that my dad was dead.

I wanted to rip the advertising boards off the wall of the airport, pull up the paving slabs and tear down the sky. In my pathetic state all I could do was crumple to the floor and sob.

The man who had given me every opportunity to live the life I wanted was gone. I'd never thanked him enough and there was so much more I needed to say to him.

I later discovered that in the confusion of trying to reach me to break the news, Mum had phoned Georgie. Mum struggled to find the words, and Georgie fell to the floor thinking I was a goner.

Dad had the last word. When I got down to sorting out his affairs I found two sets of papers lying open in his spartan apartment. A printout

of my Romanian qualifying sheet rested under his magnifying glass, alongside reviews of over a hundred prams.

The Stiglet was due in just over three months. I needed to pull myself together for the sake of Georgie and the baby. Inside I was broken.

28

LONDON CALLING

With four knackered ribs I was no use to anybody for some time. But two days after getting home I was contacted by *Top Gear* to film a race across London. I was desperate for a distraction and, since The Stig had no known bone structure, I heard myself agreeing.

The purpose of the race was to determine, in a totally scientific manner, the fastest means of travel between Kew Gardens and London City Airport.

The Stig would be taking public transport whilst the presenters proceeded by boat, car and bicycle. I duly appeared at Kew, swallowed some painkillers and eased into my white overalls and helmet in the urinals of a nearby pub. Superman, eat your heart out. Pushing my left arm through the tight sleeve of the suit made my eyes water. I finally squeezed myself in and headed across to the 'start line' for the presenters' opening piece to camera.

For the purpose of the film I was being 'delivered' to the set on a sack truck by *Top Gear*'s 'men in white coats'. Realising that the low metal frame would apply all the weight to my ribcage, Andy Wilman, in a touching moment of compassion, fitted a broom handle to extend its load-bearing structure to neck height.

Uncharacteristically, it took the presenters five takes to wheel me into the shot. Finally, we were off. We split into four mini crews and went our different directions. Whilst Jezza, Hammo and May had scripts pretty much in hand for how their journeys would appear on camera, mine would be entirely spontaneous. As the presenters voiced their opinions on road traffic and the Thames speed limits for the benefit of the camera, I fronted up with the public.

First up was a queue of school kids at the bus stop. 'Take your helmet off,' they pleaded. 'Yeeeaaaahhhhh!'

Oyster card in hand, I surfed the bus system, with Wilman directing the cameraman to pick up anything that caught his eye. As we headed into the Underground I remembered the scene in *Crocodile Dundee* where bushmaster Mick fights shy of the escalator, so I stopped, teetered on the edge and did an about face.

On the tube I picked up a newspaper with a feature on Lewis Hamilton during his F1 race-winning prime. Even anonymous robot racing drivers were entitled to a little professional rivalry, so I chucked the paper away in disgust, fuelling rumours that Hamilton's rival Fernando Alonso was The Stig.

Londoners didn't give a monkey's about a man in a white suit walking amongst them, with the exception of one guy who spat his pasty on the floor. Mostly it was like I wasn't there. After a few more changes I emerged from the Docklands Light Railway just ahead of James. Hammond had arrived first on the bike, followed by Jeremy, who had howled up the Thames aboard a supercharged racing boat at the head of a six-foot wake. James's appalling sense of direction sealed the car's fate. It wasn't the result *Top Gear* was looking for.

I fell asleep on the train home and woke up slightly out of it. I absentmindedly started texting my father about what I'd been up to. We hadn't seen each other much recently, but always kept in touch. Then a wave of sadness brought me to my senses. Dad was *gone*.

Before I had too much time for reflection, providence intervened again. A blockbusting movie stunt co-ordinator called Steve Dent rang and asked me to meet him at Pinewood Studios.

I'd always been fascinated by the movie industry. Hollywood had the budgets to do things we could only dream about on TV. I'd studied the credits of my favourite movies like *Vanishing Point*, *Ronin* and the Bond series, looking for a way in.

Top Gear gave me a cracking CV; the only problem was I could never show it to anyone. I'd put too much effort into keeping The Stig undercover to use him as currency. After numerous blind alleys and dead ends, the legendary Gary Powell had recommended me for a job on Nicolas Cage's new movie. It featured a massive car chase through the City of London.

Just driving through the stone arch of the studio's Double Lodge entrance, you felt the history of the place. Pinewood had been one of the most prolific film and television production facilities in the world since the Thirties, with a raft of blockbusters from *The Great Gatsby* to *Superman*. It remains the long-term home of the greatest of action heroes, 007.

The body of professionals producing the stunts for the movie business was a closed shop. To join them required years of training in numerous specialist skills such as fire, gymnastics, horse riding and martial arts. To be allowed to join them as a driving expert would be a rare privilege.

I was required for driving a 'pod car'. The pod was a metal cage with a set of driving controls that sat on the roof of a normal road car, in this case a Mercedes C Class. Cage and the other actors sat inside, whilst the man in the pod worked the steering, brakes and accelerator.

I met Ian, the vehicle's engineer, aka the 'big black bloke' I had been told to look for in Shed 42. His eyes lit up over his small rectangular glasses. 'Go on, climb up and 'ave a look!'

I climbed up the side of the Merc, clambered into the thick tube frame then slid into the chair like an invalid. Ian and his crew watched this palaver, then looked at each other as if to say, 'Couldn't Steve find one that's not broken?'

'Don't worry. I'll be fine in a few weeks.'

Sitting on the roofrack wasn't something I was accustomed to, but it was cool. When you turned the wheel of most road cars it would unwind and self-centre if you let go. This one didn't, because the hydraulic steering was so bloody heavy, but I could just about haul it round with my good arm. The pedals were neatly transplanted from the Merc, with the automatic gear-shifter mounted alongside the seat. It was excellently appointed, ideal for VIPs who preferred not to see their chauffeur.

Next on the agenda was to check out one of the standard Mercs with Rob Inch, another legendary stuntman who starred as the headless horseman in *Sleepy Hollow*. At over six feet tall Rob didn't look much like a cowboy. This was his first major foray into a different kind of horsepower. We drove to one of the outdoor stages, a yard of gravel with a

narrow stretch of tarmac bordered by a row of fake shopfronts. Before I could say spare ribs, Rob floored it down the tarmac alley and chucked the car right into a handbrake turn.

I could tell he had the touch straight away, if a little rough around the edges, but I wasn't about to encourage the son of a bitch. I was in agony. He powered out of the asphalt on to the loose gravel, pulled the wand again and as we slid back on to the tarmac the Merc dug in, gripped and rocked. I tensed up, held on to the door handle and bit my lip hard. The veins in Rob's arms flared as he gripped the steering and kicked the throttle to try and skid the Merc down the street.

After a number of unsuccessful runs, I explained why it was tricky to drift an automatic without a clutch to pop the tail out. The C Class was super-planted because of its stiff suspension and low centre of gravity, so it required some manipulation to set it free. He offered to trade seats. 'But you'd better not jump straight in and stick it sideways down this alley.'

It dawned on me then that this was a test. I drove quietly down the alley until I reached the gravel, then lifted off the gas, turned right and buried the throttle to produce a single powerslide at a higher speed than if I'd gone in using the handbrake. As I came back round towards the tarmac I made sure it was fully sideways and, as it hit the sticky stuff, chucked the steering the other way and used the momentum to transition slide down the alley. My ribs were killing me, but I figured it was hurting Rob's pride more, so I kept on it. I managed the whole exercise one-handed. Rob just said: 'Bastard.' Thank God for that.

With as much nonchalance as I could muster with balls of sweat dripping off my face, I said, 'Yeah, it's a good car.'

So began my life as a stunt driver for a Hollywood film. I met the rest of the fifty-strong team for rehearsals at Bovingdon outside London. Another day, another airfield. Some of the guys wore old crew shirts from mega movies like *The Bourne Ultimatum*, *Casino Royale* and *Saving Private Ryan*. These were the men who'd fallen off every horse, down every set of stairs and burnt in every inferno I'd seen on the big screen during the previous decade. The scripts were etched on their faces, bodies and X-ray charts.

One of the stuntmen was entertaining a couple of old sweats with his showreel. I watched through the cracks between my fingers as he leapt 200 metres from the top of a hyperbolic cooling tower at an electric

power station, without a parachute, to land on a modest stack of cardboard boxes. The audience nodded with approval.

The range of talents amongst the 'stunties' was remarkable. Brian was a bareknuckle boxer, shining proof that the expression 'the bigger they are, the harder they fall' was a dangerous lie. His muscles were terrifying; I certainly wasn't going to tell him that his 'Dark Advenger' tattoo was misspelt. There were ex-military folk, motocross champions, sword fighters, silent types and so on.

Remnants of black hair dye from a recent movie were visible in a few. And all seemed to have a cappuccino or fruit smoothie on the go from the onsite catering van that transformed this barren strip of concrete into a charming place to hang out.

There was lashings of the kind of black humour you expect from a dangerous profession. One boy limped towards the rest of the group with legs covered in ghoulish lacerations and purple and yellow bruising.

I'd already been introduced to the self-appointed mouthpiece of the group. Rowley had worked in film man and boy. He loved it. His full lips quivered as he saw me clock the walking accident. 'Car knockdown,' he said.

'What?'

Rowley laughed like a cockney drain. 'Got hit by a car yesterday. How's them legs, Bradders?'

Brad shot us a sheepish smile. An intense, muscular man to my left added quietly, 'Not fast enough, eh, Bradders ...'

'You mean you'd rather be hit by a car going *faster*?'

''Course,' continued Stuart, aka Russell Crowe's double from *Gladiator*. 'Only get hit once then, don't ya?' He was rolling his fingers up in the air to illustrate the higher trajectory.

'Sod that.'

The car chase we were due to rehearse over the course of a month was being billed as the biggest in London's history. A treasure hunter played by Nicolas Cage sets out on a global quest to unearth hidden treasures and discover clues that lead him into the narrow confines of London's square mile. The hero finds himself in the cross hairs of the villain (Ed Harris) and puts the pedal to the metal to escape in a high-octane pursuit.

Blocking off central London to shoot a movie was as complicated as it sounds. The stunt team had to perfect a diverse number of driving sequences on the airfield in order to hit the ground running on locations with restricted access, such as Buckingham Palace, Whitehall and St James's. Everything had to run like clockwork in order for us to race through the streets, shoot a scene in five minutes, and return the 'set' to its rightful owners. Many of the scenes left no margin for second takes because the carnage left nothing to film with.

We were also due to film in London's financial centre. If we made a mistake and trashed the Bank of England, things would turn ugly.

They used animated storyboards called 'previsuals' to bring the story of the car chase to life and develop a clear understanding of the director's vision. It also allowed them to determine what was actually achievable before the production started burning millions of pounds on location.

London's routes and intersections were painstakingly re-created at the airfield, using cones, tyres and tape. Twenty drivers took to cars, bikes and trucks, with the remainder of the stuntmen and women acting as passers-by. This was pre credit crunch, so we weren't allowed to run over real bankers.

During one rehearsal on the airfield we deployed every vehicle to simulate a scene where the Mercedes swerved in and out of oncoming traffic, whilst being chased by a supercharged Range Rover. Rob was working as Nick Cage's double in the standard Merc, so I took it in turns with him to drive the route or ride along as a passenger so that the pod could be deployed in any scene.

We tore straight into it. We overtook everything in our path at 70mph before bouncing across a pedestrian crossing, skidding past a police car and escaping down the pavement with people jumping left and right.

Of the seventy-odd vehicles we had on site about twenty were police cars, mostly Omegas. We were standing around drinking espressos from the catering wagon, the holy grail of snacking, when some chavs barrelled on to the airfield and pulled a handbrake turn in their Citroën. Our stuntmen didn't even flinch. Two of them skidded across the bonnet of their vehicles and shot off in pursuit, blues and twos blaring, cutting the Citroën off with a spectacular pincer movement. The chavs nervously produced their licences and tootled off as reformed drivers.

I seriously admired these guys and found we had a lot in common, except that I preferred not to be run over by a car or in any way set fire to or shot off a horse at 50mph. But that's just me.

We were nailing the car chase and getting to grips with the pod car. At first it felt like it would topple over every time I turned into a corner, so we built up gradually to full speed. My distance from the car's centre of gravity added a pendulum effect that clouded the normal sensation of driving and made my caged office feel like an out of body experience. I gained confidence with each run, but in the end it took a leap of faith to determine whether it actually had a tipping point.

'Can I give it the big one, Ian?'

'Oh, go on then,' he said. 'Start on those damp bits of track before you try dry land.'

The wet surface made it less likely that the car would dig in and roll over. Even inside a steel frame, if it did flip I was a long way from bullet-proof.

I blasted up the runway and yanked the handbrake. *Ooooh, shiiit.* As the suspension took the strain my metal cage wobbled and gyrated. The Merc swung through 90 degrees, I rocked around in my seat and it seemed certain that something unpleasant was about to happen until the car came to a stop.

Buoyed by this, I put the pod through its paces on the slalom course of 'Old Broad Street' and managed to get it to powerslide, which felt even stranger. It could J-turn and was actually better than the standard Merc at high-speed reversing because you had a bird's-eye view of the streets below.

It was a spooky ride for the passengers inside the carriage. With no sight of the driver or even a working steering wheel, they had no idea where the car was going, when it would speed up or suddenly come to a stop. Giving the boys passenger rides became a popular gig during down time. I showed them how to drift their front- and rear-wheel-drive police cars, and Rowley showed me how to do a handbrake turn in a 12-tonne beer truck.

I sat in the cab and Rowley nailed it until we were doing about 55, then he swerved hard right, hard left and cranked the air brake. The rear axle seized up, wallowed and spun around to fill the coned street we had marked out.

'Aha, aha,' Rowley crowed. 'Won't be quite as cosy as that on South-wark Bridge, I facking tell ya.' He wasn't lying.

Our first destination for filming was Bank tube station at 5am one Saturday morning. We brought a new kind of congestion to the capital in the form of stunt men and action extras by the hundred, scores of crew and the cast of a Hollywood blockbuster in the making.

'Today we will be smashing a lot of cars and I want everyone to switch on,' said Steve Dent, setting the tone for Day One.

Everyone was fitted into their various costumes: pin stripe suits, post office uniforms and innocuous bystander get-ups. I sported a Nick Cage wig and tan suit for the perfect 'Man from Del Monte' look. The dark brown bouffant perched on top of my head made me look like a prize tosser and Rowley let me know it.

The strongest antidote for Rowley was Pete Miles, a loveable rogue from the West Country who baited him remorselessly.

''Ere Ben, watch this,' as he pretended to harvest a giant bogey, a piece of broccoli, from his nostril. Rowley eyeballed the green matter on the tip of Milesy's finger, whereupon it was flicked onto his sleeve. Rowley dropped his cappuccino but otherwise was frozen rigid by the kryptonite.

'Get it off, *get it off, OFF.*'

The streets in and around Bank tube station were in regular Monday morning mode, except that nobody was moving. Everything was on pause. Vehicles were stationary and every face was turned in the same direction, waiting for a single command.

The first assistant director called over the loudhailer, 'Lock it off.'

'We're locked up.'

A water bowser squirted its contents across the empty streets. Continuity throughout the chase was important, and the producers had decided that it was raining.

'Stand by, cameras.'

'Rolling.'

Steve shouted, 'Stand by. *Action.*'

The engines began to rumble. A 12-tonne Fullers beer truck driven by Milesy charged into view and 'commuters' dived out of its way. There was no way the truck could stop in time for the traffic lights and a postal van was already turning across the intersection.

The clash of metal and glass made the ground shake; it was the kind of shunt people didn't walk away from.

The truck hit the van so hard amidships that they momentarily became one. It then slid into the traffic island, flattened a bollard and creased the light gantry. The driver pulled the steering hard left. There was no room for manoeuvre in the 'traffic' but it didn't stop him. Milesy knew that five cameras were recording his every move and this was a one-take wonder. He ploughed through a Vauxhall Vectra as it backed away and tore down Prince's Street towards Threadneedle, grazing the Georgian brickwork of some Spanish bank.

'CUT. Reset!'

I craned my head around the street corner and watched the show. I was ten years old again. Our immediate concern was for second-generation stunt veteran Franky Henson, the driver of the postal van. Franky climbed out grinning like a space cadet but otherwise unscathed. The first a.d. went into overtime clearing the area. Within three minutes the only sign of the crash was the broken traffic light, which wasn't in the script.

We moved on to St Paul's Cathedral, an unlikely location for a street chase and a showcase in precision driving. Fifty 'stunt priests' were roped into the act, which involved handbrake-turning the Mercedes on to the cobbled entrance, then sliding it through the bustling crowd of Bible bashers.

Mr Cage made his way over to the pod and eyed me warily as we were introduced. I tried to act like it was an everyday occurrence to sit on the roof of a car and race through a bunch of monks. He was much slimmer than I expected, delicate even, which explained why my tan suit had pinched my gusset somewhat. The actors climbed aboard, along with the movie's director. It seemed their fate rested in my hands.

The priests packed together into an area the size of a living room. Steve actioned me through my radio earpiece, and I accelerated the pod into the cobbled square. The priests were thronging around the car, waving their umbrellas and shaking their fists at me in protest. Some of the furious faces were so convincing that on the third take I thought I'd run someone down and abandoned the shot to stop and check. The next take Cage started improvising and I heard him yelling '*Stop, Stop,*' so I did. The director shouted, 'They're just acting; *keep going!*'

The pod was scheduled to work all the way through the chase, but in the end it only came out a few times. There was a scene where Cage was being shot at by the baddies in the Range Rover. The Merc drifted

through a right-hander to get away and slammed sideways into a double-decker bus. As it straightened out, it got rammed from behind by the Rangie.

Rob had perfected the transition slide on the airfield before doing it for real in front of Nelson's Column and it was on the nail. Then it was my turn to do it with the actors on board the pod. I sat on a throne of a zillion battery boxes with $2 million worth of cameras rigged to the right and front of the Merc beneath me. I didn't care about the kit, but I was a little apprehensive.

'We just want a tap,' came my instruction, 'to give the actors a feel for what's going on. Nothing heavy, but it's got to look *real*. There's money in that car, so don't screw this up!'

No pressure then.

I lined up on a side street at a right angle to the bus's line of travel. The pod was a pig to turn sharply. As I ran through the 'what ifs' in my head, the director turned helpfully to Cage. 'It's OK, the driver really knows what he's doing.'

The stunties were rubbing their hands together; everyone's ass was on the line.

'ACTION …'

We set off towards the T-junction and the double-decker barrelled straight at us. It got very big very fast. Every instinct screamed to brake and avoid it. I pitched into the corner and aimed just behind the front wheels. There was a little knock as we hit it and the sound of panels crumpling before I downshifted and accelerated away. I pulled up near the director to confirm everyone was OK and kept my job a little longer.

Some of the most intense scenes were filmed at Southwark Bridge, with little or no margin for error. Cage holds a precious artefact out of the window before throwing it into the Thames in an effort to distract the villains. Duly distracted, the Range Rover skids to a halt, followed by the pursuing beer truck. Rowley moistened his lips uneasily as the rescue divers climbed into their inflatable boats, in case he overcooked his mark. Sure enough, the bridge never looked so narrow as when his truck, laden with phoney beer barrels, handbrake-turned and skidded across four lanes of carriageway to stop with just a couple of feet to spare.

Capturing the essence of speed was essential for a film featuring cars powering through London at 100mph. To keep up with the pace we

needed a camera car with serious grunt. The Volkswagen Touareg with its 5-litre V10 Twin Turbo motor manned up to the task and I drew the long straw to drive it.

Gunshots rained down on the fleeing Mercedes and some stray rounds struck the beer truck, so the beer barrels started exploding. The pursuit ran through a police blockade and all hell broke loose. The cars weaved through four lanes of oncoming traffic, a taxi toppled on to its roof and sixty beer barrels rocketed up into the air as the stuntmen exchanged fire.

My view of the action through the Touareg's windscreen was partly obscured by a ten-foot-tall steel frame extending from the bumper for elevating the camera. Its operator sat behind me whilst the second unit director viewed the action through his monitor. The camera itself was very much in harm's way. Even though the beer barrels were made of rubber rather than steel, they were spinning towards us at 60mph.

With fake beer spurting high into the air and cars smashing into each other a few metres away, I did my best to steer a course through the beer barrel asteroid field. After five takes one of the barrels bounced curiously from the tarmac and smacked the camera head on. The director loved it, so the shot ended up in the final cut.

Thirty cars were destroyed in the course of the production, including eight police cars in a roadblock that turned into a demolition orgy.

The film was a box-office hit and my broken bones benefited from the 'time off', but the secrecy of my other life, my *Top Gear* life, was gradually being eroded. I did an interview with my local paper about the London car chase and the first question was, 'Are you The Stig?'

The rest of the interview centred on the movie, but not one word of that made it into the three-page feature they published, which was entirely about me being the man in the white suit. Thankfully the story didn't go national, that time.

There were other own goals. I'd sometimes arrive on jobs in person to discover that the people I was meeting were expecting The Stig. The all-seeing eye of the Internet and 'free press' collated rumours and every scrap of information they could get hold of, adding fuel to the flames.

I relied on the fact that there was no evidence that I had ever worked for *Top Gear*, and the white helmet was my shield. Then, one day, I was

walking across London in character to promote *Top Gear* magazine when a piercing camera flash went off ahead of me. It defeated the dark visor and snapped a clear image of part of my face.

Georgie joked that it looked like Damon Hill ...

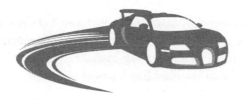

29

PEDAL ON THE RIGHT

There was an unwritten rule for The Stig that I strived continuously to overturn. He was never allowed to compete in a race in the 'real world'; his air of invincibility could never be put at risk. The frustration for me was that The Stig could have landed the kind of plum racing drives that Ben Collins had always dreamed of – and my bid to have him compete in NASCAR and Le Mans fell on deaf ears.

Then, in 2007, the rules were bent.

'We're doing the twenty-four-hour Britcar race with you and the presenters. We need you to go to Silverstone and train them.'

My only issue was that the race coincided with the date Georgie was due to give birth. I suggested staying at home but, bless her, Georgie said she would rather watch paint dry than have me hovering at home with an egg timer. I kept my phone with someone I trusted whenever I was on track, in case I had to do a runner.

Britcar was an amateur-friendly format hosting a mishmash of different GT racing categories. The bottom category was more or less for road cars. *Top Gear* got themselves a diesel 3 Series BMW. It was sporty enough – perhaps – to raise the pulse of a Tibetan monk, but on a Grand Prix circuit it was a pretty tame ride. Nonetheless, we were going racing.

First order of business was to get the boys their race licences. I called Jeremy ahead of the first session and he seemed to be taking it seriously.

'You'd better give me some proper lessons, because Silverstone is a circuit which has permanently mystified me. I did millions of laps there once and never had a clue what I was doing.'

Buoyed by his sincerity, I looked forward to the training session. After all, I knew Silverstone backwards.

I met Jeremy outside the pits and he was exuding confidence.

We climbed into a hired Lexus. Jezza coiled himself into the passenger seat with the top of his helmet jammed into the ceiling. The seat motor strained as it wound him rearwards for several minutes.

As I explained the basics of steering position and trail braking he started twitching and nodding his head as though the world might end if I didn't shut up and drive. He was staring longingly at the pit lane exit. I rolled my eyes and drove off.

I hauled the Lexus in and out of the fast sweepers and casually explained why, when and how the car would understeer or oversteer moments before it did, so that he could anticipate and feel the dynamics. This held his attention for, oh, almost a lap. Then he started talking.

'You turn in *far* too early there,' into the tight left at Brooklands. 'Why are you steering so much into that corner?' at super fast Copse. 'I don't use that line there,' through the quick left right at Becketts. Like an Olympic fencer he timed his quips exquisitely to parry my every instruction, preventing me from actually teaching him anything. Jeremy loved being told what to do the way cats love swimming.

I headed back to the pits and put Mr Smarty Pants in the driver's seat.

Whirrrrrrrrrr, went the chair.

We had our first argument before leaving the pit.

'Slow down for that hidden entrance in case a car comes out.'

He wobbled his noggin at me. 'I think you'll find I can make it out of the pits.'

Cantankerous old bugger. I tried not to smile but I couldn't help it. Jeremy was one of those rare people that never came unstuck, even when he was out of his depth. He had the luck of the devil.

Off we went, Clarkson style. He didn't hang around, but this was no pro. We moved from one corner to the next without sparing the horses. Jezza adopted a stiff upper lip and a straight arm as he pointed the car into Stowe corner, too early for my liking. Then we disagreed on the line for Vale.

'See, you slid wide because you turned in early.'

'No, I didn't.'

'*Yes, you did*. OK,' I pointed through the long fast right in case we ran wide into the gravel trap, 'watch it on the power here and let it run out gradually.'

'*Yes, yes, yes …*'

'Bridge Corner will be flat once you're comfortable. The trick is to make it back to the right side before you turn left, so *slow down a bit*.'

He disobeyed, stayed left and we ran some gravel on the way out.

'Hmm, tyres aren't up to temperature …', he muttered, mistaking our road car for a McLaren.

I was determined to teach him a safe route if nothing else, and not to repeat his legendary North Pole experience. A former sergeant from the SBS gave Jeremy a lesson on dispatching polar bears with a shotgun. He'd kicked down more doors with that particular weapon than Jezza had eaten hot breakfasts. But that didn't stop Jeremy telling the sergeant he was wrong, and taking over the lesson. They pushed Jeremy into a frozen lake later that week, but I'm sure there was no connection.

Jeremy took his late line into Brooklands.

'You won't even make the corner like that when you brake later.'

'Mmmm …' Deep concentration.

In his own way, Jeremy was doing well. All his experience of playing on circuits and airfields was paying dividends, until a sudden change of direction at Maggots sent us sideways. Instructor mode kicked in and I grabbed the steering off him, reduced our rate of turn and made horse-whispering sounds.

'Pah,' Clarkson spat, shrugging off my help. '*This* is what we do.'

Maybe I was being a sissy. The car rudely snapped one way then the other, but he kept a grip of it and made the next corner with some determined car control. I cried with laughter at his obstinacy, mostly because I saw through it. Deep down, Jeremy was a sensitive soul. Really.

I force-fed him some instruction he did his best to ignore. He started braking very late for Stowe at 100mph and I needed his full attention following a disagreement on the straight. I wagged a finger at him. 'Stop talking, *stop talking*, get ready, BRAKE, and … off and *turn*.' Jeremy dragged the Lexus through by the bit.

He reluctantly tried my early line at Brooklands. 'You might be right about that one …' Bloody hell, progress.

I dropped Jeremy at the racing school, into the hands of the very instructors who first taught me over a decade earlier. Nothing had changed: the same short-sleeve sun-tans, Ray Bans and one-liners.

'What's he like?' asked Steve Warburton, twice the size of when I first met him, but no slower.

'Difficult.'

'Oh, we like those. Makes the smell of fear so much sweeter.'

James May joined us, dressed in a brown leather Belstaff jacket. Flight Lieutenant May did indeed look like the right stuff, rosy-cheeked and ready for action. 'Morning, Squadron Leader, May reporting for duty.'

'These guys will show you the ropes, Jimbo. Don't be shy of pushing it so you can figure out the braking points around here.'

'Steely-eyed speed warriors, aye. Right-oh, let the learning commence.'

I left them all standing outside the classroom puffing away at their cigarettes. Once they passed their race licences we could go and try out the BMW.

Hammond was busy filming elsewhere. The first time he would drive the track or car would be during qualifying.

Come the race weekend, maintaining my anonymity became tricky. I had to sign on officially for the race and my pseudonym didn't cut the mustard. The organisers needed to know who was behind the helmet, and that he held a racing licence. I signed on to a separate driver sheet and made sure that I never appeared in person again for the rest of the weekend.

Jeremy had been practising in the BMW for a day before the other two turned up for the race. I stood in front of a large map of the circuit ready to explain gears, speeds and racing lines, but obviously couldn't have managed without Jeremy's help.

He soon lumbered towards me. 'Right, I turn in here at Copse in third gear, but I think it could be fourth ...' and so on.

We'd be racing alongside GT2 spec machines capable of 200mph to our 120. My main concern was that if the presenters spun in front of a field of mixed-ability drivers, they could be hurt. I pinpointed the key areas on the track where they should expect faster traffic and explained where to overtake and where the loonies would try to out-brake them. Just crossing the straights in order to line up for the next corner was a

major undertaking in a crowded race and it was easy to get turned around.

I turned my attention to our wheels. BBC guidelines prohibited us from having official sponsors, so we made some up. *Larsen's Biscuits* and *Peniston Oils* logos were emblazoned across the side of the car. Coincidentally, when the door opened during driver changes, they shortened to 'Arse' and 'Penis'.

Euphoria Racing had prepared the car, led by engineer Steve Howard. Steve was forever coated in stubble, engine oil and fag ash, and kept his butt crack on display at all times. He and his crew, whom we nicknamed NASA, were absolutely tireless.

Steve swept away his scraggly blond hair and offered me a seat aboard his baby. The racing seat was protected by a tube roll cage, and was bolted into the bare metal floor. All semblance of road car finery was in the skip, bar the stereo.

It was clearly The Stig's responsibility to post the fastest time in qualifying to position us as high up the sixty-strong grid as possible. We put the presenters out first to ensure they completed their minimum requirement of three laps. James forgot how many laps he'd done and had to make a second run, leaving me to carry the can at the end of the session.

I hopped in and got straight on it. The BMW was a wobbly old crate and the front end was numb as a brick, but she was excellent on the brakes. The constant understeer made her a safe school pony for the presenters, but without any grunt to balance it I found the experience over-bridled.

The track was packed with cars and I lost heaps of time driving around them. There was no time to find clear position, so my fastest lap put us one place from last. Worse still – piss-boilingly, catastrophically bad – was that my time was only one tenth faster than Clarkson's.

I never saw Jeremy so happy to see me. Giddy as a schoolboy, with his overalls around his waist like a pro, he declared we were evenly matched. As his driver coach it was my duty to point out that the BMW could lap several seconds faster, that I'd simply caught terrible traffic.

'So did I. Caught traffic at Priory on my best lap,' he countered gleefully.

Behind the safety of my visor, I stuck my tongue out at him. 'OK,' I laughed. 'Let's see how we get on tonight.'

Night practice was another formal requirement for all drivers wishing to participate in a twenty-four-hour event. When the sun went down on the course, you lost all familiar visual references. No trees, no grass banks, no spectators, no sky. No track either; only the narrow yellow window twenty metres ahead provided by a set of notoriously unreliable headlights. One smash over a kerb, a bump with another racer or a flying stone could easily put an eye out, and then you played a high-speed memory game. Stir in a bunch of amateur drivers with a gutful of fear, sprinkle with gravel in the braking areas from their regular mishaps and add salt and lemon to your eyeballs for the perfect *recipe du nuit*.

We all got changed in a spare blue-carpeted room inside the race control building. If only the ladies could have tuned into my view of the boys squeezing into their tight-fitting Nomex underwear. It made the *Top Gun* shower scene look like a cold bath.

May was hopping around on one leg, trying not to fall over; Jeremy's suit was four inches too short, and Hammo was turning blonder by the second.

Hammond was rightly concerned that he barely knew the track. 'I can't even remember which one is Hangar straight. I go past the pits, then it's just ... a blur ...'

I handed him a circuit map with the gears, so he could memorise them and talk each lap through as he went.

'Right. What do I do if someone wants to get past, move over?'

'No. Hold your line and sod everyone else. They will find a way around you. Oh, and you must ditch your surfing necklace, and none of you should chew gum out there.'

'All right, Daaad.'

Choking on gum was an unlikely cause of death, but mentioning it put them in the right frame of mind. Racing was *real*.

The night session was a wake-up call for them. Having fuelled their bodies with Walkers crisps and Diet Coke, they took turns to excavate Silverstone's gravel traps.

Jeremy's grin became a more poker-faced affair as he climbed into the BM and ran off a few night laps. I then slipped on my helmet, black visor and all, and, much to Jezza's amazement, knocked three seconds off our time. We were now 42nd on the grid.

Race day brought the ultimate test of endurance and mind discipline: the driver's briefing. The only useful information I ever received in one

of these marathons was in Australia for the great race at Bathurst, where they explained the warning flags for the 180mph straight: 'A single waved yellow flag means there is a kangaroo near the track. Two waved yellows means he's on the track.'

Silverstone's Clerk of the Course read the Motor Sports Association Book of Psalms to the 200 assembled drivers. Fortunately The Stig was able to sleep through the dull moments with no one the wiser. Whilst the cameras rolled on the presenters sitting next to me, I stole forty winks.

Steve's mechanics had to whip out the engine after it had crapped itself when they warmed it up that morning. The clock was ticking. If we were too late joining, we would be barred from competing at all.

Contrived TV fakery? No, it was genuine twenty-four-carat chaos.

The boys slammed home a new unit in record time. A cloud of black diesel smoke belched from the exhaust; the beast was alive and kicking. With only twenty seconds to spare, I booted it out of the garage to start the race from the pit lane exit, dead last but one.

I managed to overtake a few people but it was hardly the stuff of Stig legend, until fate stepped in. The heavens opened. Some drivers came in for wet tyres and I smoked them by holding out on slicks. The rest of the field slowed down considerably and I carved them up like Christmas turkeys.

Truthfully, it was the first time during the whole weekend that my heart rate had risen above its nocturnal state. Driving on slicks in the wet made the BMW super-sensitive. It gripped, but would suddenly let go as though it were on ice. It was all about precision and feel; every input was critical and you drove every second of every lap, just as racing should be. My stint got us past over twenty cars and into contention for a class win.

As we settled into the night my respect for the presenters grew and grew. Sharing the changing room with them, helping them with their helmets and safety gear, I realised just how little they knew about racing, and how fearful, excited and passionate they really were.

Jeremy was glued to the results screen the whole way through the race. James looked increasingly haggard. His eyes were puffy from sleep deprivation and his face was as white as a sheet. Their lap times went up and down like a bride's nightie as they strained to navigate each circuit the same way twice.

Hammond got stuck into his night stint and I monitored from the pit wall, telling him his times and keeping him going. The human contact was vital and his pace dropped noticeably when I stopped talking.

He was taking the line I'd taught him on the Hangar straight, crossing from right to left, across the front of a car he was overtaking to line up for Stowe. A much heavier, faster GT2 Mosler sliced between them and crashed into Hammond's left side at a good 140mph.

'Guys, I've binned it,' he said over the radio.

The impact broke the BMW's wheels and suspension, crumpled the bodywork and killed the engine. It was the last thing any of us wanted to see happen to Hammond.

He stayed in the car as they dragged it back to our pit and was understandably shaken, so the cameras laid off him. Typically, Hammo's primary concern was for the car that had hit him. I soon put him right on that.

Steve's merry crew swivelled their baseball caps and tucked in. Nearly three hours later I went out and drove pretty much all through the night. I kept awake by chatting to Steve and getting him to wind up Jeremy by saying that I'd pissed in the seat. Hours felt like days.

The field was too strung out to pass anyone until another gift landed in my lap. Fog descended over the circuit, and soon it was like swimming through pea soup. Visibility was zero and it was easy to drive off on the straights, which seemed longer as you counted the seconds until the corners.

We were so far behind that it seemed reasonable to take some silly risks. I overtook as many cars as I could; some were pootling along at 40mph. Their fear was our opportunity to claw back lost time. I revelled in the conditions; it was licensed madness. When it became impossible to see past the windscreen the race was stopped for safety reasons.

They re-started it several hours later when the fog had thinned a bit and, at Jeremy's suggestion, poor James was sent out into oblivion. The rules required the presenters to drive a minimum percentage of the race, otherwise I could have done the lot for them. James was cautious, but even at a fraction of my pace he fired through the gravel trap a few times. Jeremy talked at him on the pit-to-car radio the whole time: 'Drive faster ... Slow down, save the tyres ... More speed James ...' and so on. If that didn't encourage him to get to the end, nothing would.

I slept on the floor for a total of two hours. I could sleep anywhere as long as my head was higher than my chest and my knees were bent for circulation.

The morning after, the presenters looked like zombies. Their driving styles were overloading the front tyres, chewing the rubber down to the wire cords, so we kept a careful eye on them as they ran their final stints on autopilot.

James's body was present but his mind had long since gone home and was waiting for the rest to catch up. He stared vacantly across the garage, fondling an empty teacup. Hammond had the giggles and was banging out pieces to camera, his spirits lifted again. Jeremy was running on a kind of delusional overdrive and had turned a mysterious shade of purple. He brought the car home and I take my hat off to him – he'd managed a running commentary through nearly every single lap he'd driven throughout the race.

I was extremely proud when they eventually crossed the line, third in class. That the BMW finished at all was a miracle.

Georgie – equally miraculously – held on to her waters and I hightailed it home. Forty-eight hours later, she started contractions. It was time to become a dad.

Attending the birth was not the 'mystical experience' I'd heard it described as by new-age men in the media. It looked pretty damn awful to me, but the conclusion was magical. A determined little girl wrapped me around her finger on Day One and I drove our new family home comfortably below the speed limit.

As for my racing career, my recently acquired knowledge of the Square Mile wasn't helping me raise the finance needed to run a go-kart race, let alone a NASCAR campaign, but I kept my radar on.

I'd started writing for *Autosport* magazine, reviewing new and exciting racing cars. Out of the blue, they sent me to Orlando, Florida, to drive Red Bull's top-flight NASCAR at Lakeland Speedway. It was a dream ticket.

The last British hopeful who went to the States hunting for a NASCAR test was British Touring Car Champion Jason Plato. They welcomed him with a little southern hospitality.

Introduced to the legendary Dale Earnhardt in the pits, Jason waxed lyrical about the prospect of joining the series. Dale never took off his

wraparound sunglasses and his moustache barely moved as he drawled, 'This here racin' ain't for puppy dawgs. This here's where the big dawgs take a piss.' That's why they called Dale 'The Intimidator'.

On my arrival at Lakeland I was told to look for the team's crew chief, Randy Cox. It came as no surprise. On my previous visit to America I'd met Dick Trickle, the famous racing driver.

Randy bolted me into the Camry without so much as a shock and awe safety briefing. It was stuffed with so many restraints I had to wedge myself into the seat.

'Y'all set?'

I gave Randy a thumbs up.

'OK, let's go.'

I had 800 horsepower at my command in an instant and, with it, a hurricane of sound.

At the end of each short straight I leant heavily on the brakes and worked at straight-lining into and past the apex. The car nose-dived and fired in with superb accuracy and stability. I screwed the speed off, let the big girl turn through the middle and followed the test driver's advice by opening her out towards the large black tyre marks on the retaining wall as I exited. The power, the beautiful power sang and screamed on the straights as the wheels spun over invisible bumps in the asphalt.

The ever-present concrete wall would punish the slightest deviation from the racing line. It was a superb feeling, like street racing but with more grunt and grip. I drove harder with every lap and my twenty-something passes went all too quickly. It left me wanting more.

'Where do I sign?' was my first question as I clambered out of the car. If only it was that easy.

The all-important debrief with Randy took place the same evening at Hooters Bar over a bowl of chicken wings and a beer.

'When you first drove outta the pits I was takin' bets from the guys on which lap you'd crash,' he chuckled. 'But the times you did in that car, with that set-up, were really impressive.'

I'd narrowly outpaced their benchmark time on lap seven, in spite of driving on older, slower tyres. Not bad for a first drive at a new track, but that's where the honeymoon ended. Red Bull already had a driver line-up, so I thanked the team and flew back to the UK. They say it's better to have loved and lost than never to have loved at all.

* * *

Series 10 of *Top Gear* was there to console me. Jenson Button had attacked my time in the Suzuki the previous year and failed to beat it. (He subsequently won the Formula 1 title, so I seriously doubt that keeps him up at night.)

Lewis Hamilton was next in the queue. He'd just ended his first season in F1, wiped the floor with his team-mate and former champ Fernando Alonso and narrowly lost out on the title. Now it was time for the Big One: what could the lad from Stevenage do in a Suzuki fartbox?

I'd heard so much hype about Lewis that I was keen to check him out for myself. He arrived in McLaren team gear, but hanging loose. He was disarmingly laid-back and we warmed to him immediately.

I drove him around the slowly drying track to show him the best lines. Apart from Webber, I think he was the only F1 driver to let me do that. I wanted to help him adapt to the majestic Suzuki so I could see what he was truly capable of. I reminded him to get it sideways into the penultimate corner and pin the throttle, not to drive it properly like an F1 machine. The more I explained, the more he listened. This was no prima donna. Sure, he was composed, but not in the least arrogant.

The odd thing about his laps was that they didn't look special, they were neither lairy nor super-smooth, yet his times in the wet were absolutely stunning. He was doing 1.46, then 1.45 whilst the track was still greasy.

His dad told him not to spin the wheels off the start line, said it was costing him time. Their rivalry was all too familiar. Lewis reacted by sticking an extra thousand rpm on his next launch and smoking the bags. He was having fun, bouncing and jiving to a cool track he found on the radio, 'Dub Be Good to Me'.

With footage in the can from his earlier runs, we waited for the conditions to improve. When Lewis went again he produced a time of 1:44.7, just 0.3 of a second slower than my best on a fully dry run. I went and checked the track. Many of the corners were practically dry, but not entirely. I played back his in-car footage and felt that he cut some cute lines through the Hammerhead chicane; but nothing unsporting. Even so, his lap was *exceptionally* fast; he was clearly a special talent. What I admired most was the way he did it so effortlessly and with such humility.

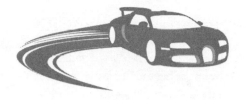

30

THE SCUD

An impeccably turned out Italian driver in his fifties picked me up at Milan Bergamo airport in an equally pristine Mercedes E Class. His immaculately honed features reminded me of Christopher Lee, aka Saruman, the slaughterer of Hobbits in *The Lord of the Rings*. From the moment he tossed my luggage into the boot until we reached our destination he kept away from the middle pedal as he guided his Mercedes missile through the rugged scenery at a cool 100. He never spoke either, apart from when a pair of construction trucks blocked our progress.

'Che cazzo stai facendo qui?' he hissed. The hapless drivers yielding their ground immediately. No one screwed with Saruman.

After that brief interruption, I dozed off whilst the best taxi driver in the world dispatched 150km and finally rounded a hairpin to reveal the picturesque resort of Riva, nestled on the shore of Lake Garda. We descended sharply into the spectacular basin hewn into the Dolomite Mountains by ancient glaciers. The sun twinkled on the vast restless pool of water below.

Riva was full of buses downloading their quota of blue-rinsed and pastel-suited holidaymakers. They joined the ranks of cool Italians wearing insect-like sunglasses and an army of Germans chomping on Frankfurters and chips.

The twisting Gardesana road, with its unparalleled views and dramatically claustrophobic tunnels, was a driver's paradise. Winston Churchill called it the Eighth Wonder of the world. I called it heaven, because it was my first day on set as a member of a James Bond stunt team to film the opening chase scene for *The Quantum of Solace*.

Production schedules for big movies lasted several months at a time and filming had become more than a part-time role for me. There was a familiar camaraderie with film crews, but I spared more than a few thoughts for my Army mates who were serving overseas with distinction.

I had reluctantly called time on my Army career when it finally became impossible to balance all my commitments, but the bond of brotherhood was unbroken. Military service had changed my outlook on the world forever; anything felt achievable, especially when you were with the right people.

Many of us brought our families out and I was joined by my very own Bond girls. With breakfast under the canopy of a fine restaurant and the water lapping at our feet, Georgie and I found Garda life very appealing. Our baby girl nodded off with the occasional point and shriek of 'Ca' – short for car in my book, but Georgie insisted she meant 'cat'. The unforgettable scenery, sharp company and Italian glamour made 'work' seem like a holiday.

Balancing multiple high-octane roles was challenging in every sense. Above all, experiencing such a variety of cutting-edge machinery was the spice of life. *Top Gear* needed me to return to England to film a 'Scud', the Ferrari 430 Scuderia. Ferrari only had it in the UK for one day and Wilman was adamant that I got on a plane.

The Scuderia edition was the super-light, super-sporting, weapons-grade version of the mid-engined Ferrari 430, itself a balanced demi-god. It was the kind of tool that founder Enzo Ferrari first set up his factory to build: uncompromising engineering excellence.

The Scud was epic. It was stripped of all but the basic functions and the weight reduction spent the horsepower all the better around the track. The soft leather wheel was chunky to grip. A flick of a dial to 'race' mode denied any electronic traction interference and upgraded the paddle gear-shift from stun to kill. Each staccato crack beckoned the next gear in just sixty milliseconds.

Schumacher had a hand in the development process that had begun with the original mid-engined Dino in 1970, before passing through the 308 to the 355, and the 430 was the ground-breaking result.

Within a lap I recognised that no supercar had ever held this level of mechanical front grip. It gave such phenomenal feedback through the steering that you felt every movement of the tyre. It was as if the car knew where you wanted it to go before you did.

There was no time to chew the fat with Ferrari before I sprinted back to the airport and returned to Italy. Just enough to say their car was magnificent and had we been on fresh tyres, rather than a set pre-digested by Clarkson, the lap time would have been much faster.

Subsequently, I tested the Ferrari 458 and for a nano-second was beguiled by its voluptuous styling into believing it was better than the Scud. But you can't improve on perfection, and certainly not by replacing a vital organ like the handbrake with a push-button fuse. That really only left the Scud with one rival for the mantle of Uber-Coupe.

The Aston Martin DBS was one of the most sophisticated machines on the market, perhaps the best all-round sports car ever built. Its graceful curves kept its brute performance covert; beneath the mature exterior was a recalcitrant wild child. It boasted six litres of devilish horsepower, totalling over 500bhp. The V12 engine responded to every millimetre of movement in the throttle, like an F1 car. It howled on full song but reduced to a whispering burble at low revs. The ceramic brakes clamped like vices but with such sensitivity that you could modulate them at the limit of grip from its fat tyres.

There was scarcely any visible difference between the DB9 and the DBS, yet the slightly lowered, delicately enhanced suspension turned the girl next door into a supermodel. Beneath her hemline, the heightened technology of the braking and traction control systems was streets ahead. Where most anti-skid systems prevented the tyre from getting anywhere near to locking during braking, the Aston's onboard computer took it to the limit several times a second and you sensed its work underfoot.

The traction control was equally aggressive on acceleration. You could leave it turned on, stamp the right pedal with a mere modicum of ability and impress your friends without decapitating them.

The scooped bucket seats wrapped around your kidneys, forging man with machine. Ergonomically, the driving position was perfect, with the centre of the helm directly in line with the shoulders, creating a natural 45-degree bend at the arms and easy legroom. The DBS had stacks of grip but she ran on the edge, reacting to the slightest toggle of the wheel, biting your hand off if you were rough. Once you stuck it sideways

though, you could spin the tyres like Catherine wheels all day long. Just as well I practised that extensively for a job that was already in the pipeline.

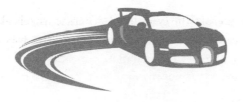

31

UNTAMED: HAMPSHIRE HEIST

Christmas gifts stuffed into already bursting bags, late-night shoppers scurried to and fro across the central promenade of Basingstoke's indoor Mall. The *Top Gear* team appeared like a team of master criminals in the final seconds before closing. We had until 5am – when the floor cleaners took over – to capture a two-car chase through the centre's tight corridors. The plan was for Clarkson to give an unusual review to the new Ford Fiesta, presenting it as the perfect getaway car – with a bad guy in a black Corvette in hot pursuit.

Security gave us the all clear whilst they flushed out the tardiest customers.

'Saddle up, big boy, bring her in.'

I pulled my baseball cap down to mask my face, climbed into the Z06 and cranked the V8. Engine growling, I edged past the line of camera phone-wielding onlookers and lined up on the marble floor to test for traction. Ahead of me lay 100 metres of glistening marble, fringed with giant potted plants. To either side a shimmering parade of shopfronts.

My shortlist for this indoor ballet came down to the BMW M3, the Vauxhall Monaro and the Corvette – all rear-wheel driven, manual with grunt. The Vette won because, surprisingly, it was the smallest.

A Corvette was on long-term loan to one of the editors of *Top Gear* magazine. He nearly had an embolism when we asked to borrow it.

'Ben, *please* promise me you won't put a single mark on it,' he pleaded. 'Basically, it's *my* car. I've had it for almost a year and I've promised GM I'll hand it back to them in immaculate condition.'

A hostage negotiator never employs a negative inflection during a crisis situation.

'Everything will be fine,' I said. 'We're only using it for one night.' I omitted to mention the part where the Corvette was supposed to crash through a concession stall.

Producer Pat Doyle stared at the rows of plate-glass windows, mentally calculating the cost of each pane. I didn't think to mention the floor; it would have been like an ice skater asking if it was all right to scratch the rink.

'Right, Stiggy.'

'*Pat!*' I swivelled a couple of eyeballs in the direction of the nearby phalanx of locals.

'Oops …' He shot me a sheepish grin as he tapped the Corvette's lid. 'Don't forget, we've got a spare Fiesta, but only one of these lads …'

I set fire to the rear wheels by releasing the clutch at 6,000rpm, windows down to revel in the sound of freedom. The Vette barely moved. The marble was like ice.

'Traction's off on that bad boy, then?' Andy Harris, our rescue co-ordinator, could barely contain his excitement. He was a big blond lad with rosy cheeks. You wouldn't argue with him if he was slicing you out of a burning wreck.

'This one's set up as the Lord intended – no stability.'

I backed up to the start point in front of Debenhams and read the shopping list in my right hand:

Approach BHS via escalator, 5 paces wide, break right at circle plinth into store foyer, hbrake, power j-turn round, kill mannequin & exit

Corvette wide slide after fwd handbrake turn past Jewellers, Onto 6 pace width track, Cars split here, concrete plinth into 2 track straight to M&S (60ft)

Head on and hbrake turn, near miss Ford Fiesta/miss window, big overhead wide shot slide uphill to tree roundabout + donut at Costa, smash tables, exit street Pizza Hut, slide and stop.

Jeremy was working his magic with the Fiesta a little later in the night, but for the initial line-ups my friend and multiple rally champion Mark Higgins was in the hot seat. His car control was phenomenal but he always licked his lips when he was nervous. He pulled up alongside in the neon green hatchback.

'That put-put is your sort of bag, isn't it, Mark?'

'Piss off, you knob. *I* didn't pick it.' He cracked a smile as he loosened the handbrake. 'Looking forward to seeing you turn that whale around the BHS lobby ...'

We broke the circuit down into sections and Andy Harris placed fire points at appropriate intervals. There was no way of rehearsing a sequence in a place like this; practising posed as much of a danger to people and equipment as doing it for real. Mark and I decided to run the chase piecemeal. Phil rolled the cameras from the moment we set off, just in case there were no second chances.

'ACTION ...'

Mark and I dropped our respective clutches. The lightweight Ford shot past Ann Summers whilst I sat there spinning. Eventually I pulled forward, wagging the Vette's tail at Abbey Bank, shifting to second at Clark's, then slithering right between two plinths towards Burton's. I slipped in behind Mark as he braked to stop under the escalator.

I followed suit, but somehow the ABS re-activated. Sensing an oil slick, the pedal crackled under my foot and refused to direct brake fluid to where it was most urgently needed. The Vette pulled up behind the Fiesta with no more than twelve inches to spare.

We reversed back to our starting point where Gavin, *TG*'s young Scottish researcher, was laughing insanely and pointing to the lines of bubbling rubber now marking the previously pristine floor. He knew full well these would become his brain-ache come Monday morning.

'Er ... Sorry about that ...'

'Don't be daft,' he said. 'Nothing you can do about it. Sounds mega.'

We popped the bonnet and wrenched out the ABS fuse. 95 per cent of the time, ABS was great. We just happened to be operating in the 5 per cent window where it wasn't. Pulse braking, modulating the brake pressure manually, was the only way to slow effectively on ice. You had to lock the tyres momentarily and release them in time to steer.

Throwing in a kiss and crotch dance for our benefit, Iain May repositioned his camera behind a hot plastic chick in the Ann Summers

window. The next stage involved gliding around the escalator, entering BHS in single file, then pulling a sharp 180 and coming straight out again.

Mark and I recced the foyer with the BHS manager. It was the size of a living room and bordered by sharp-edged platforms loaded to the gunwales with rails of clothing, mannequins and toys. There was barely enough room for the Vette to park, let alone skid in sideways.

We set up a mannequin in some racy underwear for me to wipe out and prepared to shoot. I whacked the volume up on the radio wedged into the door pocket. Phil's voice blared, 'Stand by to film, all cameras. Cars, are you ready?'

Our beeping horns echoed around the ceilings.

'ACTION, ACTION.'

Mark feathered the Fiesta, allowing me to keep up in the Corvette, then we nailed it side by side down the corridor past Iain and his plastic friend with less than a foot separating us from the kerbing of the shop-fronts and the marble edges of the central islands.

The Café Nero concession underneath the escalator loomed into view. Time to brake. Mark surged ahead. The Corvette nosed round a display of flapjacks just as the front wheel snagged from the force of braking. I released the middle pedal and carried the extra speed to avoid piling into the cash register.

Mark pulled a modest 180 inside BHS as I zigzagged towards the entrance. The foyer had seemed a lot bigger on foot. As I crossed the threshold the marble gave way to linoleum. I added a few mph and yanked the wand of plenty towards the roof.

The handbrake failed to lock the rear wheels and the car didn't turn *at all*. I sped towards the Christmas ornaments and emergency stopped, thanking my lucky stars that lino was phenomenally grippy stuff. Mark accelerated away, leaving me to make an Austin Powers three-point turn without the benefit of front-wheel drive.

I could see the skimpily dressed mannequin pointing at me and laughing in the rear-view mirror. I buried the throttle in reverse and hit her just hard enough to wipe the smile off her face, then wheelspun out of the store.

That had not gone well in my book. I walked into BHS for the verdict. Phil and six of the boys were creasing up with laughter at the playback on his monitor.

'Can we do that again?' I said. 'Just a splash of water on the deck and it should spin properly next time ...'

'Nope.'

The lino was covered in tyre marks. On closer inspection I realised that the rubber had actually burnt into the polymer. Pat, ever the optimist, called for Gavin to bring some soapy water.

The next scene was even more demanding. With a crew filming from the bridge, we needed to drive up two narrowing corridors split by a whopping marble-sided arboretum towards a large circular area bordered by M&S and Costa Coffee, where we had our unit base. The open tab there was causing quite a stir amongst the fire crews. The boys were cutting a swathe through gargantuan quantities of coffee and cake. It was not quite midnight, and they were already on the brink of serious abdominal injury.

We tore out of BHS and into the open corridor. I flicked the Vette sideways, its arse a couple of feet away from a fully stocked jeweller's window, and dived through the minute gap that separated Next from a marble island. Mark raced into the main hallway, pulled a 180 around the palm tree at its centre and we went head to head. I pulled a rapid 360, swatting aside the chairs we had planted outside Costa.

We rolled through one set-up after another. A rising walkway gave the Vette every excuse to light up its rear wheels. We flattened strategically placed Teddy bears at Clintons, boshed a stack of watermelons and arrived at the first floor gangway.

Only a wooden handrail and a thin pane of glass now separated us from thin air and the floor below – enough to stop an over-excited child but not a tonne of car. We didn't have time to put it to the test; something far more dangerous had arrived.

Jeremy feverishly thumbed his script as he walked through the atrium in his stock uniform of baggy woolly pully and blue jeans. He threw a lofty one-armed salute to us on the upper deck.

'I imagine you're a dog with two dicks in this place.'

'Oh yes.'

God bless him. The whole chase had been Jezza's mad idea, and thanks to Wilman's miracle factory, there we were doing it. I chased Jeremy on camera for the rest of the night as he skidded through the sequence we had mapped earlier. Jeremy's tongue-in-cheek review ended with the

Fiesta plunging into the sea during an amphibious assault by the Royal Marines on a North Devon beach. But that came later.

When Phil called a 'wrap' on proceedings four hours later, we were relieved and disappointed in equal measure. We'd pulled off the near impossible task of shooting a car chase through a treacherously narrow shopping centre without damaging the cars.

I took a short cut towards the car park exit and a rusty metal spike came out of nowhere to meet me. I anchored up and felt the back of my neck freeze. It was like walking out of the casino with the jackpot, only to trip and drop the lot down a storm drain. The rear of the Vette skidded across the red painted lines and the nose-mounted mini camera came within an inch of being terminally kebabed.

I handed the keys to Pat – resplendent in a Russian trapper's hat with the flaps down – without further delay.

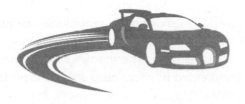

32

BUS RACING

Every now and then evolution takes a backward step. The decision to drop London's iconic double-decker Routemaster in favour of the Bendy Bus was more of a quantum leap.

I had the pleasure of driving some 'fast laps' aboard a Routemaster at Dunsfold and marvelled at its stability. Controlling something so big and potentially destructive was awesome. The giant rubber treads churned at the tarmac and emitted truly threatening groans, but I quickly figured out that it wouldn't topple over, regardless of what I did with the steering. Replacing this Goliath of public transport with a vehicle that could drift sideways to its heart's content but couldn't turn a street corner was one of Ken Livingstone's particular triumphs.

Inspired by the newt-owning mayor, we decided to measure the performance of a range of buses by racing them against each other at Lydden Hill in Kent, a one-mile track with as many frills as Ryanair. I hooked up with our Australian director, Owen, to plan the shoot. 'O' was a laid-back surfer dude from Sydney with floppy hair, big Ray Bans and a generous pearly smile. He was chilled, but took no bullshit.

The buses were heavily modified with roll cages, impact structures and toughened Perspex windows to cocoon the drivers when battle commenced. I gave them all the once-over and we decided to weld some extra mounts for the seats where they joined the rust-eaten floors. Our range of relics included one double-decker, a single-deck coach, a

Hopper and two Bendies. Now we just needed some nuts behind the wheel.

Touring car drivers sprang to mind. They were game for a laugh, didn't take themselves too seriously and had the kind of car crash control that made great telly.

In between jumping in and out of different buses to make up the numbers, I cued the drivers with specific moves. Since none of us had drifted a bus before, I climbed aboard Hammond's Bendy to lay down a marker. She was hardly top of the range. The electrics were dead, so we kick-started the thing by thumping the battery with a sledgehammer. I fired the engine and waited several minutes to build enough pressure in the system to release the air brakes and move forward.

Hammond climbed aboard and took a ringside seat just behind my left shoulder, one hand on the steel passenger pole that joined floor to ceiling. Our combined mental age: about twelve.

'Go on, go on,' he gurgled, his liquid brown eyes glinting with excitement from beneath his Tina Turner styled mullet. It was times like these I most enjoyed with RH.

I lifted the parking brake lever and arced it forward, taking up the slack on the footbrakes as I selected *drive*. Owen gave us the all clear and I floored it. I had no idea how the beast would react, but I had a basic plan.

Once the needle touched 50mph I wrenched the giant steering wheel as far to the left as I could, winding three turns of lock. The bus lolled to the left and shook on its tired suspension, then I swung the wheel fully in the opposite direction to the accompaniment of muted expletives from my pole-dancing passenger. The rear half of the vehicle switched direction and pivoted to catch up at twice the rate of the front.

I repeated the process with every ounce of my strength and the bus began to drift. I kept the steering hard right and headed off the tarmac on to the dirt section used for rallycross. Loose pebbles clattered around the wheel arches as 12 tonnes of tin careered through the curve. I turned to check how close the rear section was to the Armco barrier bordering the perimeter. *Bloody close.* I kept my foot on the gas. Hammond was bursting at the seams with laughter. Mission accomplished.

'This is such a crap job sometimes,' I said.

'Terrible … puerile. Days like this you really have to drag yourself out of bed in the morning.' RH slapped my shoulder and climbed off.

The other drivers strapped themselves into their respective cockpits, poised for action. We released them with strict orders of 'no contact' until we had some shots in the can. The days of the car football free-for-all were long gone. The boys notched up their response levels precisely in line with our instructions, but we knew something pithy was brewing.

Anthony Reid had joined the regular band of reprobates. At 50 years of age he struck you as a quaint, well-spoken gent, with neat facial features to match the ever present vintage racing cap. I've held lucid conversations with Reid, some of which have even bordered on the intelligent, but remain convinced that the compartment inside his head where his brain should be contains some kind of dark matter instead. Reid was lapping his little white coach faster than anyone.

'OK, fellas, that's enough of the boring shit,' Owen twanged over the radio. 'Get stuck in.'

The northernmost corner was a hairpin atop a sharp hill which dropped down to Paddock, a fast right-hander where the track crested a brow and joined the home straight. The main camera unit was positioned after the finish, beside the race control tower, which consisted of one cabin dropped from a great height on to another to form Lydden Hill's homage to the Leaning Tower of Pisa. I joined it as the herd of titans thundered into view.

Hammo was stuck in the middle of the throng, presenting superb pieces to camera whilst Armageddon unfolded around him. The Routemaster charged up his inside with two wheels on the grass, and the second Bendy followed suit to his outside. The violence of the ensuing collisions made everyone take two steps back, watching through the gaps between our fingers. Hammo took the hits and rolled out some spiel about disabled access and seating capacity.

There was absolutely no room for another vehicle on the track, but that didn't stop Reid. All four wheels on the grass, then teetering on to two, he speared his way up alongside the Routemaster, windows breaking like clashing cymbals.

Reid flew around the park, getting pinched occasionally between the bigger boys who otherwise trailed in his wake. Showers of broken glass filled the air, pneumatic fluid bled, radiator steam hissed and rubber bubbled. There was no such thing as a glancing blow with these leviathans; every knock sheared off a sizeable chunk of metal and spun it across the tarmac. One access panel landed right in front of us.

The Bendies slid down the main straight, tails swishing one way then the other at 90 degrees to the front deck. One stonked into the cab of Hammond's machine then swatted Tom Chilton's snail-like double-decker on the rebound, but Tom soon had an opportunity to restore his honour.

During a break in the action we set up cameras by the sharp bank at the Rally Cross intersection and told Tom to roll it. The earthen mound looked perfect for the job if he could turn sharply with enough speed. After several attempts, Tom became the first person I know of to drive a double-decker on two wheels without toppling. Luckily, we had an ace up our sleeve.

'So you want me to ram him going into that corner over there, yah?' Reid enunciated in the crispest Queen's English, as if being asked to serve tiffin.

I nodded. 'I'll cue you in on the radio so you can run up and hit him on the rear right just as he goes up the bank.' I directed his thousand-yard stare towards the appropriate point on Tom's flank.

'O … K …'

We handed Tom a neck brace and some extra Brylcreem to help ease his blond afro into his helmet as Reid started lapping well in advance of the shot, for no apparent reason.

'He's not all there, is he?' Owen said. 'I mean, even you guys reckon Reidy's a bit out there, right?'

I shrugged. 'A little crazy. He's still got it, though.'

Reid burst past the stationary double-decker one final time at terminal velocity.

'Tom, is that thing running now?'

'All set. Let's do it.'

Given the fact that he'd never rolled a bus before, Tom was a model of composure.

'OK, go *now*!'

He lumbered off, gradually building speed whilst Reid continued to circulate at full pelt. Tom reached the corner as Reid flew down the straight.

'Feather it a touch, Reidy …'

Tom lurched up the bank on two wheels and Reid pummelled into him, kept his foot down and punched the Routemaster on to its side. The top deck fell with a mighty crash but was barely damaged. The Bendies

were also – depressingly – indestructible. We sawed through the joint in the middle of one, so the front and rear sections were only held together by pneumatic hoses, and they still wouldn't separate when rammed.

The rest of the buses were toast. The freshly coiffed grass in the middle of the circuit had been shredded and seared, and the track was littered with their remains. Despite repeated heart surgery, not one was driveable by the end of the shoot. They bore fitting testimony to how much could be achieved in a single day with some nifty planning, a stellar group of drivers and a great crew. Sixty tonnes of action cut together into a great film.

33

LOOSE CANNON

Policemen develop a dark sense of humour in the line of duty. Hardly surprising given the suffocating volume of guidelines and targets they swim through on a daily basis wearing high-vis armbands.

When Avon & Somerset Constabulary arrested a notorious drug dealer, his Mitsubishi Evo 7 was seized and sentenced to death for being purchased with the profits of crime. Rather than crush it, they approached *Top Gear* for a more public execution. Happy to oblige.

We pitched up at Bovington Camp to film a final confrontation between the Evo and the British Armed Forces. The vast training area encompassed every terrain from tarmac to gravel, jumps, woods and water. The idea was for Jeremy to set off with the Army in hot pursuit – with no quarter asked for, or given.

In the *Top Gear* corner: a road car backed by our hairy-arsed technology team. In the Army corner: the Mastiff armoured vehicle, Trojan tank, Panther advanced command vehicle and Jackal hunter killer, backed by the might of British Aerospace, Supacat and the MoD.

The military were equipped with .762 and .50cal heavy machineguns capable of putting 600 rounds the size of golf balls clean through an engine block, and several more beside it. Jezza was armed with a pack of Marlboro Lights.

I took our gangster wheels for a warm-up along a closed lane to record some noise from the exhaust. The previous owner had invested nearly

£100k souping it up and we wound the turbo boost to its maximum output: a whopping 550 horsepower. It had masses of torque and all four wheels leapt from the asphalt with the engine banging off the rev limiter like a rally car. It also stank of petrol.

I checked the Evo back into NASA for Steve Howard to work his magic. We popped the hood; fuel was pouring across the hot engine from the inlet rails. It was ready to burst into flames and we hadn't even filmed it.

Steve even ditched his fag. 'Andy, better get over here, mate.'

A blur of high-vis appeared as Andy Harris covered the time bomb with fireproof blankets and began pointing his fire extinguisher nozzle with a glint in his eye.

Steve stepped back to admire the view. 'Watch out, fellas – looks like Harris might finally get to shoot his load.'

Once the fuel had evaporated, Steve fixed the hatchet job as best he could, but I had my doubts the Evo would survive until lunch.

Filming a chase like this for a movie might take weeks. We had two days.

The terrain was suitable for tanks and the hardiest 4x4 machinery. The Evo had minimal ground clearance, so we jacked up the suspension and shielded the underside of the engine with sheet steel to protect its vital organs. Standard road tyres would have spun hopelessly around the muddy ranges, so we upgraded with rally spec gravel jobs with knobbly edges.

Managing so many assets over multiple locations, communicating with the Army brass and creatively directing was murdering Phil's schedule. The boy was stressed, biting his nails back to the knuckle, and if that wasn't enough his phone kept ringing with Jeremy's last-minute changes to the script.

I'd already scouted the area with Phil. The upper plateau was strewn with lanes bordered by thick wooden posts, and a broad sweep of pale yellow dust leading to four rocky chutes dropped almost vertically to a sandy basin littered with trees, berms and jumps. There was also a minefield, several tracked forests and a live firing range for the grand finale. I hooked up with the military to choreograph some moves.

Dressed from top to toe in tan desert fatigues, full body armour and helmets, the lads looked cosy under the baking summer sun. I was sitting in a motorised Molotov cocktail, but felt substantially more comfortable in jeans and a T-shirt.

To keep it simple, the Jackal's OC would lead the other three vehicles. 'So, Jackal,' I said, 'there's a pile of rocks ahead by the fence line, over.' 'Seen.'

'I'll handbrake-turn right behind them, come back in this direction and skim past you. You all follow, over.'

'Roger, Jackal will lead.'

'Mastiff received.'

'Panther received.'

And so on.

The one I kept a close eye on was the 62-tonne Trojan tank with its spike-toothed bulldozer spade hanging off the front. The driver, who was often unsighted, was quieter on the radio than the other three. When we were parked up he had an uncomfortable habit of creeping forward. His thundering engine made your ribs rattle. He could flatten the Evo with a glancing blow and not even feel it, so I was keen to stay out of his way.

Staying ahead wasn't a problem. Even the 5.9-litre, diesel-powered Jackal, which was capable of 90mph across any terrain, was no match for the Evo when my right foot beat the floorboards. The Mitsubishi had rallying coursing through its veins. It bit into the rubble and thrust the chassis into a majestic four-wheel drift at every opportunity, leaving the Army for dust. The incredible thing with a high-powered four-wheel drive was that regardless how sideways it went, you just kept your foot flat out and the steering practically straight to drive out of it.

The deep ruts in the muddy tracks tested the steel plating. I crashed down them and listened to the panging of rocks smashing the undertray like a sumo wrestler's dinner gong. Easing off on the straights and taking longer routes around the obstacles kept them close. We were ready to shoot.

The four camera crews deployed on to an area they'd never seen like it was their own back yard. The way they could instantly assess an area and find a beautiful shot said it all. I'd explained during the briefing that vision from the military wagons was poor, but found Iain crouched at the top of a vertical cutting.

'Morning, big cock, am I all right here?'

'You'll get a lovely close-up of the wheels as they crush you. The drivers can only see ground or sky from inside these chutes so best shift further up the side of the bank ...'

'Oh, all right then.'

There was no shortage of machismo from the crew, and in some ways I had become their unofficial safety supervisor. They had impeccable standards, but I rarely slept before a big shoot like this for imagining the hazardous scenarios they might face and ways to overcome them.

A sexy, high-pitched whine rose in the background. I scanned the plateau for its source as a dust devil spun in front of us.

'Iain …'

'Got it.' His first shot of the day.

The clatter of rotor blades suggested we were about to be joined by 'Flying TV', a Robinson 44 with a gyro-stabilised camera flown by 'Q'. Quentin Smith was a second-generation stunt pilot, Freestyle Helicopter Champion and the first heli pilot to circumnavigate the world. He was late thirties and lean, with a neat quiff and a prim French moustache to complement his silk cravat and black leather boots. His thoughts regularly ran away with him, but he usually returned intact. Q more often than not puffed on a pipe, but occasionally plucked a Havana cigar from his inside pocket.

'Castro' … puff … 'makes for a bloody fine smoke, hmm, old boy' … puff.

'Sure does, Q. I'm kicking up a lot of dust out there, is that a problem for you when we get close to the trees?'

'Absolutely *no* problem, old chap. I can cut around those and come down and up, and up and down and shoot through – should be a beautiful shot, yah?'

His hands swooped and dived at the appropriate points to underscore the strategy.

'Don't big up your part, Q. All that flying's a piece of piss. The real skills are in the Evo, *right*?'

He clapped both my shoulders, gave them a squeeze and marched off laughing. Q was basically God in a flying suit.

The blue 44 pulled gently into a hover a few feet from the ground. I had UHF for talking to Phil and VHF to pick up with Q and co-ordinate our movements. The radio chattered as Phil took to the podium and began to conduct his orchestra.

'All vehicles are coming through this bumpy lane then across the big open area. Casper and Toby, if you get the big wides … Iain and Dan, get some tight edgy shots. Everyone stand by and no one else comes into this area now, I want complete lockdown.'

I lined up with the Army toys out of shot behind a ridge and signalled, 'Vehicles ready.'

'Charlie Victor standing by,' Q announced from the heavens.

With us in position, four cameras primed and a bird in the air, Phil released the Furies.

I feathered the approach to the lane, took the long route behind a pile of stone and flicked the Evo right with the Jackal cutting across my back end. We bounced along the lane; I zapped the power and dropped the entourage to head around the outside of the open plateau. I kicked the Evo into a long, sweeping powerslide, sending clouds of dust into the air. The Army vehicles punched through it and closed in on their tighter line, while Q was 50 feet above their heads, then plummeting through the air to less than 20 feet above ground and swooping across my windscreen. It made my hair stand on end.

The chalky ground looked like an even sheet of paper at 70mph, and I slammed into some hidden troughs so hard my feet came off the pedals. The car surely couldn't take it. The chutes carved into the hillside, that had each appeared so distinctive on foot, now looked identical. Only one contained a camera and I had to choose quickly to make my exit.

I spied the minute cairn I'd placed as a marker amongst a sea of stones and dived into the chute beside it. My arms went straight as my head pressed into the head-rest and my stomach lurched. I never even saw Iain's camera. The Evo shot down the earth corridor, absorbing some bloodcurdling bangs from the ruts as they boshed the sump guard. The car was a criminal; it deserved it. Shot One was in the can.

We gave Q another angle on the plateau, which involved him hovering in my line of fire near the precipice and gaining altitude as I slid towards him. Working alongside skill of that magnitude was epic; I put my faith in Q without hesitation.

We descended into the basin. I arrived from a flat section that dropped, caught some air and crashed further down whilst the Army vehicles took everything in their stride. Sand filled the wheel arches. Somehow the Evo kept going.

The plan was for the vehicles to do a frenetic Benny Hill chase in and out of the trees and knolls of the basin until we felt our sporadic routes conflict. I kept my eyes peeled as we whipped around its tighter confines, only to see a big blue hornet appear on the other side of some trees and begin mirroring my route. I spun around to accelerate through the heli's

camera frame and made eye contact with Q. The cheeky sod yawed side-ways with one hand on the collective and the other pulling at his steering handle, yet still managed to give me a wave. I returned the greeting with my middle finger.

The heli hovered so close to the action at times I could almost touch it. We kept on going until I lost track of the Army and called it quits.

Having never been a fan of either the Evo or the Subaru Impreza as road cars, I had reluctantly fallen in love with my machine. Its narrow rally tyres gave as much grip on the loose as slip on the road. The wanton grunt was addictive; its catapulting slides across tarmac or gravel were so enjoyable I never wanted to stop.

The Bovington chase unfolded largely according to Jeremy's master plan and Phil's shot list. We knocked out a bunch of 'ups and passes', speeding past camera through woods and lanes, so that we were ready for Jezza to play his part.

He pitched up in his pride and joy, the mighty Mercedes CLS Black. On seeing me he parted his legs and extended his hands to and from his groin, treating me to the 'big wanker' greeting. I held my thumb and forefinger half a centimetre apart and rewarded him the traditional 'infinitesimally small cock' response.

'What's it like?' he asked.

'It doesn't get any better than this. But you have to pull the handbrake like a demented milkmaid; the cable's knackered.'

'Good.' Jezza was on typically jovial form, in his element around a bunch of nutters with expensive hardware. He was a huge supporter of the military. In a former life he was probably a general, the kind that never got shot. He joined the story together and inserted his typically brutal humour, referring to the £400k command vehicle as a Fiat ice cream van and ad libbing with the Army boys about how he planned to give them a good dusting.

Jeremy did some quality driving between out-takes of him scurrying about on a minefield rigged with pyrotechnics, sneaking up behind the tank and being 'shot at'. He placed the Evo with absolute precision on the edge of a cliff and tore around the place with abandon.

We then waited a *Top Gear* hour (fifteen of our Earth minutes) for a deployable bridge to extend over a ravine, the gag being that Jeremy would make use of it whilst his pursuers lost sight of him.

'Stay on me, Phil. Keep cameras on me, OK?'

'Oh shit,' Casper muttered, spinning his camera in JC's direction.

I skipped over to Phil. 'If he hits that bridge at more than 15mph the engineers reckon it might shake him off.'

Phil kiboshed any *Dukes of Hazard* aspirations Jeremy might have been harbouring and we filmed him grudgingly executing a model crossing.

The Evo had the measure of the military until the live firing range. The soldiers locked and loaded with live 1:1 tracer and lubed up their respective working parts.

In spite of much lobbying from environmentalists and his fellow presenters, we decided against Jeremy continuing to drive the Evo in person. Steve fitted it with a remote control unit and Jeremy ran off some in-car footage to marry up with the external shots.

A lot was being made of the precise direction the Evo would follow. The rules of the range required cameras to film from a long way back, so the operators were keen to fix visual references of the proposed route in order to pull focus on their lenses. My experience of remote-controlled vehicles suggested it would travel in every direction *but* the planned one.

Andy had the soldiers line their vehicles broadside to the range along a raised concrete platform. They gripped the butts of their guns against clenched jaws and racked the working parts. Interspersed between them, our film crews loaded fresh batteries and aimed their weaponry with similar anticipation. A few seconds later, the Evo set off.

The machinegunners let rip. One of the Gimpies jammed within a few seconds. '*Stoppage ...*' He cleared it, but without adjusting the gas, so it jammed again.

Sure enough, the Evo soon developed a mind of its own. Under heavy fire it veered off the dirt track and took cover in the undulating heather. The car dived up and down the network of gullies, wildly out of control, giving the gunners a serious run for their money.

A sustained burst of .50cal finally tore holes the size of a fist through the engine block, steering wheel, seat and boot lid. The editors combined the footage so brilliantly in post-production that it looked like the rounds were licking Jeremy's heels. More's the pity.

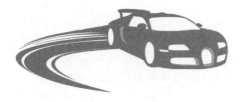

34

THE WHITE BUBBLE

Three million visitors descended on Blackpool in September 2008 to witness a million lights coming to life. They clutched dribbly ice creams, squeezed into tight swimming costumes, queued for musicals, looked for thrills and got the beers in. Meanwhile, in Basel, Switzerland, three middle-aged men were preparing to run out of fuel trying to join them.

Our heroes were aiming to make the 750-mile journey on one tankful, in a real-time assessment of fuel economy. The first to arrive would join the ranks of other luminaries – such as Kermit the Frog and Ken Dodd – to light the coastal resort's Big Candle. If none of them made it, The Stig would step into the breach.

The logistics of tracking all the way across Europe with three crews was not to be underestimated. I brought in pro drivers to pedal the crews aboard three supercharged Range Rovers. It was still a colossal workload because the whole race was effectively filmed live. There would be no pick-ups.

Clarkson set off aboard a twin turbo Jaguar XJ6 TDVI, which had a range of 655 miles on a light foot. He didn't have a light foot. May drove a Subaru Legacy Diesel with a range of 706 miles, while Hammond went for a puny three-cylinder VW Polo Bluemotion, made largely of Lycra, with a range of 740 miles.

Jeremy rightly figured he'd run dry well short of Blackpool and opted for the longer, motorway route to avoid gas-guzzling traffic jams. Hammond took the direct route, the downside being he would burn fuel traversing hills. May chose something in between.

I arrived with 'my' crew at Blackpool's central bus terminal and hopped off the National Express in the white suit. The Stig's day out in Blackpool began in the theme park. Whilst the presenters sweated traffic, I rode in a teacup through the House of Horrors. Whilst they did complicated sums about fuel consumption, I sat through a magic show, marvelling at the sparkly lights in the ceiling and the strange folk plucking rabbits from hats. Then I met a palm reader on the Pier who couldn't see my future through the white glove. She was a sweet, beautifully rounded lady with an all-year tan and mandatory headscarf.

'I can't read him,' she kept saying. 'Not unless I look into his eyes or see his hands …'

The director wouldn't hear of it. 'He never takes his gloves or helmet off. Not even when he goes to sleep.'

I lifted my visor a tad.

'Oooooooh,' she said, 'you've a bright future …'

More please.

'You'll be wealthy …'

OK …

'You're at a big crossroads. You *must leave* the old path before choosing.'

Ouch.

I snapped my visor shut before she got me fired. The truth was that I *had* been wondering what the hell I was doing with my life. Here I was, wearing a comic strip costume, having the palms of my gloves read in a seaside resort. I was having a great time – and perhaps that should have been all that mattered – but I felt like I was losing sight of the big picture. I was meant to be racing, not mincing around.

Before I could take these psychic revelations too seriously, some joss stick incense wafted across my visor, my glove's Velcro fastener got caught in a drape and I sent a cassette stall flying. All I could hear was the crew pissing themselves with laughter as mystic Meg chased after me, prattling on about the spirit world.

We moved on to the Pepsi Max at Pleasure Beach. Known as 'The Big One', it had a drop of 205 feet, a top speed of 74mph and generated 3.5G

in the corners. The fairground staff treated us like royalty; they allowed us to take over the ride for an hour. A couple of dummy runs were needed to make sure that the rearward-facing camera was bolted on securely, and then I got on with a small group of enthusiastic holidaymakers.

The ride jolted, tipped and climbed vertically. Soon the Ferris wheel below was the size of a thimble. I hated heights, but decided that if The Stig wasn't driving the rollercoaster he would be bored witless, so for his sake I pretended to fall asleep as the car began to plummet.

With my head down, all I could see through the visor was a narrow strip of the pleasure metropolis below. My stomach made its apologies and parted company with the rest of me as the car fell endlessly from the sky. Then I was hurled violently to the right as it banked hard left. I managed to maintain the same apparently nonchalant pose for the duration of the ride, never looking up but using every muscle I possessed to stay in the seat. The director was very pleased with the footage. So pleased that I went out a further four times, head down. And I got paid.

'That's a tough job you've got there, Stig,' commented the bloke behind me.

'Hellish,' I replied. 'But somebody's got to do it.'

People were fantastically patient as they waited for us to clear off their ride. We did a bunch of photos with them and headed back into the fairground. The crew were busy filming background shots when I noticed a giant chipmunk ahead. He pounded a furry paw against his chest, Tarzan-style, then pointed at me. The Stig freaked out. Ben Joiner brought his camera to bear as I froze in my tracks, turned and sprinted in the opposite direction.

The chipmunk gave chase as The Stig scarpered over a bridge, looking frantically over his shoulder until he made good his escape. Unfortunately the presenters didn't run out of gas after all, so their dreary piece on fuel economy took precedence in the edit over my Oscar-winning performance.

Next stop, the casino. The Stig won big on the fruit machines just by staring at them. We had a little help from the floor manager, who brimmed them full of coins and rigged the programme with a code I plan to use in Vegas. All that remained was to buy some candyfloss and cuddly toys for the journey to the lights.

As we walked along the pavement people jogged alongside waving their mobile phones and recorded their own pieces to camera. Everyone

was incredibly friendly. A bunch of Renault Clios started doing laps up and down the street to demonstrate how much noise they could make, then pulled a series of wheel spins. Five points out of ten, I'm afraid. If you really want to light up those tyres, Son, try using the handbrake.

We drove across to the main stage for the big moment, with an alarming number of punters in hot pursuit. I had to duck down in the back seat of the van to avoid an incident.

Radio 2's DJ Mark Goodier was whipping the crowd into a frenzy as we arrived. I walked straight through to a VIP enclosure, where celebs asked *me* how to get on to *Top Gear*. Everyone seemed to be obsessed with it.

The DJs announced the bands that would be performing live on stage to the swelling audience. When Boyzone were mentioned, they roared in their thousands. Then the DJ said, 'And we've got … *Top Gear* …' I was fully expecting to hear a pin drop.

The crowd went ape.

How could three plonkers and a storm trooper be more popular than Boyzone?

I made my way around the VIP enclosure and found the cornerstone of any social gathering: the buffet. I lined up behind Laurence Llewelyn-Bowen, lofty long-haired interior designer, and we loaded our paper plates with finger food – and I mean loaded.

'Nice outfit,' he said. 'A little impractical for dinner?'

I waved my still gloved hand in the direction of the edible pyramid I had constructed. 'It's for my cat.'

'Touché. Mind the Jalapeno peppers; could be dangerous for a man with white underpants in your line of work.'

I held the fort until the presenters finally made it at 8pm. After all that, a red-eyed Hammond won by a single minute from an excitable Jezza, the giant Duracell bunny who never slept or ate. James was nowhere in sight. His 'special route' had taken him into the back of beyond.

We three prepared to go on stage. I was deaf as a post (with my helmet amplifying the roaring crowd) and blind to boot, but I could see everyone close by was buzzing. People were happy – nodding, clapping, waving. It was an unforgettable experience.

As we walked on stage the crowd erupted. People were jumping up and down, screaming, waving and pointing. I'd never seen anything like it:

girls on boys' shoulders, banners waving, and a giant inflatable penis on a stick. No home should be without one. Jeremy and Richard went in as brazenly as ever, waving back to the crowd, taking it all in their stride. I tried not to fall over the hidden lighting cables.

I was still coming to terms with the sheer number of faces staring at us when an object on a peculiar, arcing trajectory entered my field of vision then dropped at my feet. A pair of knickers. I never knew who threw them, but I knew my life could never be the same again.

The time had come to hit the switch. Richard and Jeremy were arguing about who should.

'*You* turn them on …'

'Really, no, *you* do it …'

That was my cue. The lever sat on a big square plinth. It looked sturdy, like a beer pump. To make sure I didn't cock it up I strode across and yanked the thing hard. It turned the lights on all right; I pulled so hard the platform toppled towards me, but thankfully stayed upright. One million lights glowed, fireworks went off, hallelujah. It was Miller time.

We bundled ourselves off stage and into the crew vehicles, from where we were given a police escort back to the hotel. I got changed in the back seat, watching in disbelief as police bikes in parallel formation blocked one side junction after another to give us a clear corridor. We blew through red lights and roundabouts all the way back to the first cold beer of the day. What a night.

James and his crew arrived looking utterly ball-bagged. His hair had gone straight with tiredness, and his upper body was motionless as his legs propelled him towards the bar. Lawrence of Arabia had crossed the desert. I've never seen Jezza laugh so hard.

'*Fuck off*,' James snapped, then treated the girl behind the bar to a dazzling smile. 'Might I have a beer please, Madam?'

Three film crews had crossed half of Europe, arrived in Blackpool on time *and* captured all the footage in a single day. It was a remarkable testament to how the quirky management structure of *Top Gear* worked its magic. Our production unit was utterly extraordinary; their diet of long hours, every kind of weather and a packet of crisps made them lean, mean shooting machines. They were the unsung heroes who captured the stunning footage that brought these stories to life.

35

WHO IS THE STIG?

Without my really noticing, *Top Gear* had ballooned into a worldwide phenomenon. It was being watched by over eight million people in the UK and by upwards of 350 million in 100 other countries, generating tens of millions of pounds for the BBC. The Stig had become the poster boy for *Top Gear* magazine and led the brand's merchandising campaign on pretty much anything that stayed still long enough to have his picture stuck on it. There was everything from Stig Easter eggs to Stig soap on a rope.

Interest in the identity of the man in the white suit reached fever pitch at the end of 2008. The home team, perhaps without realising it, then managed to fan the flames.

I returned from the gym one morning to be greeted by the carpenter who was fixing our kitchen floor. He drew out a copy of the BBC's *Radio Times*, slapped it on the table and asked me to sign it.

The front cover was dominated by a photo of someone in the familiar pose, with the caption 'WHO IS THE STIG? The Nation Wants To Know, so we decided to find out …'

'Your photo's inside …'

I bit my tongue and flicked it open.

The piece inside featured the 'two chief suspects' for Stigdom and I was the only racing driver.

Text messages started raining in. People who thought I might be The Stig took the article as confirmation. Another story broke in the *Daily*

Star a few months later. A builder who said he'd worked on my house claimed I had a shrine to The Stig in my living room, complete with suit and helmet in a glass cabinet. As if. Ten days later the floodgates opened.

Georgie braved the elements – and the rumoured camera crews – to grab the day's papers.

'Oh dear, BC. You're in nearly all of them …'

My stomach lurched, but then – something I didn't expect – flooded with relief.

I rang Wilman. 'Well?'

'Well …' The minutes ticked by. 'There's no point sacking you, since we're denying it's you anyway. Just stay clear of any sodding journos.'

At the time I really appreciated Andy's loyalty. He was under a lot of pressure internally to 'get another one'.

A *News of the World* crew took photos of our old house, along with someone else's 'reasonably priced' car. Then there was a knock at our door. I was greeted by a slightly sheepish soccer dad in a checked shirt. 'Mr Collins? I think these must be for you.' He handed over a bunch of letters that had been addressed to me but delivered a couple of streets away.

'Thank you very much.'

He shifted from one foot to another. 'We've had some journalists at our place.'

'Oh really?'

'Quite a few. Photographers too. All I know is *I'm* not The Stig …'

'That makes two of us then.' I gave him a grin and thanked him for coming round.

I got a call from one of the producers a few days before the start of Series 13. I expected him to dispatch me straight to HMS *Intrepid*. 'Hope you're all set for this Wednesday. Ummm … What size overalls and helmet you use?'

'Why do you ask?'

'Can't tell you.'

'Then I can't tell you.'

'We've got something cooking for next week's guest.'

'Who is …?'

'Can't tell you that either; it might put your nose out of joint.'

We fenced for a bit until he finally admitted it was Michael Schumacher. 'We're dressing him up as The Stig to do a lap in the Ferrari FXX.

He's the only one allowed to drive that little beauty, so it throws a big smokescreen around the whole identity thing.' They hadn't yet worked out how they were going to take it from there, but needed me along for some other bits and pieces.

I couldn't wait to see the seven times F1 Champion sipping a mouldy coffee outside our decrepit cabin.

I got down to Dunsfold early for some covert filming. What happened next took my burgeoning identity crisis to another level. Schumacher had flatly refused to drive the Liana, so they wanted to film me pretending to be him pretending to be The Stig, driving the reasonably priced car.

'Have you told Michael what we're up to?'

'Oh Lord, no.'

I put on Michael's Stig suit (which had different logos on the forearms and shoulders) and brought the Suzuki to the start line. We scanned the shot list. One involved spearing off the circuit, taking out one of the cameras and probably smashing the windscreen in the process. I rubbed my hands together and got stuck into some good, old-fashioned demolition.

Half an hour later the mission was accomplished and the footage whisked away for James to edit.

I switched back into *my* Stig outfit and jumped into the new Lotus Evora. It was a fantastic little car. The intrusive understeer that undermined the bony Loti of the past was gone; it looked and handled like a little Ferrari.

I ran hard for about eight laps and then the runway was cleared of all traffic. Our star guest duly arrived in his private jet, blissfully unaware of the filming that had already taken place, and he and his PR people were driven across to their motorhome. He saw me walking by and turned, puzzled, to one of the producers. 'But I thought I am the Stig now?'

The FXX was created by dipping an Enzo in a vat of dark matter. It emerged boasting 812 horsepower, super aggressive F1 carbon brakes, slick racing tyres and additional wings to glue it to the tarmac. Who better to drive it than the man who inspired the design of the F1 car on which it was based? Of the thirty built, Schumacher's was the only one liveried completely in black and without a stripe.

I met him briefly at the start line. His skin was like velvet and he had the cocksure, carefree demeanour of someone who'd been there, won that and didn't need to wear the T-shirt. I doubt he heard much of what

I said over the high-pitched howl of the V12 being warmed up next to us, but he got the gist so we both mounted up.

I pulled my Jaguar XF alongside Alex, our producer with the bedroom eyes. 'I can't believe you pulled this off.'

'Sheer luck. He's in the UK promoting Bacardi's Drink Responsibly road safety campaign.'

Hot engines never like being kept waiting for camera crews to organise themselves and I knew Michael would want to go. Sure enough, he began slipping the FXX towards Alex, who tried in vain to stand his ground.

With a nod to the champ I led us out. I went carefully at first so he could pick out the white lines marking the course, then built up some speed on the second lap. He stayed fairly close behind, occasionally dropping back a little and doing his own thing. By the third lap I was going as fast as the Jag could manage.

In spite of my best efforts to turn its safety systems off, the XF kept trying to stabilise itself by activating its brakes in the middle of the corners. The F1 uber champ followed me patiently as I wallowed through the turns, apparently braking in all the wrong places. His Ferrari was practically idling.

At the end of the third and final recce lap my brakes were boiling, which sent the system into a complete panic. As I sped into the penultimate corner, the ABS kicked in so I couldn't slow down properly. The Jag cocked its leg and dropped two wheels on the dirt as I came out the other side. A shower of crud and stones flew into the air and my shoulders stiffened when I saw Michael's own personal, immaculate two million dollar supercar less than a length from my tail. He whipped left to miss the flying debris and I exited the track stage right to join the rescue crews at the fire station. He must have thought I was some new breed of dickhead.

He blasted around the track a few more times, came through the final bend and put on a little flurry with a spin across the line. He climbed out, had a brief discussion with the Ferrari mechanics and then strolled off to take an hour's lunch. So we all stopped too.

Michael was taking to his new role with Teutonic gusto. After interviewing him, Jason Barlow, a former *TG* presenter who now worked on the magazine, shot me an awestruck glance. 'He's taken to this pretty seriously, y'know,' he said in his Irish lilt. 'I asked him what it was like being The Stig and he told me how tricky it was flyin' back and forth from the Grand Prix circuit to make it in time for the studio.'

After the break we filmed Michael's lap proper as Stig. I hooked up with Iain, partly out of interest, but also to check he wasn't cutting across the white lines. He'd pulled a few controversial moves during his F1 career.

The Ferrari cranked up in the distance; the rasp of the V12 bounced off the fencing around the waste disposal site at Turn One. A shriek of valves, followed by staccato, bullet-like gear changes and the black rocket shot into view. Iain worked his magic, holding it perfectly in frame, focusing in on the detail then pulling the lens wide as he came closer and flew through the corner.

'Is he any good?'

'I'd say he's done this once or twice before …'

Michael drove an electric lap and it was a privilege to see him at work close up. The FXX was all race car. If anything, the setup looked too stiff for Dunsfold. The back end skipped over bumps I rarely noticed. Up close, Schumacher's turn in was very fast in the tight corners; 'Point and squirt', the way you drove a go-kart. The rest looked familiar – though he did spare his machine from hammering across the storm drain several inches beneath the tarmac at the Follow Through. Mind you, since his lap time was seven seconds faster than the record, a few extra tenths probably didn't concern him.

I had to top and tail Schumacher's introduction to the audience because I was the only person Clarkson knew who could look angry from behind a closed visor. They wanted to film me doing 'my walk' and standing in the studio before swapping me for the maestro.

Wilman was adamant that no one outside the very tight *Top Gear* circle of trust should see both Stigs at the same time, but as I rounded a corner in the production office, I bumped straight into him. Alex's eyes were like saucers. 'Two Stigs – *aaaargh!*'

It was a surreal moment. I gave Michael a crisp salute and a high five.

Wilman told him to expect a few gags from Jeremy. 'You know, he might say something like, "So if me and you were having a scrap, who would win?" That kind of thing.'

And Schumacher said, 'What does this have to do with Bacardi?'

I wasn't sure who was taking the piss out of who.

I got the nod to head for the studio. I stood outside what used to be the Harrier maintenance area. The giant hangar doors slid open and I was greeted by a roar from the audience. I stopped at my mark and looked

'angrily' around the room. 'The Stig has come among us,' Clarkson announced. 'I know exactly what this is about; he's fed up with newspapers speculating that he lives in a pebble-dashed house in Bristol ... Who wants to see The Stig's head?'

That was me done. I disappeared into Schumacher's motorhome. Once the coast was clear, I could emerge as Ben Collins whilst he 'outed' himself on camera.

As I climbed aboard the great man was tucking into a bowl of cornflakes with his female personal assistant.

I got changed, then asked him what he thought of the *TG* circuit.

He grinned. 'You call that a circuit?'

His PA chipped in sympathetically, 'Michael's just being mean.'

'Well maybe it's OK for road cars and this kind of thing, but that chicane in the middle with that bump – it's no good for *real* performance cars, I think.'

I felt myself bristling. My patch may have stunk of cabbage, but it was still my patch. Sure it wasn't Fiorano, but the bumps, curves and cambered braking areas were ideal for assessing vehicle dynamics.

'I hear that you're racing bikes now?'

His eyes lit up. 'Well, I've competed in one race of the German National Championship.'

'So you're keeping pretty busy?'

He nodded. 'I have also rediscovered my passion for karting ... And you ... what do you do?'

'Oh,' I said, 'this and that. I'm racing in GT, checking out some NASCAR. I was pretending to be James Bond last year, and today I'm pretending to be you.'

I admired the way that Schumacher operated within his own centre of gravity. He had huge inner confidence, of course, but I saw straight through the talk of bikes and karts. Like all racing drivers, he lived for the contest. We were interrupted by his cue to hit the stage. He reached for his helmet. 'How long have you been doing this?'

'For a few years ...'

'There have been many of you, yes?'

'No,' I said. 'I'm not sure how much they've told you ...' It was weird: even talking with my fellow Stig, the greatest F1 champion of all time, about to be revealed on TV, I still felt uncomfortable giving anything away.

He shook my hand as he left. 'Hope to see you later.' Then, thinking about it: 'Maybe not though?'

I wished him luck and went to find a monitor. He kept everyone on tenterhooks for a moment, then removed The Stig's helmet. The audience loved it. Cool as a cucumber, he exchanged banter with Clarkson, who'd decked himself out in a startling orange shirt.

'And do you find it a bit boring,' Jezza rolled his eyes, 'when the same person endlessly wins all the time?'

Michael responded with the kind of smile that both charmed the pants off the audience and made it clear that he didn't find that boring at all.

They kept the 'reasonably priced car' sequence for last, once he had vacated the premises in his private jet.

The Stig turned over the engine with the Liana in first, so it lurched forward and stopped. Then he stalled, restarted the motor and couldn't find the gears.

Cogs shrieking, he nudged the stick into reverse as it started crawling forwards. Once in second, he kangaroo-hopped down the road like a teenager on his first driving lesson.

The first corner approached and he skidded straight at the camera crew, half spun on the grass, made a late turn and dribbled away at 10mph towards Chicago.

The Liana understeered straight on, front wheels skidding, then careered off the track at about 50mph. Iain pegged it away, arms waving, as his camera smashed the windscreen, dented the roof and flew high into the air.

They didn't show the bit when I was texting on a mobile phone as I sped towards the Hammerhead chicane, but cut to me heading down the wrong side of the tyre wall and finally getting lost somewhere in Surrey.

Back in the studio, Jezza and Hammo grappled for a moment with the possibility that Schumacher wasn't The Stig after all. Until the credits rolled, I wondered whether I had just filmed my own epitaph. I half expected Clarkson to announce in ringing tones, 'Some say The Stig's forgotten how to drive, so we've had to get a new one ...'

'Compliments on your shitness out there, Stig,' James said. 'There's some very funny stuff here.' High praise, given the Brummy editor's exacting standards.

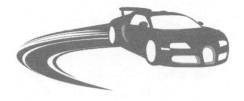

36

GIVE MY REGARDS TO DUNSFOLD

Luck had always been on my side when it came to juggling my *Top Gear* commitments, but having been asked to attend the National TV Awards to collect our prize for most popular factual programme, I had to switch at the last minute to extra rehearsals for the live show. There were plenty of willing stand-ins but fastest off the mark was Grant. 'Your loss, my gain,' he joshed as he rushed off to the red carpet. It shouldn't have bothered me, but I clung onto my helmet bag a little too tightly before passing it to him.

I spent the night perfecting a 720-degree lateral spin in a converted London Taxi whilst a suitably attired Grant collected the gong and snuck off in a limo. The paparazzi followed the wrong man and ended up snapping Will, our production assistant, as he left head office wearing an *I Am The Stig* T-shirt. The next morning, the hapless PA found himself unmasked as the man in the white suit.

I wasn't going to let anything get in my way when Red Bull needed someone to run their F1 car at Silverstone. It was due for a coat of 'glow-in-the-dark' paint, so it could feature in *TG*'s art exhibition.

'Vettel and Webber are busy,' Alex said. 'But they say they'd let Ben Collins have a go. Looks like you've picked up a fine ride, Mr C.'

I put down the phone and punched the air. About ten times. The F1 run at Silverstone clashed with the studio record several hundred miles away in Guildford, but I assured the producers I could make it.

I arrived at Silverstone the following morning. The air was crisp, with no cloud and a strong wind, and there was the big blue articulated transporter with the shiny blue, red and yellow missile parked in front of it. An F1 car never looked so beautiful as the day you drove one.

Red Bull's test team, all neatly decked out like walking energy cans, were busy running systems checks. I squeezed inside their beautiful machine and tried to treat it the same as any other racing tool.

'You might need this.' Team Manager Tony Burrows handed me the F1 equivalent of a windscreen wiper: a white rag. 'Coulthard said he couldn't see a thing through the paint once he was in fourth gear!'

Tony took a step back whilst one of the young Herberts sprayed the surface of the car with a fresh dollop of glow paint.

They threw every thermal blanket they had at the engine and gearbox to generate enough core temperature in the highly stressed systems. A hand reached into the cockpit and switched the ignition to position one. The engineer put revolutions through the motor, 'bumping', using a remote toggle. Once in ignition two, the beast awoke. The engineer blipped the throttle from his control panel.

Once the heated tyres had been chucked on I held in the paddle clutch, made plenty of noise with the gas and turned out onto the track.

I was used to F1 power from my old Le Mans racer and I'd tested a few older F1 models in the past, but nothing compared to the tautness of a 'current' machine. I squeezed the throttle and it settled into the tarmac. Enough squeezing; I dumped it. The engine howled. I flicked the gear paddle. My neck took the strain and sure enough, as soon as I reached fourth at 150mph, the gloopy paint spread across the bodywork and lashed across my visor. Momentarily blinded, I backed off a touch, wiped the *fromage* from my visor and blasted towards the Becketts complex.

From then on I kept my foot buried and wiped away wave after wave of the stuff as the car's vortex spun it in all directions. A few drops of rain made the whole process all the more interesting, with the car squirming and spinning its wheels out of the turns in third gear.

The job was done by 10.45am. I thanked Tony and his crew and hauled ass down to Dunsfold to jump into the new Corvette ZR1 and the V10 powered Audi R8.

I loved Corvettes, so I expected the ZR1 to amaze. With its supercharged V8 motor pumping 638bhp through a lightened frame, it was descended from a line of pure, simple-to-drive powerhouses that were

wonderfully balanced and deceptively fast. There was no mistaking its berserk level of power, but as soon as I reached a corner the rear end started to pitch, wobble and lose stability.

Corvettes ran on primitive-looking but superbly effective transverse leaf spring suspension, similar to that of a Land Rover. It resembled a stack of plywood, but meant you could buy something with Lamborghini performance for a fraction of the price.

The newer Vettes had sophisticated magnetic damping. Electric impulses changed the fluid's viscosity, altering its performance a thousand times every second, to absorb bumps and shift its weight. This one sensed its front wheels lifting from the copious extra thrust, considered the steering angle and automatically softened the absorption rate of the rear dampers to generate traction. I reckon it could have set the fastest time ever for a production car around Dunsfold, had it not been for the fact that the modulation between harder and softer settings cost cornering stability. In damp conditions it was only three seconds adrift of the Gumpert hypercar, a stunning result for a mass-produced model.

The Audi R8 with its 5.2 litre V10 detonator was 100 horsepower shy of the Corvette, and the Dunsfold stopwatch was pitiless when it came to grunt. The R8 relied on balanced handling to account for the shortfall and its best time came in a full second behind the Vette.

With its squat profile and sunken shoulders, the Audi looked like the Veyron's baby brother – a wolf in wolf's clothing. Dropping a V10 into it was a stroke of genius. So was giving it a four-wheel drive system with a predominantly rear-driven bias, allowing you to corner on rails or wave the tail at will. The R8 was poised and precise. The small but perfectly formed rear wing did little to conceal its front-loaded bias when you steered in, which got the juices flowing. It pitched in and you had to hang on, especially under heavy braking.

On my second timed run it bit me as I slowed for Turn One and went skidding sideways down past Iain's camera at 90mph. The lap was wasted as far as posting a time was concerned, so I dropped down a gear and torched the throttle. The R8 followed a predictable line for 300 metres with smoke pouring off all four tyres. That's what I called handling.

After a day like that, I needed no reminding of how fortunate I was. To really enjoy your job is a most desirable position to be in.

But the urge to race was nagging at my soul. I needed my sense of purpose to be defined by the outcome of ruthless competition. I wanted

to be the author of the events shaping my life, and to do that I needed my own identity back. The words of the Blackpool palm reader echoed hauntingly in my mind: choose one path over the other. I set about getting my face in front of teams in earnest and reacquainted myself with the dark art of the cold call.

I envied The Stig. He was as welcome at A-list parties as he was on the grid of the Indy 500, NASCAR and even Le Mans. With the helmet off I knew I'd have to adjust to the kind of reception Clark Kent got when he put away the cape. But to my astonishment I found that with my feet firmly back on the ground, life as Ben Collins looked a lot more interesting than I'd ever imagined.

Out of the blue, I was contacted by my old team from Rockingham, Ray Mallock's, and given the opportunity to race their car in the European Le Mans Series. I flew out to Portugal to meet both the team and the machine.

The Lola Honda Prototype, with its closed cockpit, giant fins and fat slick tyres, looked more like an F-16 fighter jet than a car.

The high revving engine whizzed over the bumpy circuit and blind flowing crests. The downforce sucked me into the tarmac as I took the corners at three times the weight of gravity. The view ahead played on fast forward, the competition was up close and personal and the impatient racing driver was home again.

RML proved why they were leading the championship by running a faultless operation all weekend. I ran the final stints into the night and took the chequered flag, barely visible through the glare of the rubber-blasted windscreen. We won the race.

EPILOGUE

Outside my little white bubble, the horizon in fact stretched away towards infinity. Replacing the constant fear that my world could unravel in the press at any moment with a ticket to ride through free space began to make sense. No more what ifs; more what's next? The world is filled with extraordinary people making things happen every day. Bigger car chases and faster races.

It was a cracking final series. Thanks to the magic of Harry Potter's best friend Ron Weasley, aka Rupert Grint, we put a new star at the top of the board in the latest incarnation of the reasonably priced car – the Kia C'eed. Rupert slammed around the newly-surfaced Dunsfold circuit in a time that was significantly faster than anyone before him. Pretty impressive for a softly-spoken twenty-something who drives an ice cream van in his half-term breaks from Hogwarts – but almost immediately under threat from a different kind of Hollywood magician.

'Stig, come and meet, er, Tom …'

Hammo and James stood chatting with a familiar figure outside an Airstream – one of three – the size of a B-52 bomber. In a loose grey sweater, jeans and gold-rimmed aviators, Tom Cruise looked ready for any mission Wilman could throw at him. Hammond was in his element too, frothing at the mouth about the *Top Gun* star's recent acquisition of one of Steve McQueen's restored 'Indian' brand motorbikes.

Tom gave me a winning grin as he shook my hand. He couldn't have smiled more broadly if he'd tried; even the big black cloud that suddenly appeared overhead failed to dampen his spirits. 'Man,' he said, 'we're gonna have a blast out there. The rain makes the car spin out easier, right?'

I nodded. 'It can be pretty extreme – like *Days of Thunder*, but without the thunder.'

Tom took a while to join me by the Kia; he stopped to greet *every single* member of the crew on the way. None of us felt starstruck, though; his excitement was too infectious.

'So nobody knows who you are, right?'

'Nope, not even my kids.'

He clapped his hands and laughed.

I normally drove two recce laps with each celeb. Tom wanted six. I eased off a touch for the superfast Follow Through at the end of my run.

'You came off it there?'

'Yes, the rain's picked up a bit.'

Tom quizzed every gearshift, studied my every move as I pushed full tilt. I ran wide at the penultimate corner on the greasy tarmac, slid sideways over the grass and gathered it to cross the line.

'Sorry about that.'

'You kidding? You're so smooth, man; the way you take those turns is incredible.'

'I've been around the block a few times – but thanks …'

He scooched deftly over the centre console and into the driver's seat. 'I'm just gonna take a look see for the first lap; nothin' too fast …'

'Exactly right. Let the place sink in.'

He kept his thumbs hooked into the T bar as per my instructions, but with his fingers pointing past the wheel. He was memorising every twist and turn.

His pace naturally quickened, so I threw down my standard test of a maximum ABS stop. He slammed on the anchors so hard we were pulling our dentures out of the dashboard, then swung hard left and right through the chicane, howling with laughter all the way.

'This is just great; it's like a vacation.'

The rain eased off and Tom was soon taking the fast corners flat out.

'The best way to picture the final bend when it's wet is like an oil slick. As soon as you steer left the car will slide.'

'Gotcha. What gear?'

'Second. And when the rear breaks away you can steer into the slide a little ...'

'Counter-steer?'

'Yes, but not for too long. And the other thing you can do – but don't ever try this in your Ford Mustang – is floor the accelerator, because the front wheels can drive it straight out of the skid.'

We launched another assault. His expression was as focused as Maverick's in a 4G inverted dive with a MiG-28. We spun on the oil slick corner and he counter-steered faster than anyone I'd ever coached. Time flew by, but complaints from the producers were noticeably absent whilst Cruise was enjoying 'the best day ever'.

'There's some people around the place making me a little nervous. Before we go can we make sure they're clear, especially the guy on this last turn?'

'Don't worry,' I said. 'Nobody likes him much; that's why he's there.'

He grinned, went solo and promptly punched out a 1.47 lap in the wet. I could scarcely believe the stopwatch. He lost it on two occasions going into that final corner, burying the throttle like a touring car driver and clipping the mini tyre wall just in front of where I was standing. Each run culminated in gales of raucous laughter.

With his film in the can Tom thanked everyone profusely and went off to be briefed for his interview.

The largely male crew found it hard not to notice the slender blonde approaching the track with Clarkson in tow. Cameron Diaz was wearing a stripy top and spray-on jeans; she wasn't short of helpers when it came to belting herself into the Kia.

I explained the basics on the demo lap, but found myself avoiding her feline gaze as she lowered her chin and looked up at me. She had this way of making you feel like you were flirting. I cranked up the AC.

She took to the driver's chair and shuffled it forwards and back until her golden ballet shoes rested precisely on the pedals. A screech of rubber and we shot onto the dried-out track.

Cameron had raced the Long Beach grand prix circuit in a Toyota Celica, so I knew she had plenty of backbone. She was pushing the Kia hard from the outset. Her trademark pout barely altered except when she bit her lower lip for her first flat out assault on Follow Through.

The slower sections were more revealing, as she discovered the limitations of the gearbox.

'God, what gear is that?' Her Valley Girl accent catapulted me back to junior high.

'That's first. Try and avoid that one.'

'No kidding, it's a raw deal. *Fuck*.'

'That's fifth; don't rush it. Swearing helps.'

'Shit. Fuckin' piece of crap car …' Her giggle did funny things to my spine.

Cameron was dialled in so we sent her solo. Grant gave her the countdown. She stalled in third gear, then nailed it.

Her times were fast. I asked if she needed any help with anything.

'Actually yes, could I get my lip gloss? Crackin' up in here.'

'Grant, she's going a lot faster than Tom,' I said.

'I think we can get him another go now the track's dry.'

Mr C had already reappeared with a helmet, itching to go back out.

I followed Cameron's progress until the Kia spluttered to a halt. After the previous week's roasting at the hands of the mighty Andy Garcia, its clutch had finally quit. I picked her up in a white Jaguar XKR and paparazzi hiding in the treeline recorded the moment for posterity under the breathless headline: *Shaken Hollywood star rescued by mysterious knight in shining armour*. If only …

Cameron took the spare car and promptly set a record time of 1.45.2.

Cruise hopped back in and I rode shotgun to dial him into dry running.

'Basically your braking markers are the same in the dry, but you brake less and carry more speed. So use third gear through here …'

'But *you said* second …' This was no laughing matter.

'I know, but not in the dry.'

Poised on the start line, Tom closed his eyes, lowered his head and rehearsed every inch of the circuit with his hands. I taught him to arc his entry to the penultimate corner and use the new concrete to boost his time. He ran wide with just one corner to go but held onto the bucking bronco by its ears and dragged it back onto the tarmac.

He kept it lit and sliced inside the border so fast that he tipped onto two wheels. For a moment it looked like he might roll and I could hear the producer's knees knocking behind me. Tom shot through the corner,

then feathered the throttle and covered the remaining 50 feet before coming in to land. It was his fastest lap.

His reward was to take out the new Bugatti Veyron Super Sport which I'd lapped earlier. The T Rex of the motor world boasted an added 196 horsepower and a top speed of 267mph. 1200bhp was enough to smoke all four wheels off the line, force your mouth wide open and keep it that way. It gripped so much in the corners that the tyres melted after just four laps. The fuel tank emptied after six. The combination of the newly-laid final corners, with surplus concrete allowing you to carry extra speed, and the Bug's atavistic grunt helped me post a new track record that I can't see being beaten anytime soon, and left Bugatti with a £20,000 tyre bill.

I've put on my helmet and the white suit for the last time; taken one final look around the pilot's changing room. Reg the beetle is long gone, as are many of the friends I made here over the years. The place is empty once more, the paint still peeling, but the memories remain.

Sure I'll miss the car park packed with Ferraris, the cabin erupting with ideas and the hangar filled by a cheering audience. Good old John Prescott's cut-out still guards the door, sun-bleached by years of service. I'm leaving Dunsfold with as many questions as I had when I first arrived, but with the answers to a whole lot more. And speed. God I love it. Wang the music up and drop the hammer. And I know that my favourite road leads home, to those I care about most: my family, my future.

I still love watching *Top Gear*, although I tell Jezza I never bother because it infuriates him. I saw him rolling a Robin Reliant onto its roof the other night; Georgie and I cried with laughter.

ACKNOWLEDGEMENTS

Georgie, my soul-mate, thank you for all your support during the highs and lows over the years. Your indomitable zest for life always reminds me what life's all about. The little ones too; more beach, less laptop, I promise.

Jonathan Taylor, Peter Sherrott and the 'A' team at HarperCollins had their work cut out keeping this project under wraps, whilst navigating some large icebergs along the way. Thank you for this opportunity to tell my story.

Mark Lucas, your verbal skewer cut me to the bone; thank you so much for all your hard work, Obi Wan!

Russ Lindsay and James Grant Media, your clarity of vision has been invaluable.

Heartfelt thanks to the Ministry of Defence for their co-operation with this project.

Special thanks to a few very good men who built and supported my racing career over the years: Klaas Zwart and the mighty 'Ascari boys'; Ray Mallock, Phil Barker and the stellar crew at RML; Graeme May, Texaco and Stuart Bassett; Jonathan France and Embassy Racing; Bill Jarnagin; Rick and Todd Kelly, Joe Bremner and the Aussie boys at Kelly Racing; Simon McNamara, Jamie McCallum and Hamish Charles at Transfrontier; Jim Wiseman; Adam Shore and JimEarl; Nigel Hassler and Donnie Graves; the members of the British Racing Drivers Club.

Every company that has ever sponsored me and notably: Hays Plc, WRM Logitics, Lynx express delivery, QR-4U, The Ministry of Defence, EFS, Elite Mobile, Jack Daniel's, Holden, Castrol, AD Group, Ridgeway Group, Alpinestars.

The *Top Gear* Team, thank you for the good times, I wish you all the best for the future.

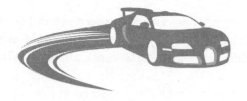

INDEX